Brock Yates

THE
DECLINE AND FALL
OF THE
AMERICAN
AUTOMOBILE
INDUSTRY

EMPIRE BOOKS

NEW YORK

Distributed by Harper & Row Publishers, Inc.
Designed by Helen Barrow
Manufactured in the United States of America
Printed and bound by R. R. Donnelley & Sons Company

FIRST EDITION

Library of Congress Cataloging in Publication Data

Yates, Brock W.
The decline and fall of the American automobile industry.
Includes index.

1. Automobile industry and trade—United States.
2. General Motors J-cars. I. Title.
HD9710.U52Y38 1982   338.4'76292'0973   82-70939
ISBN 0-88015-004-1

To my lady Pamela,
part Ferrari, part Mercedes-Benz
and, thankfully, part of my life

In 1968, I published a story which bears directly on the current dilemma of the American automobile industry. It was entitled the "Grosse Pointe Myopians" and it began:

"Imagine it this way: The year is 1870 and you march into the velvet and mahogany office of Commodore Cornelius Vanderbilt, sole owner of the New York Central Railroad and one of the most powerful entrepreneurs in Christendom. Your message is simple: you have investigated the long-range potential of the railroads to meet America's transportation needs and you can sum up your conclusions with a brief statement: 'Commodore, you're in trouble.'

"Now Commodore Vanderbilt was never one to tolerate much truck from the poor-mouths and crepe-hangers and he would quickly cite to you a few salient facts, to wit: in 1830, the United States had exactly 23 miles of railroad track. Now, just 40 years later, the mileage stands at nearly 50,000 and all reliable projections say the figure will increase to 250,000 by 1900. Having given you several seconds to digest that information, he would have you thrown into the street.

"Imagine, today, trying the same thing with General Motors. 'It's like this, gentlemen,' you might begin. 'I have made a studied and dispassionate examination of the future of the domestic automobile industry and I am here to warn you that the prognosis is grim, if not totally without hope.' They would probably listen to you with a certain amount of detached amusement and then have you thrown out of a 14th floor window of the General Motors Building."

That was written 15 years ago. In response to the article, one auto executive leveled the ultimate insult: He said I was worse for the industry than Ralph Nader. Perhaps, but no one, not even myself, imagined that the devastation predicted in that piece would arrive with such shocking suddenness.

This critique of the industry does not come from ambush. For as long as I have been writing about automobiles, I have belonged to a small coterie of writers who have been convinced that Detroit was building the wrong cars. Too often we were dismissed as obsessive "buffs" who seemed to have a fixation with tiny, overpowered European sports cars. While it was true that many imported automobiles seemed to represent a shift toward efficiency and high technology and away from the chromed land arks of Detroit, we were far from the prejudiced ingrates that industry leaders described us to be. We simply believed most American cars were too large, too heavy, too clumsy and too inefficient to meet the needs of the modern driver. Nor was our criticism singular. Erudite engineers and automotive journals had long been warning the American automoguls that unless they changed their attitudes and direction, disaster lay ahead.

What, how and why it happened, and how the situation might be improved, is the subject I hope to deal with in these pages.

Brock Yates
Wyoming, New York

January, 1983

CONTENTS

THE DECLINE AND FALL
OF THE
AMERICAN AUTOMOBILE INDUSTRY

CHAPTER I

"J" Is Not For Japanese: The $5 Billion Blunder

THE LONG TORMENT WOULD SOON END. On a bright day in May of 1981 the suffering American automobile industry would, like a powerful medieval army, heave itself out of winter quarters and begin a counteroffensive along the newly sun-dried roads. It was a moment that had long been awaited, one that would come after numerous defeats at the hands of a combined enemy force composed of Japanese, Germans, Italians, French, Swedes, and, sadly, even treacherous elements in its own government. There had been other counterattacks by the Detroit forces during the twenty-year war, but they had brought only temporary advances. Now success was imperative: The foreign invaders commanded almost thirty percent of the territory. Over half of the critical California theater was in their hands.

Robert D. Lund, General Motors vice president and veteran general manager of the flagship Chevrolet Division, was to set the tone of the campaign. Lund had the earnest, deep-set eyes and the gregarious intensity of a Presbyterian minister. This superb salesman who had given thirty-five years of dedicated service to the GM family was a first-namer, a backslapper who enjoyed the ingrained respect of Chevrolet's vast body of dealers and the corporate hierarchy. Like so many of his associates, Lund was a WASP and a midwesterner, a quintessential General Motors executive. He had worked for no other organization during his adult life. Before serving briefly as general manager of the Cadillac Division, Lund had been a "take-no-prisoners" tactical officer on the Chevrolet sales staff for twenty-five years. Bob Lund loved to sell cars, particularly General Motors cars.

But now a few months before the counteroffensive, on February 11, 1981, at a GM-sponsored press preview in Tempe, Arizona, his brand of Rotary Club joviality was muted. As Lund fingered the text of his speech at the lectern of the conference room in the sprawling Fiesta Inn, his manner was atypically formal.

In the audience were more than a hundred top automotive writers and photographers, business experts from the major newsweeklies, science magazine writers, men's magazine correspondents, and professional car testers from the automotive "buff books" who were there to witness what they knew would be a pivotal announcement.

They had come to Arizona lusting for this first look at a car that would reach the public that May. According to corporate gossip, it would be a milestone automobile, a war machine capable of repelling the invaders from the Far East. They knew it only as the "J-car." It was a GM engineering code name that seemed to designate the targeted Japanese enemy, even though the company insisted that it was merely coincidental. The J-car was to be General Motors' first serious effort to build and market a fuel- and space-efficient subcompact since the ill-fated Chevrolet Vega a decade earlier. It would be the automobile that many critics had said the American automobile industry had grown too sluggish to create. It would be an automobile that would not only recapture sales but make up for decades of eroding respect.

His preacher's eyes glistening, Bob Lund issued the call to battle in Tempe. "We are tired," he said firmly and with uncharacteristic rancor, "of hearing how the domestic industry let the Japanese take the subcompact market away from us. We need an unconventional Chevrolet—an unconventional package with an unconventional marketing strategy—if we are going to do a better job against the imports, and we spell that *Japanese*. Make no mistake about it, Cavalier [the Chevrolet J-car] is an import fighter! The whole Chevrolet organization is spoiling for a fight."

Two thousand miles away from his home base in Detroit, Lund had certainly gauged the mood of Motor City. The city was bursting with angry executives. From the paneled chambers of the Detroit Athletic Club to the oaken crannies of the London Chop House, from the glass-boxed Ford headquarters in Dearborn to the four-teenth-floor executive suite of the General Motors Building, men like Lund were ready for battle.

For years they had been the recipients of sniping fire from the media, intellectual gadflies, the government, and traitorous con-sumers in the great heartland, all of whom were complaining about Detroit's fascination with overweight, over-chromed, over-powered automobiles. These insurrectionist forces had shamelessly abetted the great imported car invasion that was threatening not only the Motor City but the economic stability of American industry itself.

Sales were the worst in memory. The Big Three—General Motors, Ford, and Chrysler (actually the Big Two and the Battered Pretender)—were emerging from a fiscal year marked by four billion dollars worth of red ink. In the quarter just past only GM had recorded a profit, a relatively thin one of $190 million. Chrysler was stalking around Washington begging loans from the government. American Motors was an indentured servant of Renault, the French automaker, which had bought 46 percent of the crumbling company for a mere $350 million. Ford was kept afloat solely by its profitable overseas operations, having suffered a $39 million loss in the home market.

The entire American car industry, once the industrial pride of the nation, was declining rapidly in size and influence. In 1950, America produced 79.4 percent of the world's automobiles. By 1981, its share had slipped below 30. But while Detroit continued to do poorly, the market for imported cars flourished. The percentage of U.S. sales taken by imports was rising each year, with the Japanese as the largest contenders.

The Japanese were selling all the 1.68 million cars they had voluntarily agreed to as a limit. That number was to represent 22 percent of the entire American market, but observers were convinced that the Japanese could capture one-third, or even one-half, of the American car business if there were no restraints. The Japanese subcompacts already dominated the field. Almost one in two of the small basic cars sold here (48 percent in 1981 and an anticipated majority by 1983) were made in Japan.

Even the perpetually optimistic leaders at General Motors were feeling the pressure. For the first time, this dip in car sales could not be attributed to a periodic slump in the economy. Detroit knew that the sharp decline had come with awesome suddenness, a symptom of some vital theoretical failure in the painstakingly developed system.

Only three years earlier, in 1978, the industry seemed to have overcome the effects of the devastating mid-70s OPEC oil embargo. General Motors had produced a profit of $3.5 billion, an amount greater than the Gross National Product of all but a handful of nations. They had employed 852,000 people in 35 nations, had enjoyed fixed assets of over $30 billion and boasted nearly $8 billion of working capital. Bob Lund's Chevrolet Division alone had produced 3.6 million cars and trucks to confirm its position as the largest component of the empire.

Yet not long before the Tempe meeting, Lund was listening to Elliott M. "Pete" Estes, who was General Motors president from 1974 to 1981, confess at a private meeting of top corporate executives: "Gentlemen, for years we figured that if we could beat Ford, we could beat anybody. But now the Japanese are outselling Ford in the American market!" Worse yet, Estes, a rangy man with an off-center smile usually bonded to his face, noted solemnly that the Japanese had displaced the United States as the number-one automobile manufacturing nation on earth.

/////

As Bob Lund was outlining his J-car battle plan at Tempe, Robert Brewbaker was laboring through another frustrating day in Michigan. After making his own presentation to the press, he had quickly returned from the opening ceremonies at Tempe to his spacious corner office of the General Motors Engineering Staff Complex in Warren, Michigan, where he faced a desk cluttered with plans, spec sheets, and computer readouts. Outside the weather was grim. The temperature was ten degrees, and the southern Michigan flatlands were layered with nine inches of snow. Tomorrow was his forty-second birthday, but Brewbaker would waive the anniversary celebration. This owlish engineer with wavy hair and steel-rimmed glasses had the job of transforming Lund's angry challenge into reality.

Brewbaker's official title was Project Center Manager, J-car, the letter designation for GM's first "World Car." The machine was to be sold in the United States as the Chevrolet Cavalier, the Pontiac J-2000, and the Cadillac Cimarron. It would also be marketed on a worldwide basis as the German Opel Ascona, the English Vauxhall Motors Cavalier, the General Motors of Brazil Monza, the Holden-GM of Australia Camira, and the GM-South Africa Ascona. In Japan, it would be under license to Isuzu. For the first time in its seventy-year history General Motors was planning to produce a universal vehicle that could be adapted to the driving environments of every continent.

The original Ford Model T and Volkswagen had pioneered the same concept and now the Japanese were circling the globe with universal Datsuns and Toyotas. General Motors had debated the merits of a World Car for years, but now the time had come to deliver. It would be a critical component of the Corporation's international scheme, but its success or failure would be measured in one market: the United States. The fifty states would be the principal battleground for the J-car, and it was Brewbaker's challenge to make it a winner.

A native of the Midwest, Brewbaker joined the Corporation after his graduation from the University of Michigan in 1963. He held a master's degree in electrical engineering and had been seriously courted by the aerospace industry. "But I'd worked for GM several summers while I was in college and they made me an offer I couldn't refuse," he recalled.

General Motors is brimming with young talents like Brewbaker. Within the five car divisions, the technical centers, and the styling studios sharp-eyed, fashionably dressed men in their late thirties and early forties wield extraordinary authority. Like Brewbaker, in his designer eyeglasses and his tailored Geoffrey Beene suits, they all seem to come from small towns like Farmington, Michigan.

Brewbaker was on what his colleagues called "the fast track" toward "downtown," a company term for the GM Headquarters on West Grand Boulevard, eight miles south of wind-lashed Warren, Michigan. The stakes for this forty-two year old engineer were enormous, as telling for him personally as the J-car was for the Corporation. While F. James (Jim) McDonald, who had replaced Estes as GM president in 1981, was publicly describing the J-car as a "five billion dollar roll of the dice," Brewbaker was looking down the barrel of a loaded corporate gun. Unless the J-car was properly launched into production his "fast track" could instead deposit him in some corporate backwater, consigned to dabbing fecklessly at a desk calculator in the engineering department of a distant assembly plant.

Brewbaker would soon know. In less than three weeks after the Tempe conference, after three years of planning and intricate coordination, the General Motors Assembly Division complex and its adjacent Fisher Body Plant in Lordstown, Ohio, were scheduled to embark on that uniquely twentieth-century act of industrial synergism known as assembly-line mass production. A $50 million advertising and marketing campaign was to move into action in the national media. Thousands of General Motors dealers across the nation had space reserved in their showrooms for the J-car; fresh order blanks were stacked in place. When the signal came, seventy-five of the new autos would spill off the Lordstown line each hour. Two weeks later a similar General Motors Assembly Division facility in Southgate, California, would begin production—provided the problems that now covered Brewbaker's desk could be solved in these last hours.

/////

Brewbaker's difficulties were being symbolically washed away in waves of euphoria in faraway Arizona. It was a four-day affair that began with a cocktail party, a buffet, and opening remarks from new GM president Jim McDonald. Donald Genord of the Fisher Body Division trumpeted the born-again Corporation's recent conversion to the "fit and finish" religion that promised a tight quality look to compete with the meticulous understated gleam of the best Japanese and German imports. Brewbaker himself had spoken in his flat Michigan tones about the car's overall engineering philosophy.

The following three days would be devoted to individual introductions to the J-cars from three GM divisions—Chevrolet, Pontiac, and Cadillac—each including a forty-minute excursion by chartered bus to General Motors' immense desert proving ground at Mesa, where brief "ride and drive" test sessions and photography setups would be permitted. The daily sessions involved prepared texts and "show and tell" slide programs by the various general managers, chief engineers, and marketing men to explain the commercial and technical aspects of the J-cars. Photos would also be taken on the precincts of the proving ground, which explains why all the early pictures of the J-cars revealed scrubby desert vistas, rather than suburban paradises, in the background.

Chevrolet would lead off the second day with Bob Lund and the Cavalier. Day three would be devoted to the Pontiac staff and their J-2000, while the Cadillac Division would showcase its Cimarron on the final day. The Cimarron was a late arrival to the program: Cadillac had been assigned a J-car just eleven months before, only after its powerful dealer council demanded a small car for their otherwise gas-hungry, oversized line. It was understood that the Cadillac Cimarron was little more than a last-hour amalgam of parts cannibalized from the Chevrolet and Pontiac J-cars and dressed up for the upper-income buyer. In fact, the visiting press was already aware of one central fact: The three cars—the Cavalier, the J-2000 and the Cimarron—were superficially restyled versions of exactly the same automobile.

The corporate public relations men understood the challenge of presenting three essentially identical automobiles to the assembled press. Most of the press were magazine staffers who were in Arizona for what the business calls a "long lead." Because of their long deadlines, some of which exceeded two months, they would be made privy to the product before the daily newspapers, which would be given another preview much closer to the time of the line's official introduction. The so-called buff books, *Road & Track*, *Motor Trend*, *Hot Rod*, *Car Craft*, *Road Test*, and *Car and Driver*, were represented, as were the craft books like *Popular Mechanics* and *Popular Science*, a number of trade publications, some men's magazines, including *Playboy* and *Penthouse*. *Time* and *Newsweek* were both planning major stories on the J-car, including a *Newsweek* cover. Within this group were several legitimate experts, auto-oriented reporters who had driven and tested virtually every automobile in the world.

In the old days most of the automotive publications could be counted on to knuckle under to the threat of advertising boycotts and anoint almost anything Detroit put on the street. But now a fresh atmosphere of candor was circulating through the business. Jim Williams, the affable young director of Chevrolet public relations, knew his Cavalier would hardly be presold to a group that included such hard-eyed skeptics. Many of them had been present at the long-lead preview in the summer of 1975 when Bob Lund had heaped the same praise on the Chevette, and a few had witnessed the euphoric "dog and pony show" that had ushered the down-sized Vega into the marketplace in 1969.

Now the fan-dancer "tease" technique was used to reveal the automobiles to the gathered press. Slides slowly brought the full car into focus while various narrators explained its mechanical and marketing nuances. A series of these tease pictures steadily increased the size and scope of the J-car until the whole image appeared. The Cavalier, the first to be presented, came in four models. In its rough silhouette and external dimensions the four-door sedan bore a strong resemblance to the Honda Accord. It was clean and boxy, with a stubby trunk and contours that made it appear rather tall and narrow. The rakish two-door hatchback sports coupe, a two-door notchback coupe, and a four-door station wagon followed. They were hardly ugly shapes, but there was nothing truly memorable about any of them. To most of the viewers the Chevrolet Cavaliers were rehashes of small car styling tricks used on Japanese cars for the last five years.

The carefully choreographed show at Tempe forged onward.

Roger Masch, a lanky native of Warren, Michigan, was the chief engineer for Chevrolet on the J-car project. Sporting a grenadier's mustache and sideburns which until recently were taboo within the Corporation, he extolled the virtues of the Cavalier from a prepared text read in concert with slides.

Following a pause written into the script, Masch announced, "When I think back about the design and development program, there are some key objectives that I think describe the Cavalier today. *Broad appeal* in this foreign-dominated market and hence this full family of four body styles; *base content* to meet foreign competition head-on and hence the most highly contented Chevrolet ever; in a subcompact exterior size our objective was to design for *maximum interior space*; outstanding ride and handling was an objective—to be better than the competition. Of course optimized performance and fuel economy was a major consideration. And *quality* was a very key objective in all of our designs throughout the program. Designs that would utilize the most advanced automotive technology to assure a quality product, not in just the fits and finishes that are perceived in the showroom, but quality throughout the car."

The press corps veterans had heard all this before. It was the all-purpose talk. Every new model introduction in memory had involved a chief engineer or a sales manager rhapsodizing about his company's newfound religion in quality, handling, interior room, and performance. Distilled to its essence, Masch's presentation was able to document little more than the fact that the new Cavalier had more rear seating room than comparable Toyotas, Datsuns, Volkswagens and Hondas and provided up to five cubic feet of extra trunk space. Just how much of Masch's comments about the car was hyperbole would have to be determined at the proving grounds and in the General Motors showrooms across the nation.

In terms of technology, there was little cause for heightened pulses. Many of those present had expected General Motors to reveal a power plant that was a tour de force: a powerful, light-alloy, fuel-injected, overhead camshaft unit that surpassed the best Japanese efforts. But as the lights dimmed and Chevrolet engine specialist John Zwerner followed Masch to the lectern their visions of a great leap forward darkened. Zwerner was the leader of the engineering group that had created the new engine for the entire J-car line. What he described was not a featherweight package of high-revving exotica, but a 1.8 liter, cast-iron four-cylinder engine with essentially the same pushrod-activated mechanism that Chevrolet had been using exclusively in its domestically designed engines since 1955.

While Zwerner bragged about the engine's lusty 88 horsepower, its relatively compact size and weight, and its modest thirst for fuel, a number of witnesses were wondering why the car was not being produced with a truly modern engine of the type being offered by the Japanese competition. But Zwerner was promising similar results from their aged equipment. Moreover, he was bragging about the car's performance. "We particularly wanted to get good performance with our automatic transmission... better than the sluggish response typical of the small-engine import with an automatic," he said somewhat enigmatically.

He pressed on exuberantly, summarizing his group's efforts. "I feel we have achieved the desired results: excellent fuel economy, good performance and innovative features. And we have paid attention to detail, quality, reliability, and serviceability, and backed it up with more test hours and more test miles than any other program."

Prepped by corporate enthusiasm, the press corps boarded the chartered buses and drove off to the proving grounds. In a matter of hours the word was out. The reporters gathered in small knots to compare notes. The evidence was irrefutable. Every stopwatch confirmed it. The J-cars were *slow*. The *Motor Trend* staffers noted that the Toyota Corolla SR-5, a conventional, year-old design with ten less horsepower, would beat a Cavalier four-speed model from 0 to 60 by two seconds. The *Road & Track* writers were talking about the "anemic thrashings" of the engine. Everybody was saying that the acceleration of the automatic transmission J-car was the slowest of any gasoline-powered automobile in modern history. It was in a class with the notoriously sluggish diesel sedans.

Otherwise the press encountered a new line of automobiles that handled creditably, that evidenced higher levels of quality control and fabrication than previous small cars produced by GM. But there was a monotonous quality to the cars, a grayness that prevented them from electrifying the gathered writers and photographers. After the years of rumors, leaks and high hopes, they had expected a brilliantly executed design and mechanical virtuosity that would make the J-car Bob Lund's true "import fighter."

Instead they found themselves riding in, driving, and pawing over cars that were at best modest imitations of the best Japanese competition. A children's crusade was being mounted against an elite force of infidels. At worst, they were "new" model cars that had arrived in the marketplace three years later than their Japanese counterparts—with dated styling and less than state-of-the-art mechanics.

At the Fiesta Inn, Jim Williams, Roger Masch, and engine man John Zwerner found themselves hectored by questions from the press. Why was the more powerful overhead camshaft German Opel engine not used? Why not fuel injection? Why not a two-liter version? Why not a turbocharger? Why the pallid, copycat styling? Where was the five-speed transmission that was practically standard on the competition? Why was the car so heavy? One question specifically not broached was price. These veterans of the car wars knew better; no manufacturer discussed retail prices until the eleventh hour. Any queries would bring the predictable response that the numbers would be "competitive."

As to the car's lack of power and performance, the Chevrolet staffers were ready. "They had their lines memorized," recalls one auto journalist. "They said they were shooting for quality and mileage, not performance, and no matter how hard we pressed them, they wouldn't buckle. These guys are very good that way. Once they reach a position, they are damn articulate in justifying it. And they glossed over the excess weight. You could sense the car was too heavy, based on the size of the engine versus the way it accelerated, but they simply switched the talk around to how they had been more interested in sound isolation and body strength than in weight saving."

As they drifted away from the Fiesta Inn in Tempe there was a certain foreboding among the press. The veterans knew that they had seen nothing with the marketing power needed to repel the

Japanese. In fact, many knew that the J-cars would be blundering into a market about to receive updated products from Datsun, Toyota and Honda, among others. Viewed in the hard light of the mid-1981 market, the J-cars were little more than modest counterfeits of machinery the Japanese were beginning to phase out and replace. Some at GM understood this, but the generally insular GM marketers had little trouble psyching themselves into believing they had a winner. No matter. Wiser men believed that Jim McDonald's five billion dollar dice roll might be coming up snake eyes.

/////

It had all begun in 1976 as a few lines on a drawing board in Ruesselsheim am Main, West Germany. Engineers at Adam Opel AG, a General Motors subsidiary, had been assigned the job of creating a successor to the corporate "T-Car," the tiny sedan sold in Germany as the Kadett and in the United States as the Chevette. Following the first fuel crisis in 1973, Chevrolet had cobbled the car together from its American, German, and Brazilian parts bins and it had served well. Then resurgent supplies of gasoline nearly wrecked its introduction in 1976 and the entire American small car market with it. By 1977, however, it was apparent that the Chevette was too crude and too cramped to compete effectively, long range, either in the European markets or in the United States.

The X-cars, GM's first generation of automobiles created by down-sizing the traditional large family sedan, were set for introduction in 1979; this would mark a major shift in emphasis for the Corporation toward front-wheel-drive machinery. But President Pete Estes believed that GM needed a stronger entry into the small car market. He envisioned the concept of a new model that would fit into a slot between the miniature Chevette and the upcoming intermediate-sized X-cars—the Chevrolet Citation, Buick Skylark, Oldsmobile Omega, and Pontiac Phoenix. It would be approximately the size of the Honda Accord, the so-called "target vehicle" in every major corporation's plans for down-sized automobiles.

In keeping with the industry's tradition of assigning a letter code to each family of basic bodies, the automobile that was formally assigned to Bob Brewbaker and his Project Center staff on August 17, 1977, was known simply as the J-car. It would be a German-American cooperative engineering effort to blitz the Japanese at their own specialty: small, beautifully engineered, well-trimmed and painted, high-quality, space-efficient, high-mileage automobiles that would sell anywhere in the world.

The J-car would of course employ front-wheel drive. This was considered to be indispensable when developing an automobile with minimum external dimensions and maximum interior room. By having the engine power transferred directly to the front wheels, the burdensome transmission "hump" would be eliminated. The system had been used periodically by carmakers for over sixty years, perhaps with the most continued success by Citroën in France and Cord in the United States. But it took a brilliant, if quirky, Englishman named Alec Issigonis to bring the concept into modern perspective. Coincidentally, it was the West's first gasoline crisis, generated by the Anglo-French military action against the Suez Canal in 1956, that stimulated Issigonis to design a vehicle that would become the inspiration of every modern front-wheel-drive car from the Volkswagen Rabbit to the Honda Accord to the new GM J-car.

Called the Morris Mini-Minor, it was introduced in 1959 to an enthusiastic British public. Minuscule on the outside, with a radical snub-nosed shape, it still contained ample room for four adults inside. Issigonis had achieved this packaging miracle by mounting the small four-cylinder engine transversely, or crosswise, which reduced the overall length of the automobile by perhaps fifteen percent. And by mounting the transmission and the differential in one compact package with the power plant there was no intrusion of the mechanical components into the passenger area.

The beloved "Mini" (which spawned an age of mini-everythings, including the famed Mary Quant miniskirts) was the product of sheer genius. Unlike the committee-designed productions of the American industry, it had been created by the energies of a single man, an eccentric who refused to travel to the United States because he thought "it was too big." Issigonis had built the Mini-Minor in a reaction against what he referred to as "those goddam bubble cars," the rounded, bloated, befinned styles that were dominating the automobile industry in the 1950s.

The Mini thrived in England and Europe for over fifteen years, during which time five million of the tiny motorized skates were sold. But it was never taken seriously by U.S. designers, who did not feel the need to create midget automobiles with drivetrains that could be loaded into an overnight bag. Quite the contrary. After brief flirtations with the compact-sized Chevrolet Corvair and Ford Falcon in the early 1960s, and the Chevrolet Vega and Ford Pinto in the 1970s, Detroit returned to what they considered a God-given mandate to produce the largest, most garish, most powerful automobiles possible.

Now, after the passage of years and the continued erosion of the domestic market by Japanese automakers, GM would again try to tap the small car market with the J-car. This time, they swore, there would be no mistakes.

/////

Despite the critical nature of their assignment, Brewbaker and his J-car Project Center staff were not initially housed in the elaborate glass and steel Engineering Staff building within the 1,500 acre GM complex at Warren. There, in what had been open farmland when the Corporation took shape prior to World War I, massive structures had risen out of the flats to house Fisher Body, the General Motors Assembly Division headquarters, the Engineering Staff and Technical Center as well as the feathery, Saarinen-created Design Center, where the flamboyant vice president of the Design Staff, William Mitchell, and his successor, Irvin Rybicki, led a team of stylists who believed, with some justification, that for decades they had set the standards by which all mass-produced automobiles in the world were judged.

Each of these vast fiefdoms within the GM kingdom is separated by wide boulevards and acres of manicured lawns accented by enough reflecting pools to rival Versailles. Across busy Van Dyke Boulevard stands the mundane ten story cement box that houses Chevrolet's advertising agency, Campbell-Ewald. On the other side of the property, huddled to the south of the Technical Center on the far side of Twelve Mile Road is an old building known as the Parts Fab Warehouse. It had been constructed for the Manufacturing Development Group to test prototype parts, tooling, and equipment, but the building had now been turned over to the newly formed Project Center groups.

It was a crude, drafty, dirty place: the antithesis of the antiseptic cubicles, large and small, that traditionally house General Motors personnel. Plans had been laid for the group to move into a fresh new West Annex being constructed at the back of the Design Staff building, but for the short term, work on the J-car would be conducted in the hulking, grimy warehouse. "I considered suing General Motors if I ever caught hepatitis in that terrible old place," commented a secretary long after the move to the new annex had been made.

Brewbaker's assignment to the J-car was not his first within the Project Center. Prior to that he had labored over a pair of automobiles that represented the older days of the Corporation's involvement with small cars. He had helped "put to sleep" the infamous Vega, which had an undistinguished tenure in the marketplace from 1971 to 1977, and had also worked as chief engineer on the Chevette program. To bright young engineers like himself, the Chevette represented old thinking. It was an aged front-engine, rear-wheel drive design being laid down long after the Corporation had begun a steady shift toward front-wheel drive and instituted a radical program to down-size throughout the lineup.

Others within the Project Center were working on more daring enterprises. Some were deep into the program to reduce the size of the "B-Body," techno-jargon for the 1977 line of Chevrolet Impalas, Pontiac Catalinas, and Buick LeSabres that had fully half a ton ravaged out of their traditionally bulky bodies without sacrificing interior room. Even more exciting was the "X-car" group, a front-wheel drive compact model which was being designed as a 1979 model import fighter. Those were challenging days for the GM Engineering Staff. The young, fresh-faced elite who manned the drawing boards and the computers were aching for a fight.

For as long as anybody could remember, the sacred cow of the American automobile industry had been the "full-size family car"—

a euphemism for an oversized ark nearly eighteen feet long and weighing more than two tons. The J-car that Brewbaker and his staff were assigned to bring to market would be four feet shorter and weigh about half as much. It would have to carry four adults in comfort and produce high miles-per-gallon figures under all conditions. The various J-car models would have different sheet metal styling, mechanical parts (including engines and transmissions) and upholstery, but the core of the cars, the inner body structures to which all the individual components were attached and which cost the most money to manufacture, would be identical.

No matter where they come from—Japan, Europe or the United States—all "new" cars are an illusion. Each is a mechanical salad made up of fresh ingredients and leftovers in a specially concocted mixture. No manufacturer, even General Motors in its halcyon days, could afford to create every bit and piece of an automobile from a clean sheet of paper. Each new model is an amalgam of some fresh additions—perhaps sheet metal, or a chassis or an engine or transmission—and a package utilizing existing parts that have been in the inventory for years.

A classic example was the "revolutionary" Ford Mustang introduced by Lee Iacocca to rave reviews in mid-1964 and one of the most successful automobiles of all time. It was, quite simply, a cleverly styled rehash of existing parts used on the mundane Falcon and Fairlane models. Apart from its razzle-dazzle external sheet metal, which has made it a style setter, it was an automobile devoid of technical distinction. Similarly, the immensely popular Chevrolet Monte Carlo and Pontiac Grand Prix "personal" cars of the early 1970s were nothing more than cleverly restyled Chevelle and Tempest intermediate sedans stretched out with a long hood tacked on to create the illusion of luxury. Like most automobiles of that era they were powered by engines that had been developed in the mid-1950s. The constant restyling of aged chassis and drivetrains was as traditional in Detroit as the Michigan-Ohio State football game.

While the basic structure of the J-car body would be entirely new, Brewbaker and his staff rifled through the General Motors parts inventory in an effort to find existing components. This would save the millions of dollars that would otherwise be needed to design, tool up, and manufacture specially created pieces. Despite its billions in corporate profit, GM, unlike the Japanese, was unwilling to reinvest a major portion of its gains in research and modernization of plants.

Brewbaker was now working for a different General Motors than the Corporation that had dominated the world markets in the 1950s and 1960s, both in sales and technologically. By the middle 1960s, GM had grown complacent and had become convinced that what looked like a perpetually growing market would be satisfied with relatively cheap annual styling changes instead of real automotive innovation. Emphasis at all the American automakers had shifted away from engineering towards marketing and finance.

The old Detroit auto men, many of whom had risen to the top with grease under their fingernails, were dead or retired. Their places were taken by financial wizards, led by GM's Frederic Donner and Ford's Robert McNamara. Soon platoons of Harvard-inspired MBAs spread throughout industry management. These "bean counters," as the engineers derisively called them, were more concerned with the bottom line than with the quality of the product. It was in this environment of penny-watching that Brewbaker was challenged to create a superior car.

Cannibalizing prior GM models was an economic expedient, if the not wisest course. In planning this cannibalization, Brewbaker's team called upon their associates who were in the final stages of the X-car project. There they found a cornucopia of items that could be transferred to the J: the steering system, the front-suspension control arms, the front-wheel-drive axle joints, wheel bearings, the starter motor, generator, power-steering pump, the radiator and air conditioner compressor, and, most important, the THX 125 three-speed automatic transmission and the FX 125 four-speed manual transmission.

Brewbaker understood only too well that these cost-cutting efforts might exact a penalty on the J-car in terms of excess weight. After all, the X-cars would weigh, if everything went according to plan, about four hundred pounds more than the J's (approximately 2700 vs. 2300 pounds) and many of the components being adapted from the larger car were beefier than necessary. Still he had no choice if he was to remain within the tight budget allotted to him by a cost-wary, dividend-conscious management.

In addition to trying to integrate a collection of old and new parts into the J-car, Brewbaker was forced to act as an intermediary between the Opel engineers—who would operate their own European Project Center to develop the version to be sold outside the United States—and the various technical men from Chevrolet, Pontiac and Fisher Body. After making a number of preliminary planning trips to Ruesselsheim am Main, Brewbaker began hosting a series of meetings in his new Warren office. It was not easy. "Some of the Pontiac engineers had never even met a German engineer, much less worked with one," said Brewbaker.

While the basic automobiles to be created in Detroit and in West Germany were similar, a number of parts and components would not be interchangeable. And most important, the national attitudes toward cars that inspired the two engineering groups were distinctly different. Germany is a nation with an elitist automotive tradition, both in terms of technical detail and demands made on the driver. Driver's licenses are more difficult to obtain than in the United States, and many sections of the vast network of Autobahns have no speed limits. The driving and auto manufacturing environment is a disciplined one, out of which have come the most technically advanced automobiles in the world.

By contrast, Henry Ford and his Model T created a nation of utility drivers who wanted little more from their cars in a mechanical sense than portal-to-portal transportation. It was an egalitarian revolution in which virtually untrained drivers handling the simplest cars were suddenly granted an unprecedented mobility. The overlay of status identified with American automobiles was supplied later by Alfred P. Sloan, Jr., longtime chairman of General Motors, and his successors. Utility and glamour, not technical advancement, became the marketing tools of Detroit, particularly in the last two decades.

It has been part of Detroit's credo that Germans, and Europeans in general, want totally different automobiles than do the Americans. The Continentals, according to this thesis, are hard drivers who prefer compact, functional shapes, stiff suspensions, tight steering and no-nonsense interiors. American buyers, on the other hand, are assumed to be obsessed with luxury, a super-smooth ride, convenience items and chrome.

Ironically, both General Motors and Ford are perfectly capable of manufacturing good automobiles in the European mold. GM's Adam Opel AG and Ford of Germany have been building taut, well-fabricated, functional automobiles for years, and comparable products have come from both the GM's Vauxhall and Ford of England operations. But the American versions of the same cars have often been less impressive. That was the story of the Chevette. The Opel version made by GM in Germany was a solid machine, but its American counterpart was over-chromed and under-suspended.

So it would be with the J-cars. While Brewbaker & Company were drifting toward the old American practice of embellishing an ordinary mechanical package with bits of glitter, the German J-car would prove to be a solid, functional performer. GM believed they were coping with a harsh reality of the American market: that without the so-called "comfort and convenience" options, their products would be left to rust in the showrooms.

Isolated in their Warren and Dearborn enclaves, the American experts continued to delude themselves into thinking that the old verities of the American marketplace would prevail. In their hearts they believed that the once-sizzling love affair between Detroit and the car buyers of the nation could be rekindled.

/////

GM's "German Connection" was to play an important part in the story of the J-car but unfortunately not a winning one. The first major decison was the choice of an engine for the new J-car. Should it be a high-revving power plant like that of many of the foreign competitors or a more traditional low-revving engine, American style?

High-revving power plants have long been in vogue in Europe, where stiff taxes and even more punitive gasoline prices have placed a premium on small-displacement, high-efficiency engines. Conversely, modest gasoline prices in America have encouraged large, low-revving engines that work best with the convenient but less precise automatic transmissions.

GM set out to prove that American drivers did not require, or want, high performance engines in their small cars. "We attached hidden recorders to the engines of a few prototype J-cars," recalled Brewbaker, "and loaned them out to a bunch of employees. We chose a broad cross section: secretaries, accountants, engineers, men and women, young and old. The cars all had manual transmissions and we discovered that very few of the drivers ever exceeded 3000 rpm, almost none went beyond 4000 and only one driver—a known hot dog—ever got near 5000 rpm." In contrast, German drivers commonly rev their engines to the "red line" (the warning mark on the tachometer) and use the transmission and brakes with much greater expertise than Americans.

These studies persuaded Brewbaker and his Project Center staff that the American driving public did not want or need the same power plant as the Europeans. The fact that hi-tech engines in both German and Japanese imports were a major selling point in the United States did not seem to register. General Motors' brief survey of a handful of its employees carried more weight than the millions of customers who were deserting Detroit to buy imports. When it came to the decision on what engine would power the American J-car, the selection seemed preordained.

There were three choices available to the GM team: the "Family Two" 1.8 liter overhead camshaft four-cylinder from Opel, a compact, high-rpm power plant being manufactured by GM in Germany, Brazil, and Australia; a new V-4 overhead valve which could be created by chopping two cylinders from the V-6 engine employed in the larger X-cars; or finally a new Chevrolet-designed four-cylinder engine with the traditional overhead valve layout. The latter boasted none of such technical advances as overhead camshafts, fuel injection, aluminum cylinder blocks and head that were attracting buyers to the Honda Accords, Audi 4000's, BMW's or midrange Toyotas and Datsuns—the very automobiles that were the targets of the J-car.

"Because Chevrolet was supplying the engines for the American J-car, it was their call," said Brewbaker. Chevrolet engineer John Zwerner was the man who headed the team which would make that vital decision. The high-revving, German-designed overhead cam-shaft Family Two engine had two disadvantages, the Chevy people claimed. One was that its displacement could not be increased much beyond its 1.8 liters and therefore it was near its theoretical limits of power output, barring the addition of expensive turbochargers or superchargers. The second disadvantage was that an overhead camshaft engine has a slightly greater external length, which is a source of potential trouble when it is mounted transversely between the front wheels. An excessively long power plant can mean a limited turning circle and other complications. "When you're designing a package like this, even ten millimeters [approximately a quarter of an inch] can be critical," noted Brewbaker.

But there was another alternative that could have been called upon. Many small-displacement engines employ a system called "Siamesing," a process in which the cylinders are joined together to conserve space. By Siamesing the Family Two overhead camshaft engine, its displacement could have been increased to about two liters (122 cubic inches) and a light, strong, high-revving, lusty little engine could have been available. But, in the words of Brewbaker, "Chevy wouldn't touch Siamesing," meaning there was little choice but to employ the older pushrod model.

GM's president seemed to favor the more powerful German Family Two engine. "Pete Estes had a gleam in his eye for the overhead cam engine," Brewbaker recollected. He was not the only one. Pontiac engineers had none of their Chevrolet associates' inbred dislike of the Siamesing process and they also leaned toward the German power plant.

But they too were overruled by the Chevrolet engineers. Although the German engine would be employed by Opel for J-cars throughout the rest of the world, it was rejected for the American market. After deliberation the new J-car engine was chosen. It would be a traditional Chevrolet design, only in miniature. It would displace 1.8 liters (about 110 cubic inches). While enjoying a 12.5 percent increase in capacity over the old Chevette engine, it would be roughly equal in size and weight. The aluminum cylinder head, which was deemed costly to produce, would not be employed.

Chevrolet had been responsible for the magnificent 265 cubic inch V-8 engine in 1955, which created the efficient lightweight drivetrains that are used up to the present day. It soon became obvious that such a system would be adapted for the J-car. The fact that it was noisier, had more moving parts, and was probably incapable of revving as freely as the more contemporary overhead camshaft German Family Two version was ignored.

A number of existing components—including pistons, valves, and valve springs—could be adapted from the X-car's V-6 engine, a cost-saving measure which insured the choice. Regardless of the gleam in Pete Estes's eye, the decision to stay with time-honored Chevrolet manufacturing technology was made final. The new engine could now easily be mated with the existing X-car transmissions, both in four-speed manual form and the three-speed automatic. Both versions would be built at GM's Muncie, Indiana, transmission plant. But a five-speed manual—a standard component in all the imported competition—was rejected as not important enough to justify the perhaps $50 million needed to create the manufacturing capacity.

Yielding to one compromise after another and saving the pennies demanded by an accounting-oriented corporation, General Motors had finally decided on an engine for the new "revolutionary" J-car that was scarcely different from ones that they had been using for over twenty years.

/////

As the basic components of the J-car were being planned, a legion of GM sales, marketing, and advertising men were joining the project to learn who would buy the new automobile and why. Small cars and the people who bought small cars had been perceived as a dark force in the marketplace, somehow linked to the anarchists, Wobblies, One-Worlders, crackpot intellectuals, counterculture revolutionaries, and consumerist zanies who had been gnawing at the foundations of the business for as long as the nation had been on wheels.

"I think there is something wrong with those people who buy small cars," boomed a GM officer in the late sixties. Executives lunching at the Detroit Athletic Club after the 1972 Presidential election had laughed scornfully at the news that over 90 percent of the Saab owners in the USA had voted for George McGovern for president. To Detroit, the Saab represented the kind of quirky, anti-establishment thinking that seemed to infest the campuses and threaten corporate stability. In much the same way, the VW Microbus came to symbolize the Haight-Ashbury hippie lifestyle.

The insulated American automotive executives divided the imported-car market into three distinct and equally distasteful groups: the pinkos and the avant-garde who were vehemently anti-American; the Marin County, Fairfield County, and Main Line snobs who drove Mercedes-Benzes and Jaguars simply because they were made in Europe; and the largest bunch, the tightwad Consumers Union acolytes who were prepared to do penance in small, drab automobiles in the name of high fuel economy. Since World War II, Willys and Studebaker had gone out of business and American Motors was in desperate shape after trying to cater to that latter collection of skinflints. The Big Three had long tried to sell small spartan machines to them without real reward.

While Detroit recognized the snob appeal that generated sales for such brands as Mercedes-Benz ("It's the old thing about California wines versus French wines," stated a senior GM public relations man), they minimized the strength of that appeal in the subcompact market. Instead, American car makers attributed the rise of the Japanese manufacturers solely to their ability to import high-mileage cars with low price tags.

The evidence seemed irrefutable to Detroit. Every time there was a recession or a gasoline panic, small car sales boomed. When things returned to normal, Detroit's "family-size" machines gained customers. Yet the facts defied such schoolboy reasoning. The Chevette, for example, was as economical as most of the Japanese competition. It was as tiny, as inexpensive, and certainly as spartan. Yet, like the Fiesta from Ford and other efforts from Chrysler, its record of "conquests" (theft of customers) from the imports was terrible.

It had long been the case in Detroit. Big sellers often succeeded only in stealing customers away from another brand within their own corporate families. This was what was happening with Detroit's forays into the small car field. Its own customers were buying, but very few people were deserting the imports. A classic example of this "conquest paradox" was articulated by a Ford executive, who mused: "Since 1960, the Ford Division of the Ford Motor Company has had three sales bonanzas. First came the Falcon, then the Fairlane and finally the Mustang. When we started, we had a 23 percent share of the market and now, after all the hoopla, we've got 20 percent. So what the hell did we prove?"

If the desire for more miles per gallon was the primary motivation, how could the boom in powerful $20,000 to $50,000 Mercedes-Benzes, BMW's, and Porsches be explained, or the jump in sales of $15,000 Volvos, Saabs, Audis, Peugeots, and a number of high-line Japanese sedans which had neither the low price tags nor the mileage figures of many American cars?

Simply, it was because large segments of the market were deserting Detroit. In order to make a real determination of what was going on, the marketers did what they always do when the situation gets murky. They headed for Detroit's Metro airport and boarded a plane for Los Angeles. Southern California is to Detroit's automotive trend watchers what the Olduvai Gorge is to paleontologists. In this lotusland of car crazies and six-lane freeways, they believe, lies a Mother Lode of Truth. Detroiters periodically travel there to examine the latest automotive totems and taboos.

"They think we're all cuckoos," says a Southern California automotive journalist who has guided numerous tours for the expeditionary forces from Michigan. "They come out here once or twice a year and they shuck their gray suits and their silk ties and get on their wild plaid slacks and their Lacoste shirts and act as if they're in some nutball land of sybarites. Sure, they see all the Japanese cars, and they take note of them and mouth all the right things about California being a bellwether of trends. Then they get on the plane and go home and tell their wives what a wacky place Southern California is. They simply don't think we're part of the same nation as Michigan."

Despite their patronizing attitude, the midwesterners recognized that California was the center of the small-car culture in the

United States. They could see a prototype for the automobile of the 1980's emerging from the smog of the Los Angeles Basin. It looked for all the world like an automobile built in a smallish (the size of California), congested nation of 115 million nonwhites in another hemisphere 5,300 miles across the open sea.

It looked like an automobile that these people had decided would better fit the needs of Californians than anything being produced by the midwesterners. It looked like a Honda.

/////

In a four month span during mid-1976, Japan, Inc. had unleashed an invasion of new products on our shores: Datsun, Mitsubishi (for Chrysler), Isuzu (for Opel), Mazda, Subaru and Toyota introduced *eight* fresh new body styles and over a dozen different models for sale in the United States. But it was the Honda which sent the true import shock through the Tech Center in Warren and placed the GM engineers on the defensive. The Japanese were not only leapfrogging in small-car technology but were upgrading state-of-the-art automotive design at all levels. By the summer of 1976, when thoughts of a J-car were still embryonic, the stunning Honda Accord reached the U.S. market.

It was, by any rational measurement, a masterpiece, the work of a small Japanese firm that had not built its first car until 1962 and had essentially ignored the world arena for a decade afterward. It was a brilliant design created by the Japanese motorcycle manufacturer Soichiro Honda. His first major assault had come in 1973 in the form of the Civic, a powerful, nimble, well-built update of the Issigonis Mini-Minor. Three years later Honda introduced the Accord, a larger version of the Civic that incorporated every desirable component of small car technology. Exquisitely fabricated, with a transversely mounted overhead camshaft, high-efficiency aluminum engine, and Germanically detailed interior appointments, the Accord was immediately recognized by everyone in the business as the ne plus ultra of small cars.

It also embodied a great irony. Although the car was produced in a country where roads are the most congested of the advanced nations and where the maximum speed seldom exceeds 60 mph, the Accord was clearly inspired by the best German engineering. Its type of engine, independent suspension, five-speed transmission, disc brakes, and radial tires were superfluous in the home market, yet Honda included all of these high-technology components.

The GM technical personnel were, of course, familiar with the work of Soichiro Honda. They recognized that his Civic model, with its minuscule external dimensions, advanced-design engine, and ruggedness far out of proportion to its size, was the finest mini-car on the market. But they smugly rationalized it away as a machine too miniature and too segmented from the mainstream of the market to command their attention. Some also remembered, with irritation, how Honda had politely borrowed a Chevrolet Vega in 1974 and had returned it to GM six weeks later with Honda's own special cylinder head installed. So fitted, the Vega performed better. It would now meet the stringent EPA emissions standards, regulations so rigid that General Motors was protesting loudly in the press and in the halls of Washington that they could not be attained with the current technology.

Such setbacks were viewed as flukes by the GM engineering staff. After all, they reasoned, the Honda people had years of experience fiddling with high-output, small-displacement engines in motorcycles and tiny racing cars. Their displays of thimble-sized technology were interesting in an academic sense but were of little relevance to the big leagues of American automotive sales.

Then came the Honda Accord. This was the automobile that shook the secure base of the business from Michigan to Stuttgart. The Japanese were obviously no longer limited, either by national perceptions or commercial intentions, to the small, low-priced segment of the car market. The Accord indicated that the Japanese had not only shed their image as manufacturers of rolling tinware, but proved themselves capable of mass-producing automobiles that rivaled the quality once considered to be the exclusive property of Mercedes-Benz, BMW and Porsche.

The Accord looked exquisite even to the most unpracticed eye. Its painted surface shimmered like a miniature Rolls-Royce. The minimal chrome brightwork trim fit perfectly; the body panels appeared to have been aligned by a surgeon's scalpel. The interior upholstery and vinyl trim had the look of functional elegance normally associated with expensive European cars and executive jet aircraft. The instruments had black, high-tech faces and sharp-edged, sans-serif letters and numerals. The switches and controls worked with the precision of a fine automatic pistol. There was no evidence of the old Detroit styling tricks—phony chrome bezels, fake burled walnut instrument fascia, logotypes inspired by resorts on the French Riviera. The American "art moderne" instrument layouts that seemed to have been modeled after 1940s vintage console radios were conspicuously absent.

Although the Honda Motor Company's styling department was numerically outmanned 1700 to about 20 by the General Motors staff, they had created one of the most aesthetically pleasing car shapes in automotive history. Many critics argued that the style of the Accord had been filched from the Volkswagen Scirocco, a rakish three-door sports coupe created by the Italian design genius Giugiaro. But it was quickly shown that the Accord had been on the Honda drawing boards long before the Scirocco was introduced in 1975.

At a time when small cars were by nature tall and narrow, with skinny tires suspending stubby, bobtailed coachwork, the Accord had near-perfect proportions. This was partially a brilliant illusion. It looked larger that it was without resorting to the hoary Detroit deceptions of long hoods, chrome spears, overhanging trunks, and bulging door panels. The Accord, in fact, had very little wasted space. Its front-wheel-drive engine was mounted sideways, or transversely, to preserve interior room. While its wheelbase was half an inch shorter than the Chevette's, the Accord measured nearly two inches longer overall, which again provided additional interior room.

The Accord was also fully two inches broader in the beam than the Chevette and most other subcompacts of the day. This provided both added interior room and lent the car a substantial, somewhat brawny external appearance that belied its modest dimensions. The Accord could accommodate four adults in uncramped comfort, and thanks to its hatchback "third door" and a rear seat that could be folded down, its cargo capacity rivaled a small station wagon.

In a styling sense everything fit on the Honda, which cannot be said about much of its Detroit competition. Too many American automobiles seem to have oversized bodies perched atop four skinny wheels that protrude like chair legs from beneath the automobile. These shapes often look appealing in the styling studios, where they are sculpted in clay on flat podiums, but fail when they move toward production and wheels are put on.

The wheels on most American cars are a part of this "platform"—an existing frame containing standard suspensions, engines, and transmissions. Countless "new" automobiles can be created by dressing the same platform with different sheet metal. Sometimes these altered outfits are aesthetic triumphs; other times not. When the scheme fails, it produces car bodies that look as if they have been mistakenly draped over the wrong set of wheels.

Because it had been created as a unit, the Accord's wheels huddled inside the fender wells where they belonged. The distance between the wheels, the "track," was fifty-five inches, almost four inches wider than a Chevette and nearly as wide as some intermediate-sized models. This, coupled with four-wheel independent suspension, produced an automobile that handled well around corners, tracked straight and was relatively immune to crosswinds. If there was an automotive confirmation to the old designer's adage, "what looks right, is right," it was the Accord.

The Honda Accord was greeted with editorial huzzahs and touched off an immediate sales boom in spite of what veteran Detroit marketing experts considered to be unforgivable sins of omission. There were no options: no climate control, no interior luxury lighting group, no power radio antennas, no vinyl roofs, no automatic headlight dimmer, no station-seeking four-speaker stereo radio, no lighted vanity mirrors, no power door locks, no opera windows, no monster engine, not even an automatic transmission or air conditioning system in the early models. Honda did later relent and offer a two-speed automatic the following year and came out with air conditioning on its fancy LX version in 1978.

But the original Accord did have some thoughtful fillips that entranced the newly sophisticated public. It offered touches like a small coin tray, complete with a wire loop to hold stray bills; an indoor release for the hatchback and an electronic dashboard panel that warned against unlatched doors and burnt-out taillights. Other instruments notified the driver about low fuel, the need to change the oil and oil filter as well as to rotate the tires. Subtle refinements that seduced the automobile lover—the equal foot pressure needed to operate both the brake and clutch pedals, the silence of the four-cylinder engine, the solid latching of the doors—became evident only after longer periods of ownership. But it was obvious at first glance that these automobiles, manufactured in faraway cities like Siama and Hamamatsu, were superior manifestations of the industrial age.

There they sat, hunkered down in the showrooms like half-scale Mercedes-Benz clones, available in three solid hues of silver, red or blue and equipped exclusively with five-speed manual transmissions, mysterious devices that the Detroit marketers believed the American motoring public viewed with aboriginal suspicion. Yet unlike most domestic manuals, which were crude, tractorlike contraptions that demanded a truck driver's strength, the Honda five-speed was a mechanical symphony. Even a ham-fisted motorist weaned on the mindless glories of the Hydra-matic transmission could learn to drive it in an instant. And once acclimated, drivers easily attained consumption levels of 30-32 miles per gallon with the five-speed Accord. All this came for a list price of $3995, slightly less than the cost of a Chevette.

Not since the upper middle class and the academic community took the Volkswagen Beetle to their bosoms in the early 1950s had a small car enjoyed so much cachet. The Honda Accord was a brilliant amalgam of automotive philosophies and it was attracting an influential, upscale group of customers. J.D. Power & Associates, a highly respected California market research group, would confirm in 1981—the year the J-cars were introduced—that of the 370,000 Honda customers, 58 percent were college graduates, 20 percent held master's degrees, 7 percent were doctors of one sort or another. Moreover, over 45 percent of them belonged to households earning between $30,000 and $60,000 a year. Pecksniffs and bohemians be damned. Honda owners were real Americans, even super-Americans.

Although early models suffered from head gasket problems, fading paint, and rusting in the front fenders, demand still rose to fevered levels. The small group of Honda dealers, operating with the bare-fanged avarice that has blighted the franchised system since its origins, responded to this booming market with price-gouging. Accords were suddenly loaded down with after-market gewgaws and bolt-ons to boost their base price despite angry threats from the Japanese parent company. But the Accord was so desirable that it seemed capable of transcending any sales obstacles: bloated prices, six-month waiting lists, and minor mechanical failings.

It was a milestone automobile. As the hazy outlines of the J-car formed in the minds of the GM Engineering Staff, it became clear that if the subcompact market was to be entered, this extraordinary car would be, in the vernacular of the Project Center, the target vehicle. Brewbaker's goal was simple but unstated. Copy the Japanese mini-miracle.

The notion of regal General Motors slavishly aping an automobile designed in Japan would have been unthinkable ten years earlier. In the mid-1960s the Japanese car industry was pitiful, groping along by making bogus replicas of shopworn British designs with garish overlays of American-inspired fins and chrome. Ten years earlier everybody was copying the Americans. Even the small Mercedes-Benz 230 sedan sported vestigial tail fins until the late 1960's.

But times had changed. With the decline of the big car, Detroit had drifted into limbo and had meandered aimlessly until it reached the sorry moment, in 1976, when a group of GM engineers sat down to duplicate a Honda. A number of Accords had been purchased by General Motors and examined with the curiosity that might be devoted to an alien spaceship. Across town in Dearborn, Ford engineers were doing likewise as they laid down their somewhat smaller "World Car," the Escort, which would more closely resemble the Honda Civic. A Honda executive would later recall, "The guys in Detroit were scooping up so many Accords we finally had to cut 'em off. They were digging into our dealer allotments."

/////

There were thousands of challenges to face in competing with Japan's best, but the basic layout of the J-car was relatively simple. There are only two feasible ways to package the drive-train and the passengers within minimal external dimensions. The conventional front-engine, rear-wheel-drive arrangement consumes too much interior space. Either everything must be stuffed up front with a front-engine, front-wheel-drive setup, or the back end must be loaded with a rear-engine, rear-wheel-drive configuration. The latter had been tried with the Chevrolet Corvair in the 1960s and the gruesome memories of failure were still vivid.

The J-car would have a front-wheel-drive setup, with a transverse engine. The chassis and drive train would be laid out in a relatively conventional manner. The suspension at the front would be a MacPherson strut, which combined the coil springs and the shock absorber in a single unit to save space. The Accord used the same setup. But to save money, the rear suspension would be a solid beam axle, not an independent unit like the Honda's. It was to be still another of several myopic attempts to save petty cash that would result in a fiscal failure of enormous proportions.

At least the styling did not have to be compromised. The design would begin with a clean piece of paper. Because the car would come in four body styles—four-door, fastback, coupe, and wagon for Pontiac and Chevrolet—there was a fair amount of flexibility. The car was to ride on a wheelbase about eight inches longer than the Honda's in order to provide more interior passenger room, 101.2 inches versus the Honda's 93.7. It was to be nearly eleven inches longer overall than the Accord three-door, totalling 173.5 inches overall against 162.8 for the Honda.

With a smallish car where interior space is at a premium none of the old long-hood and overhanging trunk tricks could be employed. Conservatism was the rule. The final styling of the J-cars came out in the clay models as rather nondescript shapes in the four-door and coupe styles, featuring stubby trunks and tallish glass areas. While the fastback looked good on paper, in reality the long wheelbase coupled with the short overhang at either end gave it a strange tubular appearance that offset any aspirations to rakishness it may have had. GM had decided to play it safe. They succeeded in that, but they had failed to produce a classic, something Honda had seemingly accomplished overnight. The new J-car style, even as viewed by insiders, did not measure up to the sheet metal sleight of hand of Iacocca's ten-year-old Mustang.

The Pontiac and Chevrolet styling departments were told to add interior trim and their own grille and bumper treatments to the car. The Chevrolet grille was pleasant enough, well-integrated, and thoroughly forgettable. Pontiac took a more daring course, choosing to adapt the horizontal, twin-nostril split grille that had been a trademark of the division since the 1959 Catalinas. It was a debatable addition to the J-car, but made up in vividness for what it lacked in aesthetic appeal. Arriving as late as they did, the Cadillac stylists had little choice but to tack an innocent egg-crate effect onto their Cimarron, giving it the look of a miniaturized version of the Chevrolet Caprice.

For lack of a better idea, the interiors would be made to appear more European. The old Atwater-Kent console radio look would give way to a contemporary design, featuring dials and switches Detroit had previously reserved for sporty cars. More instruments would be used. Most domestic dashboards featured only a speedometer, a gas gauge, and a row of cheap, essentially useless "idiot lights," but the J-cars would carry space for an optional tachometer, temperature and oil-pressure gauges, and a voltmeter. These components were considered useful only to the more frivolous buyer, not to the traditional, All-American customer anxious to spend his money on lighted vanity mirrors and power door locks. But Detroit knew it would have to fight its own instincts if it was going to beat the Japanese.

Finally, after years of ignoring the carping of the automotive press, GM gave in on another Detroit holdout. Adjustable seat backs would be offered. It was Detroit's custom to equip cars with dreadful straight-backed seats and make plush power-units available only as expensive options. Ratcheted, manually operated bucket seats of the type preferred by the Europeans, and expertly adapted by the Japanese, were not considered acceptable for the American market.

GM seats were designed for what was called "the ninetieth

percentile human," a composite body style that presumably excluded only the more bizarre human shapes. In fact, these seats were ergonomically unacceptable, a deficiency that was compensated for by optional, high-profit adjustable steering wheel columns and an assortment of power seats. Finally, in the J-car, adjustable seat backs would be installed in mass-produced American cars, ten years after they had been in widespread use elsewhere.

The Accord's paint job was a source of distress to its American imitators. It had stimulated customer admiration in the showrooms, but the Fisher Body people considered it something of a "con," a brilliant patina created by a final coat of clear acrylic over the regular paint. Why not duplicate it on the J-car? Again, the consideration of cost, and lack of modern technology prevented this attractive detail from being incorporated in the J-car.

Some stringent air quality laws also made the painting process more complicated than in Japan. In the Southgate, California, plant, for example, the California Air Resources Board regulations forbade the use of anything but water-based enamel. This required more power sanding and final finishing without producing a visibly superior result. The Lordstown, Ohio plant, which was less subject to complex emissions laws, did have the capability of using two different painting processes, but, as it turned out, did not have the technical ability to duplicate the Honda finish.

As the J-car developed, the Fisher Body engineers worked hard at modernizing their painting system. They experimented with "batch painting," running a mass of cars through the painting galleries and applying the same color to all of them. These efforts, plus the decision to reduce the color selection to a relatively sparse (for Detroit) fourteen hues, helped to enhance the paint quality. Pilot models indicated that the finish on the J-car would be better than anything previously seen on smaller domestic autos. But it was evident that it would not match the external surface of the little Japanese jewel.

"Manufacturers like Honda use a clear coat, which gives them a deeper shine. We don't have that capability yet," admits Paul Tosch, who was in charge of the J-car within Fisher Body. He knew several ways to improve the paint quality on the J-cars, but all would

require additional assembly line space and of course, more investment. That was something the accounting-oriented GM management was peculiarly unwilling to do—even at this crucial point in its
corporate history.

Brewbaker and his staff took some comfort in the fact that their
undertaking was of a far greater magnitude than that of the Honda
Motor Company. If all went as planned, the Accord's entire model
run would be but a fraction of the J-cars produced worldwide. The
J-car, which was to be manufactured in a number of countries in a
multitude of permutations, involved a much more complicated
organizational infrastructure than Honda's small, single-source
manufacturing system.

Once the basic planning for the J-car had been completed, the
American Project Center and its counterparts from Opel slowly
drifted apart. The Germans would coordinate the J-car design and
production outside the United States, while Brewbaker's group
would create the basic automobile that would ultimately be sold by
all five General Motors divisions under various nameplates. First
would come Chevrolet, Pontiac and Cadillac, with Buick and Oldsmobile to enter the market with their Skyhawk and Firenza versions
in 1982. Aside from exterior styling and interior trim, the entire line
would be identical, but the sheer magnitude of coordinating production within the numerous GM Divisions created a management
nightmare for Brewbaker and his small staff of twenty-seven.

/////

Everywhere the GM executives went, they were assaulted with
accusations that cars weren't built "the way they used to be." Weary
of the complaints, they vowed that the J-car would be built right. In
the old days a flawed part could be either quietly replaced or ignored,
but with the intrusion of the consumerists and a curious government
into Detroit's midst, recalls of automobiles to replace unreliable or
unsafe pieces had become media events that qualified for the evening television news.

It was apparent that the consumer would no longer tolerate
shoddy workmanship in the domestic auto industry. Recalls, spiral-

ing maintenance costs, and rapidly decreasing used car values all tended to amplify the surge towards imports, which in the public's mind at least, were perceived to embody higher quality and workmanship.

Some of GM's old guard still failed to receive the urgent message. The General Motors front-wheel-drive X-cars were hits when first introduced in mid-1979, but they were later criticized for careless workmanship and performance flaws. The X's were recalled several times to correct weaknesses in the carburetors, steering systems, clutches, and brakes. Yet as late as 1981 Howard Kehrl, the crusty General Motors vice chairman and a thirty-three year veteran of the Corporation, thundered to *The New York Times*, "The real index of quality is what the customers say, and we've sold a million and a half of them [X-cars]—all we could make. I don't understand what this flap is all about."

But others in management did. These GM officials realized that the publicity surrounding the recalls, plus the gas station and cocktail party chatter about declining American auto quality was seriously affecting sales. It could not continue. The line would be drawn with the J-car. That automobile would represent a drastic shift in General Motors' thinking and would, come damnation, reach the marketplace with higher levels of quality than any car in recent memory. The tone of GM's campaign was set by Jim McDonald, then GM executive vice president. By the time Bob Lund delivered his Tempe introduction speech, McDonald had succeeded Pete Estes as GM President. But during the creation of the new car, he had gone on the road to repeat the message: "Business as usual is not acceptable."

New standards of what the industry called "fit and finish" would be imposed. Survey after survey, dealer input, and simple observation made it clear that American cars, especially in terms of paint, body fit, interior trim, were inferior to the best Japanese and German products. Major steps were now being taken to correct the situation.

With Brewbaker at his side, Jim McDonald, the steady corporate servant from Saginaw, Michigan, traveled to the GM plants in Lordstown, Grand Blanc, Kalamazoo, Grand Rapids, Columbus,

Flint, Saginaw and Dayton to deliver the new quality dogma. They talked to the Fisher Body staff and foremen, trudging through the noisy production galleries, looking at parts and dies and watching the line thump and hammer the bits and pieces into an endless line of car frames. Suppliers outside the Corporation were hauled into the engineering staff auditorium and given one-day seminars on quality.

At Fisher Body, Paul Tosch, a local Detroit boy large enough to play middle linebacker for the Lions, took the mandate seriously. As the chief engineer for Fisher on the J-car project he was responsible for the proper design and manufacture of a number of pieces—everything from body panels to window trim to seat springs. New manufacturing techniques were being developed: laser-beam scanners and gamma-ray inspection devices, as well as thirty-six new robot welders to assemble the bodies. The subassemblies had been radically simplified to eliminate bad fit and misalignment. For example, the four-door body side panel (called a "ring") was to be made out of a single piece of sheet steel rather than the old patchwork of three to four stampings employed on most Detroit-built automobiles.

The J-cars would have "unit bodies," built in one integrated package rather than the traditional rail chassis upon which the body is mounted. While the manufacturing process is more complicated, the technique produces a stronger, lighter, more rigid container, less prone to rattles, and with improved crashworthiness, the ability to withstand impact. There would be more automation used in the construction of the J-car. It was intended, as Tosch put it, "to eliminate operator sensitivity," technocratic jargon for worker carelessness that results in sloppy welds, badly misaligned panels and ill-fitting doors.

"The Japanese have no advantages in a technological sense," Tosch said. "In fact, both the Japanese and the German workers do lot of 'messing.' For example, jockeying with a door skin to make it fit. With the J-car, tools will do it." The new car was also designed so that body panels would be joined with a silicone bronze technique which eliminated the old grinding marks to be found in lead solder. That in turn meant more precise joints and smoother paint.

Tosch and his Fisher engineers were trying hard to eliminate the sloppy trim that seemed to disfigure so many recent American cars.

The stylists had cooperated, shucking the traditional brightwork that surrounded the windshield and replacing the old chrome bumpers. The stainless steel trim around the side windows was mitered at the corners rather than overlapped, a time-honored Detroit trick that cut costs and tolerated less precision. The so-called end caps, separate pieces of plastic or metal mounted on the end of the rear fender quarter panels to hide bad fits, were rejected. The new and costlier die-stamping machines would have to produce perfect panels.

These new methods for better fit and finish on the J-cars were first tested at Fisher's Plant 21 in the Warren complex. Small numbers of Cadillac Fleetwood stretched limousines were normally built there, but they had been displaced by a small pilot production line to test the new quality system for the J-car. The underbodies had been built at Lordstown, where 100,000 square feet of extra production space had been added to accommodate the special presses and welders for the J-car.

The initial run of 125 units was then trucked to Plant 21, where Fisher jigged, welded, trimmed, and painted the complete car before sending it along to the GM assembly facility at Flint to have engines, transmissions, individual divisional labels, and interior upholstery attached. These pilot automobiles, built two years before introduction, would be used for sales and marketing evaluation, government safety and emission certification, advertising photography, and endless test runs at the Corporation's Milford, Michigan, proving ground.

But before they were released from Tosch's grip in Plant 21, each piece underwent an unprecedented, merciless inspection. Although suppliers had been repeatedly warned, some were still shipping in shoddy, badly fitted components. These parts were yanked off the cars and tossed on the floor, where they lay until the manufacturer sheepishly appeared to scoop them up and haul them home. "When we told the suppliers we weren't going to compromise on quality, some of them believed us and some of them didn't," confided a senior engineer.

Sadly the system had been so lax for so many years that it could not be changed by edict. Not only were hundreds of suppliers inured to the old ways, but General Motors itself was swollen with personnel who seemed mystified by the notion that quality could be improved. For all the preproduction rejections and the cajoling and the endless lectures and pep talks by McDonald and others, Bob Brewbaker knew that more production delays due to sloppy workmanship lay ahead.

/////

Regardless of the mountainous problems that were involved in getting the J-cars into actual production, final approval of the preproduction prototypes had to come from top management. It came at the Mesa, Arizona proving grounds in February of 1979, two years prior to the J-car's press preview. It was a pivotal moment in the checkered history of the automobile. A planeload of General Motors brass was flown out from Detroit, and, after being delayed by bad weather and a rainstorm that lashed the Phoenix Sky Harbor Airport, they were driven to the complex east of the city. Heading the entourage was Pete Estes himself, a gangling, swarthy man who, with his cropped mustache and firm manner, more closely resembled a retired brigadier than the president of a motor company.

They liked to say that Pete had "gasoline in his veins," a standard industry cliche which distinguishes the product-oriented men from the financial experts who traditionally sit in the Chairman's seat. Accompanying Estes and McDonald were two division general managers, Bob Lund of Chevrolet, and William E. "Bill" Hoglund of Pontiac, and Frank J. Winchell, engineering staff vice president, a crusty career engineer who in defending the American auto industry and its steadily weakening position could marshal a brilliant battery of facts and figures in support of why exactly the opposite should be taking place. Like so many men in Detroit, Winchell was a gritty conversationalist who could bludgeon doubters of General Motors' ultimate wisdom into submission. In recent years he was more often called upon not to trumpet its victories but to justify its defeats.

Eight new J-Car prototypes equipped with everything except nameplates were awaiting the delegation at Mesa. The "ride and drive" would be a six-hour tour of the mountains to the north, over the Mazatzal Range and through the Fort Apache Indian Reservation. Stops were made and drivers were switched. Everyone got a chance to drive the various models, the sedans, coupes and wagons that Brewbaker and Masch and the other engineers had so carefully prepared for the journey. Only the representatives of Cadillac, who did not enter the J-car program until a year later, were absent.

Following the ride and drive, the group retired to the Scottsdale Hilton for an evaluation session. "There was no major concern. Everyone was quite pleased," recalled Brewbaker, who was relieved that the expedition had gone off without a breakdown or other crisis. "There was some sensitivity to the level of performance," he said, but noted that in the winter of 1979 the Iranian crisis was at full pitch and everyone was distracted by the challenge of maximum fuel mileage. "Two years later, when the car was introduced, gasoline prices had stabilized, consumer attitudes had changed, and people were more 'foxy,' you know, a little more aggressive about the way they drove. But then the whole emphasis was on fuel economy," Brewbaker added.

Because of that fact, and Estes' repeated satisfaction with what he enigmatically called "the feel of fuel economy," the generally flaccid performance of the J-car was forgiven. Moreover, the engineers present assured the executives that the Cavaliers and J-2000's they had just labored up the grades would outperform the rival Datsuns of the day and even the target vehicle, the Honda Accord.

What they did not consider as they sipped their vodka and tonics in the Scottsdale Hilton, was that Honda was planning to introduce an eye-popping little four-door sedan with internal and exterior dimensions almost identical to the J-car four-door, and an up-sized (from 1.6 to 1.8 liters) version of its four-cylinder engine that would easily outperform the J-car with no penalty in fuel economy. In addition, a whole new line of Accords now in the prototype stage in Japan would enter the market less than six months after the planned J-car introductions.

This self-assured group of American executives was expressing their satisfaction with an automobile which, had it been introduced to the public that very day, would have represented, at best, barely contemporary small car thinking. They failed to anticipate the energy of the Japanese, who would produce such dazzling entrants in the small-car wars as the Nissan Maxima and Stanza, the new Accords, the Toyota Cressida, Celica, and Tercel, and the Mazda 626, in the intervening two years before the J-car's introduction, or shortly thereafter. The GM brass in Scottsdale was unknowingly toasting an automobile that was, in essence, already obsolete.

/////

How did they come to be so deluded? One reason is the self-congratulatory market research technique called "Product Clinics," which seem arranged mainly to justify marketing decisions already made by top management. At the Tempe, Arizona, introduction of the J-cars in 1981, Chevrolet general manager Bob Lund told the assembled press that the Cavalier was the perfect response to the dreams of a great cross section of potential buyers.

He had the data to prove it, at least the type of faulty research data car manufacturers had been using for years. "I'm sure you know about product clinics," Lund began, addressing the press. "You bring specially selected people together and ask them in a lot of different ways what they think of the product. You line up a selection of cars, and you ask these people what they like or dislike about them.... It's a very scientific operation.... We've had three Cavalier clinics in the past two years, involving some seven hundred buyers, and we'll do at least one more before the car goes to market. That's twice as many as we had for Citation. The participants represented a very carefully selected cross section of the Cavalier market. Equal numbers of men and women. Half of them currently own foreign cars. Median age about thirty-five. Income ranges upward from $25,000 a year. These people tend to know cars. They read your magazines, they know what they like and don't like. And if I may say so, they love the Cavalier.

"In a clinic last month, for example, right here in Phoenix, ninety-nine people were exposed to five Cavaliers and five competition vehicles, including a Datsun 310, a Toyota Corolla, and a Honda Accord. They were asked to rate every car in some three dozen categories. And to say we were gratified with the results is an understatement."

What Bob Lund did not reveal was that at no time during the three Cavalier clinics (the others were held in San Diego and Houston) did any of the participants ever get a chance to *drive* the cars. And no one was told how much they would cost. A captive audience had been exposed to a group of imported cars, most of which they had seen on a thousand streets, and a few sparkling new Cavaliers which were the central source of excitement. Primped and highly polished, pre-production prototypes are vastly superior to off-the-track vehicles. Is it any wonder they got high marks, especially when none of the examiners had the vaguest idea how they behaved in the real world or what they cost?

"To do a really proper clinic, you need several hundred people on site for four or five days, with all of them driving the cars for extended periods of time," confesses a senior GM researcher. "A program like that costs at least $200,000 and we didn't spend that kind of money on the J-car." Had this been done, it is possible that there would have been valuable feedback on the lack of power and acceleration in the Cavalier. As to the price of the automobile, it was only noted that, like its performance, it "would be competitive" with the imports. As it turned out, neither claim was true.

By the time the car was actually driven by GM management, and discussed at the Scottsdale Hilton, Pete Estes's "feel of fuel economy" had become an absurdity. But no one at the meeting wanted to make such an admission. "High mileage was a major factor in creating the car the way we did," said a senior Chevrolet marketer later. "It got greater emphasis than performance, because of the world condition in 1978-79, when major development was being finalized. We got the mileage, but not the performance."

To be sure, the Environmental Protection Agency's much-repeated mileage estimates for the J-car looked impressive: 26 mpg for the city, 42 mpg for the highway. But the EPA figures for all cars were being widely denounced by everyone who understood automobiles. The statistics had, in fact, originated as by-products of the EPA emissions tests, in which all automobiles sold in the U.S. must be certified by a simulated drive on the EPA's special dynamometer at its Willow Run, Michigan, test facility. The test involves mounting the automobile on a stationary stand and "driving it" by computer, which accelerates, slows down, brakes, and stops over a simulated 7.5 mile route to determine the level and type of exhaust emissions.

When the busy bureaucrats discovered that the emissions test run also produced a miles-per-gallon readout, they began publicizing the results, although nothing in their mandate gave them any such responsibility. The EPA mileage figures became a kind of impartial benchmark for the industry even though they were unrelated to real-world driving, ignoring as they did wind resistance, tires, suspensions, driving techniques, weather, altitude, and other variables. The advertising agencies quickly embraced the EPA numbers because they were generally fifteen to twenty percent better than anything that could be obtained by all but an expert driver in a flawlessly tuned automobile.

By those measurements the J-cars looked magnificent. But the realities of the highway produced different results. Because of their lack of power, the J's had to be driven with substantially more vigor in order to obtain reasonable levels of acceleration, which in turn produced lower mpg figures. The testers, operating on the open road as opposed to the artificial confines of the EPA laboratories, later found that the J-cars would produce more in the range of 25-28 mpg than 42 mpg. *Road & Track* received a reading of no better than 22 mpg with a fully loaded Cadillac Cimarron J-car that had the decidedly un-subcompact weight of 2885 pounds.

The official General Motors specifications listed with the Motor Vehicle Manufacturers' Association showed the weights of the various J-car models to be in the 2380-2500 pound range. But these were numbers for "base models" not equipped with automatic transmissions, air conditioning, and other common options that could easily add several hundred extra pounds.

Weight is the implacable enemy of performance and economy. The more bulk to be accelerated and stopped, the more power and fuel to be consumed. Judging by figures for the Honda and other rivals, the J-cars were from 300 to 400 pounds overweight. That, coupled with their anemic engines, resulted in an automobile that was neither fast nor frugal.

Brewbaker and his staff chose to celebrate their failure in a strange engineering cant. They reached deep into their thesaurus of techno-jargon and began talking about "mass efficiency" and "mean efficiency curves," a brave corporate effort to deal with the excess bulk of the J-car.

"This is a complex issue," said Brewbaker. "For example, we didn't use aluminum wheels or cylinder heads for cost reasons. Our piece costs forced us to use off-the-shelf parts—steering units, alternators, transmissions, control arms—that were somewhat heavier. Then the individual divisions loaded their cars with different options and acoustic levels. But in terms of weight we are lighter than a BMW 320i [a German sports sedan priced from $15,000 to $17,000 that is much faster than the J's, while being about as economical in gasoline consumption]. But," he added, "we have trouble stacking up to a Honda Accord."

Brewbaker insisted, however, that the chassis strength, the reduced road and wind noise and greater trunk and interior capacity of the J-car were offsetting features that equalized the two automobiles in terms of overall mass efficiency. "Actually we're about 60 kilograms [132 pounds] over what they are and what we want, but if you take all the competition, we're right on the mean efficiency curves."

Despite the jargon, the J-cars were too heavy and everybody knew it. Brewbaker & Co. were planning to equip the heavier Cimarron and some Cavalier models with aluminum hoods to reduce their bulk, but the inherent design of the J-car simply precluded much in the way of serious slimming. "Sure, the car is heavier than we expected," admits Roger Masch at Chevrolet. "It was a cumulative problem." He speaks of the need to add special components to the bumpers to comply with Federal standards, as if this were a unique burden laid on Detroit alone. While bemoaning government intrusion into the auto business as a reason for its overall troubles, the American car industry has ignored the fact that imported car companies had to develop the *same* emission and safety components for their automobiles.

"I guess you could say the Japanese have been more mass

conscious than we have," admits Brewbaker. He describes their tradition of building small, light, efficient cars, noting that Detroit has had to change its philosophy of design—one in which weight and size were not as critical. "It's a lot easier to make a component larger than it is to reduce it in size. That's what we're having to do, and it doesn't happen overnight."

/////

In spite of its weight problem, the J-car would have to be built, and built in large numbers, if it was to become Lund's weapon to drive the imports into the sea. This meant a complex operation that would have to begin at Lordstown, Ohio, where parts from hundreds of suppliers would be funneled into both the Fisher Body plant and the adjacent General Motors Assembly Division facility, which would turn out the completed product.

Accumulating an inventory of parts from all over the country, even overseas, was a nightmarish task involving a vast transportation network and a warehousing operation that placed GM at a distinct disadvantage with the Japanese. Engines had to come from Flint, Michigan and Tonawanda, New York; transmissions from Ypsilanti, Michigan; power steering units from Saginaw, Michigan; bumpers, lights, and plastic bits from the Guide Division in Anderson, Indiana; hoses and engine mounts from Inland in Dayton, Ohio; carburetors from Rochester Products in Rochester, New York; radiators from Harrison Radiator in Lockport, New York; radios and electronic engine controls from Delco Electronics in Kokomo, Indiana; bearings from New Departure-Hyatt in Sandusky, Ohio, as well as manual clutch components from as far away as Brazil.

In addition to the parts produced within the General Motors empire, dozens of components—from tires to body side moldings to emblems—were manufactured by outside suppliers. Chevrolet alone had contracts with 7500 other companies; the Corporation with over 30,000. Although not all these firms provided parts for automobiles, the sheer magnitude of purchasing control was a burden for GM, even at the best of times. Compared with the Japanese way of conducting business, which placed most of the suppliers cheek-byjowl with the manufacturing facilities, the setup was grossly inefficient.

The Lordstown facility had to keep a ten-day supply of components on hand, which entailed added costs in handling and storage. "Some of the parts are handled up to thirty-two times before they actually end up on the automobile," said Masch.

Such disadvantages had been built up over a period of almost half a century and they could hardly be altered in time for the new J-car. Brewbaker's manufacturing strategy involved going into production at Lordstown on March 2, 1981, with Southgate to begin two weeks later. Leeds, Kansas would start producing Pontiacs early in October. Cavaliers and J-2000's would be assembled at Lordstown while Cimarrons would be manufactured exclusively at Southgate, where Cadillac had erected a building to give its cars a final primping before being shipped.

Lordstown was a modern plant which had been radically updated in the late 1960s in order to produce one hundred cars per hour, courtesy of large automatic spot-welding rigs and other advanced mass-production technology. In the late 1960s, John Z. DeLorean, then Chevrolet general manager and nearing the height of his reputation as the industry's Renaissance man, had instituted a rigid quality control program at Lordstown involving banks of computers and a sizable staff of inspectors and line workers. The car was to be the Chevrolet Vega, GM's first small-sized "import fighter." Although he privately denounced the Vega as badly designed, it was DeLorean's intention to overcome its intrinsic weaknesses through excellent fabrication.

A general UAW strike cut early production of the Vega when it was introduced in September of 1970. A month later the Lordstown plant was taken out of Chevrolet's control and transferred to the General Motors Assembly Division. Although GM denies it, some observers speculate that this was done to intertwine the Division with the Corporation more deeply so that they could not be separated by government antitrust action. GMAD quickly fired seven hundred blue collar men, mostly DeLorean's crew of inspectors and extra line workers, immediately converting the Lordstown plant into a national media symbol for the dehumanizing aspects of the modern automobile assembly line.

The UAW screamed about a work speedup with seven hundred fewer workers. The press spoke of the "Lordstown Syndrome," and the union responded with an acrimonious three-week strike in early 1972. From that point on Lordstown was a disaster. The cars being manufactured there set new standards for low quality.

A Chevrolet dealer recalls a tour he took through Lordstown in 1976, when the plant was producing the Monza, a fastback derivative of the Vega. "It was unbelievable. Nobody was working very hard. Dozens of people were just standing around. I saw one woman on the line who was supposed to be attaching trim molding. She was putting it on behind her back, like a basketball player. Just slapping it on as if she didn't give a damn. Which she didn't."

This time it would be different. More robots and a newly instituted labor relations program would ensure that. This program, being touted by GM as QWL (Quality of Work Life), was intended, like the Japanese system, to give the workers more decision-making power in the manufacturing process, thereby stimulating loyalty and pride. The planned production rate for the J-cars would be reduced to seventy-five per hour, and DeLorean's obsession with inspection would be carried a step beyond with the use of lasers and gamma-ray probes. If components were not correct, there would be no more "running changes" as in the old days. The assembly line would be *stopped* until things were fixed.

The first delay in production involved the engines. The initial batches arrived from the Flint engine plant with some serious imperfections. This was difficult to comprehend, since the engine men had ostensibly instituted their own quality tests, including running the units at operating temperatures as well as electronically checking bearings, valve clearance, and ignition. The Flint assembly line had also been modified to accommodate full engine teardowns, a first in the industry. Still, batches of engines arrived in Lordstown with major flaws. Connecting rod bearings did not fit properly, bolts were incorrectly torqued, pistons slapped noisily against the cylinder walls, and thermostats were faulty. All these units were quickly quarantined and sent back to Flint by the freight-carload.

Tosch and his people at Fisher Body were in the meantime

rejecting the ratchet mechanism in the seat recliner as being too noisy and sending badly designed rear window wipers for the station wagons back to the suppliers. Worst of all, the polyurethane nose-pieces for the Type-10 Cavalier CL Hatchback (named with an obvious reference to sex symbol Bo Derek) were lumpy and rippled. This was the sportiest car in the line, designed to compete against such Japanese models as the 200SX Datsun, the Honda Prelude, and the Mazda RX-7. But the moldings were so crude that production of the model was delayed for over a month and the car did not arrive in quantity at the dealerships until midsummer.

The front-suspension grease fittings were imperfect. In the past, this would have been corrected by a running fix, that latter-day manifestation of American know-how that had made it possible for the nation's farms and automobiles, even its World War II war machine, to operate on baling wire and a legendary streak of Yankee ingenuity. But running fixes would not do this time. With each discovery of a flawed part the Lordstown assembly line shuddered to a halt. Trucks were loaded with the rejected pieces and the workers waited patiently until the correct components were ready.

It was a slow, frustrating, alien experience for the managers and foremen who had been used to seeing the assembly lines operate like runaway freight trains: unstoppable torrents of steel and plastic roaring through the factory. In the old days the line could only be stopped by a strike, a recession, an annual model change, or the outbreak of war. Now the day had come when the assembly line was shut down because a side molding didn't fit.

/////

The J-cars were being sold under different trademarks, but they were actually products of "nameplate engineering." The Cavaliers and Pontiacs coming down the line were virtually the same automobile with different brand labels. GM, Ford, and Chrysler had been doing this for years, but it apparently did not upset most consumers who were used to paying several hundred dollars more for a Mercury, Buick, Oldsmobile, Dodge, or Chrysler than for a clone from Ford, Chevrolet, Pontiac or Plymouth. But it did complicate the manu-

facturing process and multiply the chances for shoddy workmanship, including such practices as installing a piece incorrectly, then
bashing it into place with a blunt instrument.

Specifically, the Chevrolet Cavaliers and Pontiac J-2000's would
receive different front end treatments, interiors, external brightwork, suspension bushings, stabilizer bars, shock absorber settings,
and in some cases, steering ratios. Otherwise they would be mechanical twins to be separated not by technology or design, but by
image advertising and, most important, by that final arbiter of the
marketplace, the price of the car.

As Lordstown was gearing up to make the cars, corporate marketing and financial experts in Detroit were trying to set prices.
Through the magic of research, the marketing experts believed they
had discovered a new generation of car buyers who didn't like to shop
"price." These consumers had somehow transcended the age-old
contest between the silver-tongued salesman, resplendent in his
exploding supernova tie and houndstooth sport coat, and the crafty
consumer haggling over the cost of optional opera windows.

The Japanese were once again the model. The Honda was being
sold in American showrooms as a "complete car," with an option list
you could write on a book of matches. It sat there completely
trimmed with only a few extras available from the dealer—air
conditioning, custom wheels, and fancy radios. This Japanese marketing concept had accidentally come about by the exploitation of a
major weakness in their distribution system. The five- to eight-
thousand-mile gap between Japanese factories and their U.S. dealerships made it necessary to ship complete automobiles to the
United States. Delivering a specially built car with an optional
tufted-brocade interior, moon roof, and remote control trunk lid,
would have taken months and led the Japanese down the same
garden path as the Detroiters. It would have required the creation of
a manufacturing and distribution system that dealt in literally
millions of different varieties of the same basic model.

It was quite a departure from the traditional American technique
of offering a low-priced "base" car with enough high-profit options
to nearly double the price, and quadruple the profit. A Yale physicist
whimsically calculated that a 1965 Chevrolet, offered in 46 models,

32 different engines, 20 transmissions, 30 colors, and 400 options, could be purchased in almost as many permutations as there are atoms in the universe. And here was the Honda Accord carving out a large niche in the marketplace in a few basic styles and three colors.

As a result, GM marketing men now reasoned, the public was learning to buy cars differently. Seeking to analyze Japanese strengths and to cushion top management from their failings, the experts managed to produce data that turned upside down everything GM knew about marketing. The Japanese imports ostensibly enjoyed a major advantage because of their higher sticker price, fully loaded cars, and modest availability of models. The fact that the domestic industry had let its lineup proliferate to the point that there was no brand loyalty (What is a Citation? A Mirada? An Electra?) and no cohesion in prices (a loaded Chevrolet Caprice Classic could cost more than a base Cadillac Coupe de Ville) was somehow ignored. It was determined that the solution was quite simple: The Japanese experience showed that small car buyers wanted high-quality complete cars which they could buy without wasting valuable time poring over option lists. If GM was going to imitate the Honda, why not pick up its marketing tricks as well?

The J-cars would, in theory, be as simple to purchase as the Honda. But even that was not to be. In the case of Chevrolet and Pontiac the theme was instantly compromised by the presence of four body styles and five different trim levels, two for Chevy, three for Pontiac. Only the Cadillac remained relatively faithful to the import concept by offering a single four-door version.

Ignoring the harsh message sent by consumers to the Chrysler Corporation when it introduced its initially high-priced K-cars in the fall of 1980, GM chose to purge the J-car line-up of the traditional base model, a shameless, bare bone loss leader which could be advertised purely for its bargain-basement price. Chrysler had quickly learned that customers experienced "sticker shock" when they encountered the early well-equipped K's, and speedily reverted to the old sales technique of offering an inexpensive, stripped model as part of the line. But GM forged ahead, choosing to promote and sell complete J-cars for relatively high base prices.

The launch was set for May 1981, specifically the fourteenth day of the month, when the aromatic breezes of spring would prompt buyers to end their hibernation and head for their nearest dealership in a buying frenzy. Introducing cars out of the normal autumn season had happened twice before. First Ford broke the hallowed tradition by launching the Mustang in May 1964 to an unprecedented response. Then the X-cars received a joyous reception when they were unveiled in the spring of 1980. GM hoped to duplicate these off-season successes. The marketers considered the spring to contain a six-week window from mid-April to late May when a new model could be successfully thrust into the public arena. During that period, men—and now a growing body of women—would be on the prowl, their wallets bursting with the rewards of dark winter's labors and their heads mildly fevered by nature's rebirth.

As with a space shot, the timing was critical. Launch too soon and the malaise of winter would keep people inside. Delay too long and the eager buyers would be replaced by frugal legions of June bargain hunters who knew that dealers would soon be discounting current models in preparation for the new lines due in autumn. Any major sales promotion had to be wedged in between. The J-car would have to be rolling off the assembly line in quantity by mid-March in order to fill the pipeline with the necessary levels of dealer inventory and spare parts.

Lordstown and Southgate would need to pump out perhaps 50,000 cars to assure that the approximately 9000 dealers (6000 Chevrolet, 3000 Pontiac and a small quantity of exclusive Cadillac dealers) would have sufficient inventory. If the introduction missed the May deadline and had to be postponed until autumn, the assembly plants would have to be closed for the summer, or a glut of cars would be created in the interim.

Because of the manufacturing delays, the choice was clear: either introduce the car in May with insufficient dealer inventory or wait until September when there would be too much. It was standard Detroit theory that automobiles had to be present in the showroom in order to make sales. Buyers appeared to have no patience or vision. Detroit was convinced that American consumers insisted on instant gratification, ignoring the example of thousands of devoted Honda buyers who were patiently waiting six months or more for their small silver chariots.

The Lordstown line moved along spasmodically through March until the situation became critical. While the public announcement date had been set for May 14, it was now apparent that not enough cars could be built by then to even minimally stock the dealers. Television time had been reserved, and more press previews had been scheduled. Internal postponements began to multiply. Jim Williams changed the date of his daily press preview invitations three times. Finally he told Bob Lund, "You sign the invitations. You're the only one they'll believe at this point."

While the final pricing and production policies were slowly evolving in Detroit and Lordstown, the sales organizations of Chevrolet, Pontiac, and Cadillac were revving up for yet another round of cheerleading designed to put dealers into a selling mood. During April, each of the Divisional National Zones (42 for Chevy, 27 for Pontiac) conducted special "ride and drive" clinics in which each dealer was exposed to several days of tub-thumping to generate enthusiasm for the automobile.

"This system is so archaic as to be laughable," says a major Chevrolet dealer and a former General Motors executive. "Here's the way it works. The zone people will usually rent some big suburban hotel—a Hilton or a Marriott or something—and haul all the area dealers in for several days. The whole thing is scripted in Detroit. So you'll get the zone merchandising manager, who was probably just transferred in from the truck division somewhere and who knows less about the automobiles than the dealers, standing up there *reading* a prepared script against a slide show. You know how it goes... the guy is reading 'and the new car features optional bucket seats' and then he comes to a place where it says 'Pause' and waits for his assistant who's running the projector to flash up the next slide. They've been doing it for years, with practically the same scripts. The only surprise is whether you get the meat loaf or rubber chicken for dinner."

The J-car was hardly excepted from this banal procedure. "At least Pontiac ran some tough seminars and testing on their salesmen to make sure they were well versed on the technical aspects of the J-2000," says one dealer. "They recognized that the import buyers were generally much more knowledgeable about the mechanical parts of the automobile. But Chevrolet completely dropped the ball. Their presentations were awful. Stilted beyond belief. It was all they could do to keep people awake."

After driving the automobiles one dealer reported what he considered to be a case of self-delusion. "The reactions of many of the dealers seemed forced," he reports. "They appeared to be behaving the way they felt they should. Some of them who hadn't been exposed to the imports were excited, but the ones who understood the Hondas and Toyotas could put the J-car into perspective." Said another dealer, "It was the best job GM had done in a long time but was still three bricks short of a load."

The price of the J-car was still a corporate secret. The trade press—including the weekly *Automotive News*, the industry bible, and *Ward's Reports*—had been hinting that the base price of the Cavalier would be in the range of $6,800, with the J-2000 several hundred dollars more expensive. This figure would have placed the cars in direct competition with the target vehicle, the Honda Accord hatchback. In January, another trade magazine, the generally reliable *Ward's Auto World*, had guessed, probably with the aid of hints from GM, that the base Cavalier would cost about $5,900. As it turned out this number was utter whimsy.

By early April it was obvious that not enough cars could be manufactured to meet the May 14 deadline. Corporate communications writer Alvie Smith and his staff prepared a major news release for corporate public relations vice president John McNulty. Datelined April 7, it would deal with President Jim McDonald's breakfast speech that morning to the Engineering Society of Detroit on the subject of GM's born-again faith in quality. According to the release, McDonald said: "GM is slightly behind its planned acceleration schedule for building its new J-cars—to be introduced next month—because we just weren't satisfied with the quality of materials coming into the plant. Quality is so important that we've rejected entire shipments even though it meant slowing down production. And we'll continue to do that because we can't afford to tolerate below-standard effort."

What he did not tell his breakfast companions was that a press statement was ready for release the following day in which GM would announce the postponement of the J-car introduction a full week, to May 21. It would also admit that Lordstown production was thirty percent behind schedule. The release quoted "General Motors spokesman" Harold Jackson, who was in fact a public relations staff member in charge of sales and marketing. The reason for the delay, the release repeated, was the Corporation's new commitment to quality: The rejection of numerous components had slowed early production.

A one-week delay did not sound significant. How could seven days effect the introduction of an automobile that had been seeping into the public awareness for over six months? In reality it was very serious. The General Motors Executive Committee was faced with a hard choice: either launch the car on May 14 as originally planned and have the dealerships practically bare of cars or wait a week until the pipeline could be more nearly filled.

The risk of waiting was obvious. A national and regional media campaign was set for the fourteenth. Chevrolet's advertising agency, Campbell-Ewald, and Pontiac's D'Arcy-MacManus & Masius were poised with advertising blitzes designed to have every man and woman on the North American Continent salivating over the J-cars. Cavalier would literally honk its way into every American living room with Campbell-Ewald's plan to "roadblock" network television by purchasing the same televison commercial slots in prime-time viewing hours on CBS, ABC, and NBC. This made it probable that about eighty percent of the viewing audience—or perhaps as much as forty percent of the entire population—would be simultaneously exposed to the virtues of the Chevrolet Cavalier.

Chevrolet would use the "Complete Car" theme, while the Pontiac pitch was centered on the rather vague concept that a J-2000 buyer would be opening the door to all manner of "excitement" in his otherwise mundane life. The Corporation lumped the sizable marketing and advertising expense into a budgetary gunny sack labeled "consumer influence," which included everything from $200,000 per minute television spots to printed matchbooks for dealers.

Both *Time* and *Newsweek* were planning major coverage in their

May 11 issues, as were other first-rank magazines and newspapers. Television and radio commercial time had been blocked out and contracted for; newspaper and magazine ads were scheduled; direct mail and point-of-sale promotions were set for the week of May 14 and would be carried out whether there were cars in the showrooms or not. GM faced the risk of lathering up the population a full week before there were cars available, but it was considered a better alternative than further delay.

The big transports that rolled into the dealerships across the country were loaded not only with shiny new J-cars but with packages of harsh, unpleasant truth. Only about half the dealers would have J-cars in stock by May 21, and larger allotments were being given to the higher-volume franchises while many of the smaller franchises (called "stores") would have to wait even for their floor models.

The dealers, like the customers, were about to face more than delay. There was a traumatic case of sticker shock. The cheapest Cavalier would hit the dealerships with a tag of about $6,800, meaning that by the time a customer paid taxes, registration fees, and dealer prep, the car would cost well over $7,000. Even these prices might have been competitive, but when the trucks were unloaded there were no $6,800 Cavaliers or $7,000 J-2000's. There were $8,000 models without air conditioning and plenty of heavily equipped high-line four-doors and station wagons for over $10,000, but nothing in the range to vie competitively with Honda.

In May 1981, a Honda three-door with a list price of $6,999 could be driven home, licensed and full of gas, for about $7,200. The exquisitely styled Accord four-door, which had been introduced after the J-car was in the development stage, cost about $7,800 to $8,200, depending on options and dealer markup. In general, this handicapped the J-cars by $1,500 to $2,000 for comparably equipped models, and even more against the somewhat less elaborate Datsuns, Toyotas, Mazdas, and Subarus.

In fact, a completely equipped Cavalier CL sedan or Pontiac J-2000SE could easily command $11,000, and a Cimarron, with a few options, could nudge $14,000. To American car buyers, whose cortexes were branded with the notion that quality and prestige can be weighed by the pound, numbers like these were bound to be a shock. Some skeptics fretted that buyers would instantly notice that the somewhat larger X-car Chevrolet Citations and Pontiac Phoenixes could often be bought for less than the J's. After years of yammering about how big cars were the best buys, how were dealers going to sell these expensive dwarfs?

Much of the problem was of their own doing. General Motors had put themselves in a trap through their worship of the old option game, the trick that had once made them rich but that was now backfiring with a vengeance. By 1983, a sporty Chevrolet Cavalier Type 10 Coupe J-car could have come to market with a base list price of $6549 which would have been in striking range of its Japanese rivals. But GM could not resist loading up its J-cars with extravagantly priced, high-profit extras that boosted the vehicle's cost to often-astronomical levels.

A "well-equipped" Type 10 delivered to the showroom might well include air conditioning ($625), a "custom-interior package" ($696), power windows ($180), aluminum wheels ($272), stereo radio and cassette player ($455), power steering ($199), and cruise control ($170). Along with other small amenities—tinted glass, color-keyed floor mats, intermittent windshield wipers, rear window defogger, sports striping, comfort-tilt steering wheel and a heavy-duty battery—this new subcompact came to $10,937.36. It was now a "complete car," but one priced out of the market.

Ironically, the two options that are the most popular with import-minded buyers—a five speed transmission and an improved suspension system— were not made standard equipment on the J even though they were available at minimal cost. The superior transmission cost a mere $72 and the improved suspension, which provides a much firmer ride and more precise steering, was only $49.

While the national media blitz for the J-car was still reverberating around the country, the faint odor of defeat began to infiltrate the showrooms. "It was obvious. Floor traffic was down. And the customers who did come in were appalled at the sticker prices," recalls one dealer who handled both the Chevrolet and Pontiac J-cars.

"There was no base car," says another dealer. "Sure, there was one on paper, and it was full of all those standard features they were crowing about. But do you really think you can sell against a Honda by telling a customer that the standard features include bumper rub strips and bright rocker panel moldings?"

The quality of the fit and finish was generally good. For the first time in memory, salesmen could point with pride to the fit of the doors and hood and to the properly mounted trim and improved, if not exceptional, paintwork. But the J's were still not up to the standards of the Japanese. Again, the dealers who had no direct contact with the imports were impressed. But those who were "dualed"—who owned franchises for both imported and domestic lines—were less than overwhelmed.

"Let me put it this way," says one Honda/Chevrolet dealer, "in the old days it looked as if the workers tossed the pieces on the Chevys from a distance of about four feet. With the J's, they moved in to two feet." That was possibly overharsh. The extra four hundred pounds of mass had paid off in durability, strength, rust-resistance, and crashworthiness which exceeded that of the Japanese imports. The problem lay elsewhere. Firstly, the stiff price repelled American buyers who were accustomed to seeing only large movable arks in the $8,000-$10,000 range. Secondly, the "conquest" customer, the person who was expected to trade in a Honda for a J-car, was disappointed by the absence of what were standard items on most good imports. The J-car had no five-speed transmission, no overhead camshaft engine, no independent rear suspension, no standard tachometer, and no sense of a hi-tech motoring environment, or the *illusion* of it, that was present in the imports.

/////

By the first of June it was clear that the J-car was a flop of enormous proportions, the Edsel of the 1980s. Sales were at a standstill. The J-car was suffering, the corporate line insisted, from two unexpected evils: the shortage of cars in the showrooms, caused, GM said, by their pious conversion to the new quality-control religion; and a steady worsening of the economy which was slowing down car sales of all kinds, at least in the domestic sector. By July, two months after the hoopla, only 19,000 Cavaliers and J-2000's had been sold, a mere fifteen percent of the four-month sales goal of 125,000 units.

Even the irrepressible Bob Lund was faltering. "We're running a bit behind," he told *The Wall Street Journal.* That was obvious. But to attribute the J-car's failures to short supply and a sagging economy was disingenuous at best. The essential problem lay with the product itself. In this sense the J-car was symbolic of the problems endemic to the entire American automobile industry. "It was a disaster," reports a dealer who sells Hondas and Cavaliers in the same showroom. "I had to move the Accords outside because they made the J's look awful."

Propelled by the speed with which bad news is transmitted, the failings of the J-car became almost universally known within weeks of its introduction. Realizing that the "Complete Car" campaign was a travesty, Campbell-Ewald changed its advertising course in midsummer and began concentrating on the Cavalier's quality instead.

It had taken this long for the Corporation to determine that the 1.8 liter engine was, in the words of *Road & Track*, "short on power and painfully slow"... "stalls constantly when cold and occasionally when hot"... "doesn't rev easily." *Motor Trend* was somewhat more tolerant in its appraisal: "The new 1.8 liter pushrod has only acceptable responsiveness.... Performance-minded buyers won't be excited by [the car's] rather lackluster straight-line abilities." The fact that these deficiencies had been evident two and a half years earlier, during the executive "ride and drive" at Mesa in February 1979, makes it all the more disheartening that the J-car was permitted to reach the marketplace in such a handicapped condition.

"I don't know how these people have become so isolated from the real world," comments a large Chevrolet dealer. "For the past four or five years there has been a steady lessening of the impact of new car introductions of all kinds. For example, when we had the grand-opening day for our 1982 line of Chevrolets, we counted *less* people in our showroom than on an average day! It was the same with the J-car. Floor traffic at that time was slow anyway, essentially because of apprehension about the economy. The J's simply created no stir.

No stir whatsoever."

If an aggressive salesman was able to get a potential customer to ignore the price tag long enough to take a test drive, the car's feeble performance became an issue. The automatic transmission in the J-car was stupefyingly slow. It had so little power that even slight undulations in the highway while cruising at 55-60 would cause the three-speed automatic to downshift crazily between second and third gear. Acceleration from 0 to 60 mph was in the eighteen-second range, comparable only to the slowest diesel sedans. Suddenly, in the real world of automobiles, the "Complete Car" was uncompetitive in the two critical areas: performance and price.

The problem was equally grave with the Cadillac's small car entry. Its J-car, the Cimarron, was the stepchild of the program. It was to be sold either to young marrieds who formed a major part of the BMW/Volvo/Audi/Saab market, or to suburban Caddy-owners' wives as a second car. Given such an abbreviated time schedule, the Cadillac engineers and stylists could do little more than provide their J-car with a grille treatment that seemed borrowed from a Chevrolet and to coat the seats with Mercedes-Benz-inspired leather upholstery.

The car was aimed at the upscale market, but the Cadillac product planning staffs appeared to lack the vaguest notion of what buyers in this class were seeking. For $12,000 to $14,000, BMW, Volvo, Audi and Saab customers expected mechanical sophistication: fuel injection, five-speed transmissions, as well as vivid performance. Cadillac was blundering in with what was basically a well-detailed Chevy Cavalier. It was doomed from the start. A BMW 320i, for example, would accelerate from 0 to 60 mph in about eleven seconds, which was *five* seconds quicker than the Cimarron. It would produce better fuel economy as well. The same was essentially true for the Audi 4000, Saab Turbo and Volvo GLT Turbo.

The Cimarron was out of its price class. While some engineering young lions recognized this failing and urged improvement, upper level management seemed oblivious. A journalist recalls witnessing a product planning meeting at Cadillac during the final stages of the Cimarron program. "The staff seemed to be divided between the progressives and the conservatives," he recalls. "The big issue was whether or not to put the traditional Cadillac ornament on the hood."

The Cimmaron episode was a dismal chapter in the Cadillac saga. Surely one of the great brands in automotive history, with a long list of proud engineering firsts including the self-starter, the synchromesh transmission and the modern overhead-valve V-8 engine, the Cadillac division had seemingly been anesthetized for the past twenty years, existing as a symbol of upper middle-class kitsch while Mercedes-Benz seized the high ground of automotive status. Cadillac's original 1976 Seville (actually introduced in mid-1975) was not much more than a dressed-up Chevrolet Nova. Now Cadillac further degraded itself by coming to market with a slow, overweight derivative of a tiny car created for the Chevrolet crowd.

Robert Templin, chief engineer of Cadillac Division and one of the real progressives in the corporation (which, cynics say, explains why he has been mired in the same job for nearly a decade), takes a rather sanguine position on the subject. "You've got to understand that there are still a number of people here at Cadillac who cannot envision the words 'small' and 'luxury' being in the same sentence," he comments. "The Sevilles got rid of the visible excesses but did not remove the need for even more compact, space-efficient Cadillacs. But as long as the Seville was selling well, it was hard to sell the idea of an even smaller Cadillac."

It was not until the big car market collapsed in 1979-80 that the 260 exclusive Cadillac dealers in the nation, a select group that accounts for over 60 percent of all the Division's sales, began demanding a subcompact. GM reacted. "At that point we had to pick *something*," shrugged Templin, who had been urging such a move for years. With only eleven months to work on the J-car, Templin and his staff were able to make only superficial modifications and fell far short of the announced goal of producing a car that could be pitted against the prestigious German BMW.

Complained a Cadillac loyalist after the damage had been done, "In the old days Cadillac designed and built its own cars. The Corporation left us alone. Now cars are created in massive committees centered around each of the involved car divisions, the Project

Center and the Corporate Design staff. Like somebody said, 'A camel is a horse designed by a committee,' and that's what you've got with the J-cars."

Despite its weak performance and the fact that even former GM president Pete Estes complained that it looked too much like a Chevrolet, the Cimarron sold proportionately better that the Cavalier and the J-2000. It reached nowhere near its sales goals, but the Cimarron did end up as the second car of some traditional Cadillac families and helped to edge the division's graybeard median ownership age to a fraction below fifty years. Contrasted with other J-car failures, this was a modest accomplishment.

GM refused to accept total defeat. By early autumn of 1981, the electronic chip in the J-car's Computerized Command Control system, which electronically monitors the engine's spark and air-fuel mixtures to minimize emissions, was changed to produce better low-end throttle response. Optional gear ratios were also offered for both manual and automatic transmission models to improve acceleration.

These were stopgap measures, while more radical fixes were being readied for the 1982 models. In January the engines were increased in displacement to two liters and boosted from 88 to 90 horsepower to improve performance. Pontiac was permitted to install the Brazilian-built overhead camshaft Family Two 1.8 liter engine as they had requested in the first place. Work was accelerated in conjunction with Isuzu in Japan to modify the Muncie four-speed manual transmissions to the much-missed, much-desired five-speeds being offered by most of the competition. Rear-seat contours were altered to transform the car from a strict four-passenger vehicle to one that would theoretically transport five people, in cozy proximity, for short distances.

While these improvements were being rushed into production the J-cars were dealt another blow. When the winter descended over the northern half of the United States, it was discovered that the Cavaliers and J-2000's had a cranky habit of failing to start under special circumstances. If the cars were used on days when temperatures ranged much below 10° Fahrenheit, they would drive a short distance, then stop. Sometimes the tempermental J-cars would stubbornly refuse to restart at all.

Some last-hour machining inside the carburetors (manufactured by Rochester Products, a division of GM) was responsible for the glitch. A change had been made during the race to meet production deadlines in the warm spring of 1981 and the part had not caused trouble until the frigid weather arrived. "The problem just snuck up and bit us," said a Chevrolet spokesman. "We just weren't aware of the situation until the cars hit the field." It was hard to understand why three years of intense testing had not rooted out such a potential problem. The trouble was quickly corrected by the dealers, but the incident only further shredded the car's tattered reputation.

To reduce one great negative factor, the sticker price, Chevrolet made a silent admission that the "Complete Car" pricing policy had not worked. It introduced a "Cadet" low-line Cavalier model with no-frills packaging. Apparently convinced that security lay in numbers, General Motors also injected Buick and Oldsmobile into the J-car lineup, announcing that the Buick's Skyhawk and the Oldsmobile's Firenza versions would reach the market in March 1982. Outsiders puzzled over the decision, wondering why the marketplace should be cluttered with even more J-car clones.

A confidential market summary which circulated at the advertising agency of one of GM's major competitors discussed the winners and losers of the 1981 model year. It cited the Ford Escort/Mercury Lynx as the big domestic sales triumph, noting that "It is the only domestic front-wheel-drive econobox coupe actually competing against the real import strength: Toyota Corolla, Datsun B210, Honda Civic, and Volkswagen Rabbit. The car is honestly represented in its advertising and is priced competitively."

The same report was hardly as kind to the J-car: "Without question, the biggest loser of the year has to be the much-heralded GM J-cars. Only ninety days after their introduction as the latest in 'world technology,' these cars have come off as being overpriced and underpowered, which indeed they are. Chevrolet learned that the American car buyer was not looking for a Toyota in the Chevrolet showroom, and Pontiac learned once again that you can't put a split grille on a Chevrolet and sell it as a Pontiac. Both cars were overpriced, oversold and woefully underpowered. When put into a direct comparison with comparable Toyotas, Datsuns, or even German Audis, *they lost.*"

Neither were the buff books impressed by the later 1982 modi-made in the J-car. Commenting in January 1982 on the second-edition improvements, *Road & Track* noted that the two-liter engine version "still lacks the acceleration to fit its image." It also cautioned, "By 1984... Honda will be producing 12,000 Accords per month in its Marysville, Ohio, factory. Then, perhaps we'll see a proper battle between the champion of small sedans and its most prominent rival. And I hope GM will have been introspective enough to honestly answer the question of how it fell into the J-car trap and didn't have a complete anti-Honda right from the start."

"GM's excuse that the J-car failed because there were not enough cars in the showrooms during introduction just won't wash," says a Detroit marketing consultant who fears to drop his anonymity. "People waited months for cars like the early VW's and the Honda Accord because they were worth it. Americans aren't stupid. A good product creates word of mouth and its own sales promotion. The car simply didn't have the performance or the sophistication to make it in the market it was attempting to penetrate."

"Penetration" is a key word. It is a synonym for the "conquest sales" which were intended to blunt the import invasion by stealing customers back to American cars. As with Detroit's earlier small autos, the J-cars simply did not capture significant numbers of buyers from the imports. The statistics were clear. In spite of individual successes, such as the Chevette and the Escort, the percentage of import registrations continued to climb, which meant that the industry was merely trading sales among its own brands while failing to resist the inroads of the Japanese and some European makers.

While successful, the imports were hardly unblemished, either in their marketing and distribution systems, or even in the quality of their often excessively praised products. Fiat, Citroën, Alfa Romeo, Peugeot, have been generally inept in organizing effective sales efforts in the United States. Moreover, any number of foreign products—among them the Audi 100LS and Fox, the early Mazda rotary engine cars, the Volvos of the middle 1970s, the Datsun F-10, the Volkswagen 411, most of the Fiats, and most recent British cars— have been cursed with reliability problems.

If the imports have gained a reputation for infallibility, it is far from deserved. But as mightily as Detroit tries, it has not been able to cut into the foreign car market. Every countermeasure, particularly the J-car, has failed.

/////

How did it happen? How did the world's largest automaker, backed by years of experience, billions of dollars, and armies of bright young men and women, fail so decisively in the seemingly straightforward enterprise of making and selling a practical small car? This was hardly a moonshot or even such a major gamble in consumer marketing as video recorders or microwave ovens.

Unfortunately, there was nothing original about the J-car, which was an amalgam of proven, widely used components and concepts. To put it uncharitably, it could be seen as a mediocre Japanese copy, although it truly deserves more credit than that. But the cruel evaluation of the marketplace dubbed it a loser, and only time will tell whether General Motors can save the car from oblivion.

Of course the J-car was in short supply at the beginning. Of course the car was overpriced. Of course the car was underpowered. These shortcomings contributed to its failure, but they are merely symptoms of an underlying industrial malaise. The reality lies elsewhere. And so does the blame.

People—highly paid people at General Motors—built the J-car that way. *They* built it with too much weight and too little power. *They* botched the job of getting it to market in time, and selling it with inept policies that dated back twenty years. *They* created a system so infected with overhead and excessive profit per car that the product was overpriced in a free world market. All of the post-game analysis, computer readouts, reasoned explanations, true confessions and in-depth examinations cannot obliterate one salient fact: General Motors *people* made a bad mistake with the J-car.

Yet there were precious few repercussions. To be sure, Bob Lund, the Chevrolet general manager and fiery loyalist, was moved upstairs. Almost a year to the day after his introductory speech in Tempe, he was made corporate vice president in charge of the Sales and Marketing Staffs. Though he was hailed with perfunctory congratulations, it was clear that he was no longer in charge of GM's key division.

His successor was Robert C. Stempel, a forty-eight-year-old former general manager of Pontiac who had returned from an eighteen month tour as managing director of Adam Opel AG to take Lund's place. Lund left Chevrolet after losing 305,000 sales in 1981, with the division in a confused market position. Despite his tireless efforts, Lund was only the second man, along with John Z. DeLorean, who, since 1967, had not used the Chevrolet post as a stepping-stone to the corporate presidency. Robert Brewbaker remained as head of the J-car Project Center, assigned to the job of updating and improving his unpopular offspring.

Those who suffered the most from the J-car debacle were hourly workers and lower echelon administrators who soon appeared in the unemployment statistics. Scores of General Motors plants including the J-car factory in Southgate, California, were shut down temporarily, or closed permanently, and many lost their jobs because management thousands of miles away had made a series of blunders. For the most part, it was business as usual. Business the Detroit way.

CHAPTER II

The Detroit Mind

THE MEN WHO MADE THE J-CAR and wasted billions of dollars for the American auto industry live in magnificent isolation in Bloomfield Hills, Michigan, the center of the affluent northern suburbs of Detroit.

Bloomfield Hills, population 4000, is the richest little city in America. Richer than Palm Springs, Palm Beach, La Jolla, Scarsdale, Greenwich, Carmel, or any Houston or Dallas suburb. According to the U.S. Census, every man, woman, and child living in wooded, Waspish splendor in Bloomfield has an annual income of $40,000. Taxes are ridiculously low. Half the $2.5 million municipal budget is used to maintain the fire and police services in this obsessively private community whose lanes are carefully lined with No Parking signs, warnings to intruders that this is the preserve of the princes of the auto industry.

Success for the automobile executive lies on a Bloomfield lakefront, literal pay dirt for his forty years of exquisitely complicated living by the code. It arrives in the form of property on the shore of Square Lake or Orchard Lake or any of the half-dozen modest ponds nestled in the hardwood-topped hummocks northwest of Bloomfield Hills. There he, his loyal wife, and his architect have cut out the land, pioneer fashion, on which they have erected a half-million-dollar, five-thousand-square foot monument to his labor on behalf of the American automobile.

The home may be either modern or traditional, so long as it is not ostentatious. This will not happen, because any man staking his dream house in the soft loam of a Bloomfield Hills lakesite has memorized the canon of behavior for an automobile executive, tattooing it on his brain as he climbed up through the system to general manager, executive vice president, or the equivalent rank within one of the four major automobile manufacturing companies or one of its satellite industries. The only ostentation in his life is reserved for the gaudy American cars he designs, builds and drives.

The private road leading off the winding, heavily patrolled public street will probably be dirt. Dirt roads have meaning in Bloomfield Hills, as a symbol of the spiny individualism that originally built the auto industry. After all, he hogged out the road with a D-9 Cat bulldozer, and now the trail lays there in dusty witness to the fact that he has not forgotten his origins. Though virgin dirt has meaning in Bloomfield, to outsiders it is a strange anomaly in men who have grown rich building cars for the continuous ribbons of asphalt and concrete that stretch from coast to coast.

The auto prince's home is simultaneously a monument to his new power and to the hard years spent edging up the ladder: the twelve-hour work days, the endless rounds of golf, the at-home study sessions, the incessant travel, the Byzantine search for the right coattails to perch on, membership in the right clubs and ordained churches, and the perpetual inner struggle never to say or do anything that might separate him from his peer group.

Now that he has arrived on the Bloomfield lakefront, he will likely drink too much scotch or white wine and perhaps be on his second marriage. But the trip has been worth it. The bonus system and the stock options are starting to deliver opulent dividends. He owns a boat, a sloop in the 30-35 foot range, and at least three cars, all American-built. The company has provided him with a large sedan: a fully loaded Cadillac, Lincoln, or Imperial, or other flagship machine of the division he represents, painstakingly maintained by his firm. His wife drives a somewhat smaller but equally effective American-built image vehicle. Stored in the garage is an American antique car, a collectible that immediately identifies him as a member of the Detroit fraternity: "a car guy."

Bloomfield Hills and the neighboring town of Birmingham are worlds of gilded provincialism which boast few of the chic characteristics normally associated with wealth. The main shopping area, Somerset Mall, is a smallish, rather prosaic suburban bazaar anchored at opposite ends by Saks Fifth Avenue and Bonwit Teller and containing only a scattering of prestige shops, including small Gucci, Bally, and Brooks Brothers outlets. In Dearborn the Fairlane Mall houses a Lord & Taylor but little that might differentiate it from a hundred other shopping centers around the nation.

"At any given moment you can find several dozen wives of senior executives from GM and Ford shopping in Somerset, but you'll never see them buying anything that might be construed as faddish," says Howard Kenig, a Detroit broadcaster who has long studied the habits of the automotive executive. "Fads are extremely dangerous in this business. If one day you are still wearing Lacoste shirts when everybody has switched to Adidas running suits, you're in serious trouble. Remember, the secret here is *never, ever* get separated from your peer group."

There is no Bloomingdale's or Neiman-Marcus in Somerset, and no successful art galleries in the small, exclusive Birmingham business district, which from a distance vaguely resembles Palm Beach's Worth Avenue. There is no Tiffany's, no Cartier's, no haute-couture dress shops, no Elizabeth Arden and no exotic car dealers, save for a Mercedes-Benz agency in Birmingham, which caters mainly to a nonautomotive industry clientele. Only Roche-Bobois, a fashionable furniture shop, punctuates the mundane independent and chain shops.

Why doesn't a community with such industrial and financial clout exhibit greater signs of taste? "The answer is simple," states a New York advertising executive who spent several years in Detroit working at Campbell-Ewald, Chevrolet's advertising agency. "The place is packed with people who have upper-class money and middle-class minds. They simply don't know how to spend their money, except the same way the guy next door spends his money. That's likely to be a motor home he stores in the driveway or a dirt bike for his kid. The way they live and the way they design and build their cars is a dead giveaway of their taste."

Life in Bloomfield Hills is a group activity, played out in lush cultural isolation from the nonautomotive society. "They live together, they work together, they drink together, they play golf together, they *think* together," said a former GM executive. He was speaking of the highly structured life-style of General Motors management, which insists on weekends of golf and gin rummy games at the Oakland Hills Country Club and back-lawn barbecues dominated by conversation about the automobile business.

"It's like entering the priesthood," remarks another local observer. "They get out of college and go into the system at the zone level. From then on the Corporation takes care of everything; it sells their houses when they move, invests their incomes, provides them with new cars every few thousand miles, gets them memberships in the right clubs, and so on. They even retire together in GM colonies in the South and Southwest. You talk about a cradle-to-grave welfare state. The farther they advance, the more monastic they become. They simply have no concept of the real world."

Fortune was prompted to comment on this unique group existence. "GM officials," they noted, "are products of a system that discourages attention to matters far outside the purview of their jobs. And they are captives of a camaraderie that keeps them much in one another's company—on the golf course and around the card table as well as in the conference room. While this generates an *esprit de corps* that constitutes one of the organization's great strengths, its effect is to insulate GM's managers from many contemporary currents of thought."

"If they weren't isolated in Bloomfield Hills, driving their Cadillacs and Lincolns and Imperials, they'd understand why imported cars sell so well," says another corporate expatriate, referring to executives of the three major automakers. "Their automobiles are built to their life-styles, and they have no comprehension of why people in Los Angeles, San Francisco, Scarsdale, or Fairfield County, Connecticut, want Mercedes, BMW's, and Hondas instead of Buicks and LeBarons."

As the auto prince stands beside his lakeside home, he is not aware of his isolation from a rapidly moving world. He is proud of his life-style. His children are in college, most likely at the University of Michigan or another large midwestern university. His golf game is strong, even though he now puffs as he moves about the racquet-ball court. He remains a resolute jock despite the flab that rings his midriff even after endless hours at Vic Tanney's in Southfield, a gym that has replaced the downtown Detroit Athletic Club as a fitness center for the younger, more aggressive auto executives. He can recite the starting lineup of the Wolverines' varsity team for the last decade and knows the inner politics of the hapless NFL Lions by rote.

Once his roots are put down by the lake, he knows that he has made it and that the perquisites of his power will flow. He can walk to his golf club for the Sunday afternoon games after church. His colleagues live nearby. The good wife is at his side wearing all the right clothes from the shops in Somerset Mall, not the esoteric fashions of New York designers or the radical styles of chic boutiques. He also owns a cottage in northern Michigan, but makes use of it less than before. The vacation home was once an indispensable status symbol in the auto industry, but even higher status is now awarded to those who leave a portion of their vacation time unused, whether at the cottage or elsewhere.

As he looks back on a generation of service, the prince represents the prototypical automobile success story: a man whose intelligence, appearance and behavior patterns have destined him for membership in the Bloomfield Open Hunt Club and the Orchard Lake Country Club, an environment of pure fantasy for someone of his humble origins.

The automogul was born in a small to middle-sized midwestern town in Michigan, Indiana, Ohio, Illinois, or Iowa. He is a white Anglo-Saxon Protestant, with Catholic allegiance occupying a close second place. Jews are tolerated, but not encouraged. One Jew, Gerald Meyers, reached the presidency of American Motors, but, like other minorities, Jews must work under such close scrutiny that their general absence from the heirarchy of Detroit is to be expected.

There are few role models other than WASP males, and the idea of someone of minority stock striving to rise to the top in Detroit is not unlike a black man seeking to become a Mormon elder.

As a boy, the Detroit executive was a robust, well-rounded lad: a Boy Scout, football player, newsboy, with solid if not outstanding grades in mathematics and science. He entered the University of Michigan, Purdue, or Ohio State schools of engineering or business, or the industry's own degree-granting university, the engineering-oriented General Motors Institute in nearby Flint. Traditionally the presidents of General Motors, the organization which sets the economic and social patterns for the entire industry, have had engineering backgrounds, while the chairmen of the board have been financial men.

The "fast track" to the top is in engineering; the MBA lies ahead as an obligatory second degree for anyone who has potential. It is possible to succeed if one graduates from such "plow jockey" colleges as Michigan State or one of the out-orbit Big Ten schools. Even the distant coastal institutions of MIT, Harvard, and Stanford are now gaining in vogue, but the magic imprimatur still comes from the old Maize and Blue, Michigan's mega-university in Ann Arbor.

The management man has made it through the demanding system that has shaped his entire mental and spiritual physiognomy, giving him an internalized set of attitudes, thought patterns and work habits that has brought him to where he is today. Collectively it is what may be called The Detroit Mind, a way of thinking that is also responsible for the precarious position of the American automobile industry.

/////

For the loyal auto prince there is comfort in the knowledge that out beyond the lakes and skinny maples there are thousands of younger bare-toothed, pulse-pounding men learning the arcane sociology of the great automobile industry, groping through the unwritten rule books to find the lever that will get them to that same lakefront. It is a brutal game based on the system that builds a Superbowl pro team: a tragic one for those who can't play the game;

a bountiful one for those who can.

Like the chief resident of a great teaching hospital, he can help those below to avoid the pitfalls that almost tripped him up on his way to the top. Like all executives, he has his favorites, sanctioning rapid advances for young loyalists. But for the most part he has encouraged the system's open warfare. According to his own standards of excellence, he has permitted the superior men to rise to the top.

"This is the residency system, pure and simple," explains a longtime GM engineer. "This is a cut system that goes on for your entire career. If you find at age thirty-five that you've been in the same job for three years, you're dead meat. It's relentless pressure. Even after retirement these guys keep going as consultants. They have been on the run with their hearts going 180 beats a minute for forty years. They can't stop. What's more, it's a sign of weakness if they go lie in the sun."

Once a recruit has joined GM, or the somewhat less disciplined Ford, Chrysler or AMC organizations, he is given two or three years of specialized training, perhaps receiving a few temporary assignments in glamour locations at the big proving grounds or one of the research laboratories. All the while he is gaining strength in several of a thousand engineering specialties.

During this period the novice is expected to ease his way into the system. He has, it is hoped, married a pretty, intelligent midwestern WASP who will be supportive, even maternal, during his years of trial. They will first move into a garden apartment, perhaps in the somewhat modish Somerset Park Apartments in Troy (which at one time was reputed to be the center of suburban Detroit's sexual revolution) or into an entry-level ranch home in a modest suburb such as Sterling Heights or Farmington Hills on the perimeter of Bloomfield and within commuting distance of the massive General Motors complex in Warren, the nucleus of the Ford empire in Dearborn, or the Chrysler headquarters in Highland Park.

Sensibly cut gray and brown suits and a drawerful of perma-press shirts will be purchased from the big middle-grade chains of Hughes and Hatcher, or Jacobson's. Bizarre ties, French cuffs, radical styles and any footwear other than decent, stolid brogues will be avoided.

"A young GM engineer learns quickly that a raised eyebrow over a piece of too garish wearing apparel can be the kiss of death," says a twenty-year veteran. "There are those risk takers who'll push the system. Some radical behavior can be tolerated *provided* his pay-backs to the business are immediate and apparent. But he's running on a very dangerous track if his performance flags for a minute."

By the time he has reached his late twenties, the aspirant has become a specialist, a manufacturing or marketing technician molded to the system. He will now likely have a modest title: an assistant managership of sorts. He has moved into a slightly larger house in the deeper reaches of the suburbs, but still far from the magnificence of Bloomfield. By now he may have a pair of children and his wife is learning the skills of entertaining, mostly to impress their peer group, but with occasional special domestic exhibitions for her husband's immediate boss. There is little time for frivolity and little interest in the consumption of culture that is so important to life in the New York or West Coast suburbs.

Outings to suburban mall movie theatres and steak and chop dinners in chain restaurants like the Magic Pan or Bloomfield Charlie's are about all that is feasible at their junior level. Foreign food is not popular. There was a brief fascination with Szechuan food a few years ago, and there is a Mexican cooking vogue among the more bohemian advertising and styling types, but the Detroit suburbs are not entranced by haute cuisine, nouvelle or otherwise. Legitimate theater, other than the Broadway road companies that come to the downtown Fisher playhouse, is practically unknown, as is live music, except for a few shoestring jazz clubs. Though the fifth largest metropolitan area in the nation, Detroit lies in cultural tall grass. "They've said it for years; Detroit is a great place to make money and a lousy place to spend it," muses a Chrysler executive and a native of stuffy Grosse Pointe, where the old money of the last generation still molders.

The young prospect is now settling into the system, awaiting the next career leap. If he gives evidence of being a "team player," and has developed rigid, twelve-hour-a-day work habits with plenty of take-home weekend assignments, and has made no serious enemies, he may be ready. He has learned to be at his desk at seven o'clock in the morning and to remain until at least seven in the evening. He tries to be professionally well read, which means the *Wall Street Journal, Business Week, Forbes, Time, Newsweek,* and several of the car magazines. "At this level if you show up at the coffee machine a few minutes late and the subject of discussion is a piece in the *Journal* you haven't read, count that as a defeat," says a GM expatriate. He attempts to be broadly conversant with world affairs and to absorb the necessary political line, which is to identify himself vocally as a solid but progressive Republican.

Graduate school is next. This translates into prosaic night classes at Michigan State's Troy campus for the ordinary candidates, full-fledged sabbaticals at Harvard or Stanford for the anointed. "This part of his life will break his balls, and very likely his marriage," says Howard Kenig. "The loyal helpmate will lose the faith. At this point a lot of screwing around will begin. There is a lot of sexual adventure among the young marrieds in the northern suburbs, most of it traceable to the tremendous pressure of the jobs. Divorce used to be absolutely taboo, but since John DeLorean [the fallen angel of GM] and Ed Cole [the ultimate engineer who became president] did it in the late 1960s, it has become acceptable, almost expected."

Now in his early thirties, the young superstar will arrive back in the fold with his MBA and possibly a new wife. She will be a more spectacular woman, more visible, more self-assured than his former hausfrau. "Believe it or not, Jewish-American Princesses, or at least women who behave like them, are becoming very popular in Detroit," says Kenig. "They are tough, talented, but completely dependent upon their husbands in a professional sense." With his flashier new wife and a newly-decorated home whose furnishings proclaim inoffensive good taste, he now faces another major professional decision, whether to push on toward the top.

It is presumed that he has all the physical prerequisites. He is lean with fair skin and darkish hair, and tall. "Take a look at the top management," says an industry observer. "They're all big guys, physically imposing in one way or another. Slight ethnic types haven't got a prayer." His eyes are clear, but he has none of that high-cheeked, narrow-faced, triangulated-jawbone look of the eastern Brahmins. He is a meat and potatoes midwesterner who can blast a five iron 170 yards out of the deep rough of a good mid-level golf course like Bloomfield Hills and articulate a catalogue of detail on his tightly focused phase of the business, all the while lacing his discourse with such techno-jargon as "data bases," "maximization of mean efficiency curves," "on stream," and "factorization of variables."

He is a loyal team player and known as a nice guy among his cohorts. The mean or obsessive variety of management is not popular in Detroit. His subordinates and the staff public relations man will begin to pass his name along to the media as someone to watch. His manner is forthright, and his eye contact is good. He prides himself on a folksy way of chatting on a first-name basis, using occasional mild locker-room profanity to convey a feeling of earthy sincerity. In private conversation and in any public forum, he makes it clear that he loves automobiles, particularly American-made ones. Regardless of his private thoughts about cars, and the fact that he took little interest in them prior to joining GM, it is important that he become known as a "car guy."

At this point in his career Bloomfield Hills, or its affluent suburban rival, Birmingham, becomes a reality. Not a custom built place on one of the lakes, but a $250,000 four-bedroom, mauve-brick modern with an in-ground pool and a small circular driveway in one of the new tracts near Wabeek, or in one of the older wooded sections where the houses all seem to have emerged from plans in a 1968 issue of *Better Homes*. There, for acre after forested acre, the land is dotted with precious center-hall colonials, mock French Provincials, flashy raised ranches, bogus Tudors, and bold but inoffensive moderns. This first step into Bloomfield is a major move in the desired direction—northwest, closer to the lake country and miles away from the middle income Southfield zone.

Home base is in sight. The executive is now approaching the final decision point: his forty-second year and his twentieth anniversary with the Corporation. Life is good by all measurements. Barring a major peccadillo, getting fired is out of the question. For a GM executive, a lateral transfer to one of the outback divisions like AC Spark Plug or Rochester Products (in Rochester, New York) would place him in a career purgatory from which there is no recovery. The same banishment from Detroit might send a Ford executive out to its Motorcraft (ignition services) Division, or a Chrysler man all the way to Syracuse to wile away his time at the New Process Gear Division.

But that is unlikely if he is promising material. Further advancement to the vice-presidential and general manager levels is possible, but it requires further risks on his part. More personal alliances must be sought; careful probes into the higher managerial strata must be undertaken. Subtle assaults must be waged to undermine, yet seem to openly support, his superior, while simultaneously fighting off the determined attacks of certain of his own subordinates. Success here will one day be commemorated by an original oil portrait in the lobby of one of the GM administration buildings, or at Ford or Chrysler headquarters.

His kids will now attend such private schools as Cranbrook or Kingsbrook or Country-Day at Eleven Mile and Franklin. God forbid that he should send his child to Roper, with its colored geodesic domes and its avant-garde curriculum. "The kid is weird, and since he comes from his father's gene pool, that means he's a little weird, too," says one GM executive. Roper is left to the children of designers and ad men who are considered "arty" and therefore entitled to a modicum of nonconformity.

By now a number of candidates for the top have run out of breath. The track to the executive suite of GM, Ford or Chrysler has become too fast. They make a decision that for the next twenty or twenty-five years, until they reach mandatory retirement age, they will coast, waiting until the men ahead of them catch up. Some movement is still possible but the reach for the top—with its mandatory overseas assignment, the acquisition of a personal public relations man, the currying of favor with a key executive vice president, the risk of another divorce and a brief exile in the expensive Moon Lake apartment complex in Bloomfield—is forgone for a future of guaranteed security. That security is not a myth. One study shows that of the top 6000 GM executives—two-thirds of whom have never worked elsewhere—less then one percent will be fired or defect from the company during their entire working career.

Those who drop out of the race to the summit will sit out their lives in their well-fortified homes on the serpentine avenues off Long Lake and Orchard Lake Roads, safe from both the blacks of Detroit and its white-collar drones. They face a life of seven-to-seven paper shuffling, worrying about the new door handle mechanism for the 1986 models or a zone marketing survey to determine if velour upholstery can be sold to unmarried heads of household. The northwest lakes are now a distant vision on the other side of Crooks Road. It is all what might have been had a little more fire burned in the executive belly.

Life will wind down, perhaps ending during a monthly meeting of one of the Big Three retiree clubs in Sarasota or Naples, Florida or Scottsdale, Arizona. With any luck the final play will come at the bridge table or on the tee, or possibly during one of the annual talks by a key GM official who comes down to retirement land to update the old-timers on the Corporation's new plans. The end will come more than a thousand miles from the old stomping grounds in Bloomfield and Warren. Like his life, the passing will come while he is among his peers, and it is likely to be as orderly as was his career. Others will be remembered as being more successful, but perhaps both the snails and sharks alike in Naples and in Bloomfield Hills have been quietly dying for years anyway.

/////

The Detroit Mind has placed a premium on cultural conformity, which helps explain the auto industry's inability to maintain parity with the Germans and the Japanese even in the apparently simple area of design. Auto consultant and car customizer Bill Mitchell [no relation to former GM design chief William Mitchell] went to work at the Oldsmobile Division in the mid-1960s naively believing that he was about to be involved in the ultimate in design creativity. Instead, he discovered what he considers a backwater of executives obsessed with playing the arcane game of career advancement. "I graduated from Purdue as a mechanical engineer and went to work at Oldsmobile as a wide-eyed car freak," recalls Mitchell from his Cheshire, Connecticut, shop. "When I first started I worked on front-end sheet metal and then was assigned to design dashboard Kleenex dispensers. I wanted to do new and creative things. That was my first mistake, because there was no reward for creativity or initiative. Everybody was slotted into a specific job description and spent most of their time keeping their desks clean."

Like other rebels who have left the Detroit fold, Mitchell counts himself a "car person," an individual who cares passionately about automobiles, both aesthetically and conceptually. At GM, he found himself in a minority, overwhelmed by those who were unconcerned about the cars they were making. "They hired a guy from one of the defunct government space programs at a level slightly above me in the engineering department and asked me if I would give him a tour of the manufacturing operation in Lansing," Mitchell remembers. "We got into the engine plant and as we were walking along, he nudged me and said, 'Excuse me, I wonder if you'd explain how one of these things work.' The *thing* he wanted me to explain was an engine! He had just been hired as an engineer by the world's largest automobile company and he didn't have the vaguest notion about how a four-cycle internal combustion engine worked! It was then that I knew I was in the wrong business."

Mitchell recalls how each annual model change was evaluated against one major standard—last year's car. "They never, ever considered the competition of foreign cars. The senior engineers and management would all go out to the Milford Proving Grounds and first they'd drive the previous year's Olds model. Then they'd try the upcoming model. If it was slightly better than the old one, they were satisfied."

One adventure in car testing at GM shocked Mitchell's automotive sensibilities. The Toronado front-wheel-drive car, introduced in 1966 as a two-ton behemoth, was originally intended to be a rakish sports coupe. Oldsmobile purchased several sports cars for evaluation, including a Corvette, a Jaguar XK-E coupe, and a Ferrari GT. Somehow a limited-production ultra-fast Porsche 904 coupe was borrowed from the collection of GM styling chief William Mitchell to complete the competitive array.

"It was unbelievable," recounts Bill Mitchell. "None of these guys had the foggiest notion about what these cars were for, much less how to drive them. They had the poor Porsche and the Ferrari lugging along, bucking and heaving in fifth gear, at 20 mph! They complained about the cramped cockpit in the Corvette and engine noise in the Jaguar. Here they were surrounded by four of the most advanced automobiles in the world and they universally agreed they all stunk! Needless to say, the Toronado eventually turned out to be closer to a two-door Olds 98 than one of the world's greatest sports cars."

The isolation that characterizes the Detroit Mind not only precludes intimacy with the best cars in the world, but does not even permit the rising car executive to become familiar with the domestic competition. Another young turk, now an executive with a major imported-car manufacturer, recalls his days as a junior marketing expert at Cadillac. "I told my boss about a weekend experience in a sporty new model being built by Ford. He ripped me apart for having the temerity to discuss in a positive way automobiles built by the competition. My loyalties were to Cadillac, and he didn't want to hear me talking about, much less praising anything else!"

Even the top brass are not immune from this medieval edict. One General Motors division manager was determined to get a realistic handle on the competition by driving Ford and Chrysler rental cars on business trips. When this was discovered, word quickly came down from the Fourteenth Floor that he was to be seen behind the wheel of his own division's cars and no others.

The isolation imposed on automobile executives extends even to the media. Stories in the local *Detroit News* and *Free Press* or in the industry's weekly trade paper, *Automotive News,* have more impact than coverage in the *New York Times, Washington Post* or the *Los Angeles Times*. A mention on the lively J. P. McCarthy morning show on radio station WJR is considered to be akin to a presidential citation.

The industry that once dominated the world markets is run like a local business. Its environs stretch from Bloomfield Hills on the north to Grosse Pointe on the east to Dearborn on the west. Judgments about cars are made exclusively within those perimeters, except for the occasional intelligence gathered from Southern California. Cars are designed essentially to meet three critical criteria:

(1) to ride comfortably on the area's wide, billiard-table-flat streets and highways, (2) to start and stay warm in the murderous Michigan winters and to keep cool in the humid summers and (3) to carry a family and their gear on summer vacation trips.

This last arises from the auto executives' tradition of owning summer places or visiting hunting camps in Michigan's Upper Peninsula (the "U.P.") and regularly hauling wives, offspring and fishing rods up and down the state. The Detroit executive views a car's ability to do this heavy-duty chore as the standard by which all Americans should measure an automobile's usefulness.

This myopic marketing viewpoint mirrors that of the movie industry in Los Angeles, where it is known as the "Westwood Syndrome." The Hollywood film community, which is often as insular as the carmakers, is always anxious to know how a newly-released picture is doing in the Westwood theater district on Wilshire Boulevard. They endlessly recite the reactions of their sons, daughters or secretaries to a new film. Crowd figures, laughter, post-show comments are all monitored in Westwood, in the false belief that the reaction of this enclave of hard-core film enthusiasts can somehow be extrapolated to include the entire American population.

The same conviction dominates Detroit, where executives incessantly discuss how their relatives or close associates like or dislike the new models they are driving. Neither the cost nor the maintenance of these cars reflect the realities of the real world. Many of the cars have been obtained through special management buy/lease programs, or they belong to vast corporate pools where autos are painstakingly maintained on a routine basis. Judgments made on the basis of such input are about as valid in evaluating car performance as it would be for the President of the United States to judge commercial air travel from the cabin of Air Force One.

/////

A stiff, small-town, essentially Calvinist work ethic dominates an industry that now demands originality and daring to succeed against foreign competition. The suburban Detroit life-style, like its cars, is the ultimate expression of the same small-town bourgeois ideals its inhabitants absorbed while growing up. It is the central reason why the Detroit Mind missed the entire point of the small car revolution. While the auto moguls deluded themselves that sub-compacts were being sold to crackpots and skinflints, they failed to comprehend the most salient point of this phenomenon: it was the less isolated, more sophisticated *upper and upper middle classes* of the nation, economically and intellectually, who first embraced imported cars and thereby endowed them with social credibility.

Locked defiantly in Bloomfield Hills, the car executives failed to appreciate the reasons for the shift to small cars. Rising internation-alism after World War II stimulated interest in travel, European clothing, Eastern religions, French cooking, English rock groups, Japanese cameras, Scandinavian furniture. And German cars. With this came a booming interest in high technology, stimulated by the space race, the birth of computer science, and the transistor. Sud-denly the trendsetters of our society were tossing out their old Kodak Brownie Hawkeyes and buying 35mm single lens reflex cameras from Nikon and Pentax and Canon. Seemingly exotic air-cooled, rear-engine, four-speed Volkswagens and Porsches were the status rage.

The public's fascination for hi-tech in the 1960s passed the executive staffs of the Big Three automakers by, as did the acceler-ated enthusiasm for the trend during the next decade. With hi-tech came its natural offspring: miniaturization, in cameras, computers and cars. It was this triad of internationalization, miniaturization and hi-tech that established the basis for the small car revolution. It was *not*, as Detroit would like to believe, a simple lust for better fuel mileage. To be sure, once the imported car had been given credibility by the trendsetters and the middle classes had begun to follow them into the small-car market, sensitivity to gasoline prices became a factor. But in the beginning it was the urbane, educated, more adventuresome segment of the nation—not the gasoline pinchers—who discovered the imported car and gave it cachet.

How could the Detroit Mind, nourished in isolated splendor in Bloomfield Hills, Michigan, understand why a wealthy doctor in Palm Beach, or an advertising executive in Darien, Connecticut, or a successful novelist on the Monterey Peninsula, or a university professor in La Jolla would crave a Mercedes-Benz or a BMW rather than a chromed behemoth of a Cadillac or Lincoln?

The foreign car revolution was in many ways an American one, using overseas design and manufacturing skills to make a domestic protest against Detroit. "Everybody thinks it was the Japanese and the Germans who revolutionized the car industry in America and brought Detroit to its knees. That's utter bull," asserts a former Oldsmobile advertising and marketing executive who is now working in the imported car field in California. "The fact is, dissidents from Detroit—guys like myself who couldn't stand the stifling conformity and the discouragement of anything that smacked of nonconformity—we're the ones who made the imports work. Sure, the Japanese and the Germans built the cars, but *Americans* set up the dealer networks, built the distribution systems, created the advertising and marketing campaigns, and put the merchandising in place. We could have done the same thing for Ford and GM if somebody had given us a little latitude and freedom of expression."

/////

South of Bloomfield Hills lies the great brawling city of Detroit. The word generates a flood of stereotyped, only half-accurate images: a dark city somewhere in the great midwestern interior crammed with sooty auto factories and sprawling slums. It is the home of crazed blue-collar sports fans, and of an offshoot of rhythm-and-blues music known as the "Motown Sound," icebound winters, and meaty ethnic heritages.

But more than anything else Detroit is synonymous with big automobiles, those Veblenesque aberrations of capitalism gone wild. In this context Detroit is a state of mind that embraces the excesses and greed that we associate with the manufacture and sale of the chrome-soaked, two-toned, two-ton leviathans which, like their ancient cousins, the Cretaceous reptiles, became extinct in the face of a radically changing environment.

By most demographic measurements, Detroit is the fifth largest metropolitan area in the nation. Despite its periodic agonies of auto industry unemployment, it ranks ninth among major cities in median family income. Yet as Chicago is cursed in reputation for its brutal winds; Los Angeles for its smog; New York for its crime; Buffalo for its snow; Philadelphia for its dullness; and Dallas for its nouveau-riche ostentation, Detroit carries the stigma of seemingly witless isolation from the cultural mainstream.

Residents live in a steady state of apology. Their defense mechanisms are tuned to stoically absorb, rather than repel, the incessant indictments of the city's filth, racial problems, weather, and general intellectual bleakness. This has produced a rather mordant brand of self-mockery, one which reached an artistic peak a decade ago when the heavily Polish neighborhoods in the industrial suburb of Hamtramck began flagellating themselves with witty insults that soon swept the nation as Polish jokes. But, heads down against the arrows of sophisticates from both coasts, Detroiters trudge ahead, armored with the conviction that their city is stronger, more vibrant, even more intelligent and cosmopolitan than outsiders realize.

The city is hardly a ghetto of unassimilated Poles, poor blacks, and unenlightened petty bourgeoisie. But it is true that Detroit has long been dominated by an ethic. It is the American auto ethic, one fashioned by a subspecies of Detroit industrialists who have implanted a set of antediluvian notions about cars in our national consciousness. Unfortunately, those ideas are no longer valid and are economically disastrous to Detroit, the Midwest, America, and the world.

Directly and through its suppliers, the auto industry employs one in twelve Americans. Because of the ripple effect of car purchases on the economy, the industry's solvency, or lack of it, is usually a barometer of the nation's financial stability. The car is also a cultural artifact with an impact unrivaled in the history of technology. By revolutionizing our life-style, the men who built them became oversized figures in American folklore. Some, like the first Henry Ford, have been revered. Others have been reviled. But collectively they have created for America the preposterous socioeconomic phenomenon known as "Detroit."

The Detroit Mind may thrive in magnificent isolation in Bloomfield Hills but it comes in daily contact with the outside world on one street. It is Woodward Avenue, a road which drives flat and true from the edge of the Detroit River all the way to Pontiac, twenty-four miles to the northwest. It is a wide, brash thoroughfare, lined with the defeats and triumphs of the great city. A block to the west is the formidable General Motors Building, celebrated as the largest office structure in the world when Albert Kahn created it for $20 million in 1919-20. Towering above its flat-topped parapets is another Kahn creation, the joyously baroque Fisher Building, one of the most architecturally elegant commercial structures in America.

Far to the east lie the remains of the once-great Packard plant, where in 1903 young Kahn, a native Detroiter, created a modern factory with expanses of windows and sprawling, unencumbered work areas. In Hamtramck, several miles to the north along Woodward, Kahn designed the Dodge Brothers factory, but it was soon overshadowed by his masterpiece in Highland Park, where, fronting the great avenue, he built for Henry Ford the complex that would mass-produce the Model T in 1913. If there is an historical center of the twentieth century automotive revolution, it is at this four story brick and stone complex that now stands as a memorial to the eccentric visionary from Dearborn who made the automobile the emancipator of the working classes of the world.

The thoroughfare is named for Judge August B. Woodward, a pioneer thinker whose devotion to Pierre L'Enfant, the Washington D.C. planner, prompted him to create a similar wheellike pattern of grand avenues and boulevards for Detroit. The fact that the city was then a rutted patchwork of cabins on the edge of the endless timberlands and Michigan not yet a state does not diminish his vision.

As Judge Woodward's Avenue probes northward away from hard-edged monuments of the new industrial age, the flat Michigan landscape begins to soften to the eye. Royal Oak looms up. It is a midwestern middle-class suburb, beholden to the automobile and the past glories of the full dinner pail. It is a stolid, decent city, but demographically a no-man's-land separating the outer regions of Detroit's spreading black neighborhoods from the splendor of Bloomfield Hills.

For decades the leaders of the American automobile industry have transported themselves up and down Judge Woodward's Avenue as they journeyed between their offices, clubs and watering spots downtown, then back to the sanctuary of Bloomfield Hills. There is limited Amtrak commuter service, but the small parking lot in Bloomfield's railroad station is generally half-empty, indicating there is no need, either practically or socially, to ride a train to work.

Each morning thousands of executives climb into their corporate-owned and maintained Fleetwood Broughams, Continentals, Imperials, Electra 225's, Bonnevilles, New Yorkers, Caprices, and other vinyl and fake-burl-walnut-applique monsters and make the big trek south to work. (The Ford people actually veer slightly west, to Southfield Road, in order to reach their headquarters in Dearborn, but the basic experience is the same.) Like their drivers, these cars are flawlessly manicured and run like expensive watches. No matter what the weather, the big machines plow down Woodward like a mighty river of steel.

Yet real life is moving around them outside their tinted power windows. During the 1960s Woodward Avenue became the home of the so-called "muscle car" phenomenon. As a part of the youth uprising in the later part of the decade young men turned to smaller than average but monstrously overpowered automobiles and began ripping up the pavement in impromptu street races. Woodward Avenue, with its drive-ins, fast food parlors and wide lanes, became a nighttime racetrack. As fat-tired Chevys, Fords and Pontiacs began snorting under the neon shimmer, the more aggressive marketing men in the auto industry recognized the trend and sought to capitalize on it. Rumbling Dodge Hemis, Plymouth Road Runners, Chevrolet Corvettes, Ford Mustangs, Olds 4-4-2s and brightly-hued Pontiac GTOs were created specifically for this market and Woodward Avenue became their proving ground.

The Pontiac muscle car was actually an overpowered, stylized version of the mundane Tempest intermediate coupe. It was the work of three rising automotive stars, John Z. DeLorean, then the chief engineer at Pontiac, his assistant, Bill Collins, and a flamboyant advertising marketer, Jim Wangers. By wedging the powerful, 348 horsepower "Tri-Power" V-8 from the larger Bonneville into the lighter, smaller Tempest and renaming it GTO (a direct steal from a limited production Ferrari model), they created the fastest and most rakish of the muscle cars then entering the market. The "Goat," as the teenagers immediately labeled the car, was a giant hit. The following year Pontiac raised the horsepower to a thumping 360, and the sales continued to climb. Pontiac even went so far as to have a semiofficial "factory team," based at their Royal Pontiac dealership in adjacent Royal Oak, racing on Woodward.

At the peak of the GTO madness James Roche collared Pontiac General Manager John Z. DeLorean in the GM executive suite and said, "I am sick and tired of hearing about GTO Tigers!" That comment signaled the turnabout that would end the muscle car era in the first years of the 1970s.

The muscle car business boomed until shifting social attitudes, crippling insurance rates, the Clean Air Act and the fuel crisis removed the cars from the market in the early 1970's. But they left a vivid message etched in the Woodward asphalt: A segment of the younger American market was hooked on smaller, more agile automobiles. The muscle cars had mainly been compact and intermediate chassis carrying oversized engines, but their attraction lay not only in their numbing acceleration but in the shift toward advanced technology that they represented.

The muscle cars never reached over ten percent of the domestic market, but they had made an impact on the nation's attitude toward small cars, one that was beyond the comprehension of the Detroit executives who saw the muscle car revolution on Woodward Avenue as nothing more than a teenage quest for thrills. It was accepted that the import buyer and the Pontiac GTO customer had nothing in common; they ostensibly represented two different markets. On the surface this appeared to be true, but it proved to be a near-fatal fallacy.

Muscle cars, with their highly tuned engines, improved handling, better braking, and more flexible four-speed transmissions, represented a missing link between the ostentatious land arks Detroit was building and the smaller, more maneuverable, technically sophisticated imported sports and economy automobiles that were beginning to arrive on our shores in the mid-1960s.

Had they looked beyond their hood ornaments, the Bloomfield Hills contingent might have recognized that the so-called teenage punk street racers and their bouffant-haired girl friends could tell them more about the shifting tastes in cars than all the stultified market research being produced to satisfy the preconceptions of the Detroit Mind.

/////

These decent, upstanding citizens, managers of the American auto industry, were born into the culture of rural and small town Middle America between the great wars. They remember the Depression and served in the struggle against the Japanese and Germans. They participated in the glory years of the American dream, when hard work and ingenuity could repel any adversary. They joined the auto industry and gave it a lifetime of unquestioning devotion, watching it gain unprecedented stature and power. From the moment in their childhood when they first witnessed Henry Ford's Model T crabbing its way through the cold Michigan winters to the proud day when they received their first Cadillac, Lincoln, or Chrysler, the ideals of the American automobile industry became imprinted on their brains.

Henry Ford had unleashed the automotive age by providing cheap, reliable transportation. General Motors chairman Alfred P. Sloan, Jr. then embellished the notion by exploiting the universal urge for status. He developed a carefully layered lineup of cars based on price, styling and perceived status, beginning with Chevrolet at the bottom and the Cadillac at the top, and layers of Pontiac, Buick and Oldsmobile in between. It offered a perfect way for a restless, upwardly-mobile society to express its newly won affluence. Through the innovation of the annual model change, manufacturing decentralization, brilliant financial management and flawless administration by a series of committees, Sloan created the infrastructure and sales credo of the American automobile industry. It was this philosophy that enabled succeeding GM administrations to carry on after his death in 1966.

Sloan's passing symbolically marked the end of an era at General Motors. A year later, the last of the breed, Frederic G. Donner, retired as chairman of the board, thereby ending the nearly fifty year tradition in which principal corporate business was carried on in New York City rather than Detroit. Like Sloan, Donner was an ice-blue businessman, calculating, intensely private, and totally devoted to the Corporation. His departure opened the way for a cadre of executives who were more oriented, by upbringing and philosophy, toward the Midwest than the East.

They steadily began to migrate from the old elephants' graveyard in Grosse Pointe, where the early moguls were rooted, to the more contemporary precincts of Bloomfield Hills. It was a slow exodus, however, and business life still centered around downtown locations like the Detroit Athletic Club, the Detroit Club and such traditional eating places as the London Chop House and the Caucus Club. As the years passed the business took on a seemingly eternal quality, as if the Vatican had been transferred to the shores of Lake St. Clair. The world was rich, smug, and midwestern, and it would last forever.

As the younger gunners of the industry flooded toward Bloomfield, remnants of the great auto families—the Dodges, the Chryslers, the Fords (including Henry II) and others—remained in Grosse Pointe, where they have slowly come to adopt something of a fortress mentality. A few blocks to the west, across Alter Road, the multitudes of East Detroit's jobless blacks press against their back fences. The transition is instantaneous and shocking. One block will be lined with gaping slums; the next will blossom with the shiny palaces of the upper middle class. There are five major components of Grosse Pointe: Grosse Pointe Park, Grosse Pointe Farms, Grosse Pointe Woods, Grosse Pointe Shores and Grosse Pointe. All are affected by the same paranoia—the gripping fear that the black multitudes will one day break across the imaginary boundaries. The move toward Bloomfield Hills, away from aging and threatened Grosse Pointe, has enabled the auto executive to maintain his supreme isolation, both intellectually and sociologically.

/////

The myopic behavior of many General Motors executives can be traced to a complex of buildings on Chevrolet Avenue in Flint, Michigan, a city of 150,000 that may stand as the ultimate embodiment of the "company town." It is the headquarters of GM's Buick division, as well as five Chevrolet plants, a pair of Fisher Body factories, seven AC Spark Plug facilities, and several warehousing operations.

Flint is the nominal birthplace of General Motors, being the home of carriage maker William Crapo Durant, the erratic entrepreneur who erected the original framework of the Corporation. In 1978, before GM's great collapse began, more than half of Flint's citizens were working in the corporate vineyards and enjoyed the second highest wage scale, behind Anchorage, Alaska, of any municipality in the nation. By 1982, GM had slashed 18,000 jobs from its work force and the city was burdened with a 23 percent unemployment rate, the highest of any major metropolitan area.

Despite the automotive depression, one unit of the GM empire in Flint has continued to operate virtually at full strength. This is the General Motors Institute, a company university that has helped shape the Detroit Mind by institutionalizing the industry's isolation. Old-timers still call it "GM Tech," and *Fortune* magazine has termed it the "West Point of General Motors." For years most of the company's top brass were graduates of this unique institution. Alumni still command a strong respect, but GMI's power has recently tended to diminish as a frightened General Motors management attempts to broaden the background of its executive roster.

"Outsiders" are now rising in higher corporate ranks, but General Motors Institute still remains a prime source of the middle and upper-middle-level managers who operate as a vast private industrial civil service. Like state and federal bureaucracies, GMI graduates tend to behave as a separate, uncontrollable element within the system, often unresponsive to true corporate needs much less the demands of their customers.

GMI is a fully accredited university that has everything except the academic independence that makes for true higher education. As Paul Goodman explained in *Community of Scholars*, it is the "foreign" nature of a university that separates it from the community and makes it able to understand the culture objectively. GMI is far from foreign; it is an inherent part of the Corporation.

School begins each year for about 500 eighteen year old freshmen (selected from approximately 3500 applicants) who achieve the highest Scholastic Aptitude Test scores, especially in math and science. GMI is a technical school, with the single purpose of creating General Motors managers. There is little interest in abstract thought and even less devotion to the humanities. The curriculum is almost purely technical, with major emphasis on engineering, applied science, and advanced technology.

Some attention is given to management-labor relations and other nontechnical subjects valuable to the Corporation, but liberal arts courses in the homogeneous, nonintellectual atmosphere of GMI are as rare as campus riots. Many GMI graduates, 95 percent of whom immediately join the Corporation with salaries ranging up to $24,000, will have taken only a single course in art or literature or foreign language in their four years at GMI. This unbalanced curriculum is one of the failings that leaves GMI graduates unable to comprehend why the Detroit Mind shaped by the school is lost in the complexities of the modern internationalized world.

In a sense, General Motors Institute is older than the Corporation itself. An outgrowth of the evening classes run by the Flint Vehicle Workers' Mutual Benefit Association before World War I, it evolved into a well-organized night school for local production workers and supervisory personnel. By 1926 it had grown to the point that the vibrant young Corporation was asked to take it over and expand its curriculum. It did, first as General Motors Institute of Technology, then as General Motors Institute.

For years the school was an incredible bargain, offering students low tuition and good pay during their lengthy periods of on-the-job training. In recent years annual tuition for the five-year program, which alternates three-month shifts of classroom courses and actual work, remained at $1200, which was more than offset by the $8000 salary paid to senior students. However, as the economy squeezes the GM budget General Motors Institute has been transformed into a privately endowed college, a move which might raise its tuition as well as enrich its curriculum.

The indoctrination of GMI Corp-think has exerted immense influence, most of it negative, on the recent history of General Motors. Its emphasis on empirical problem-solving, rigid discipline, and undying loyalty to the traditional Corporation has produced a breed of executive whose outstanding qualities have been a slavish commitment to whatever job was assigned to him and a tendency for non-creative "team play" that is ill-suited to today's intensively competitive market.

/////

The effect of the General Motors Institute education can be found in the career of GM's former president, Elliott M. "Pete" Estes, who retired in 1981 as president and chief operating officer after 47 years with the Corporation. Estes was a small-towner in the story-book success mold. Born in tiny Mendon, Michigan, population 900, he graduated from high school in nearby Constantine, a town of less than 2000, and in 1934, at age 18, he trekked northward to Flint and entered "GM Tech." Save for two years at the University of Cincinnati, where he received a degree in mechanical engineering in 1940, Estes would never leave GM.

In 1956 Estes was hired by Pontiac's new division manager, Semon "Bunkie" Knudsen, the son of former GM president William S. "Big Bill" Knudsen, who sits in the pantheon of corporate deities beside Chairman Alfred P. Sloan, Jr. and the legendary engineer and inventor Charles F. "Boss" Kettering. At that time Pontiac was in desperate shape, so weak in the market that only its foundry was generating a profit. Rumors were circulating that GM was considering the removal of this fossilized "maiden aunt's car" from its lineup. With little to lose, young Bunkie set out to revitalize the Pontiac image. Estes, who had been a member of the Kettering team which developed GM's revolutionary high-compression V-8 engines in the late 1940s, came to Pontiac from Oldsmobile, where he had advanced to assistant chief engineer.

Knudsen, with Estes as his new chief engineer and John DeLorean as his new director of advanced engineering, managed to turn around Pontiac's image in as stunning a fashion as the Marlboro cigarette transformation from a ladies' filter tip to a symbol of the western frontier. By 1961 the "Wide Track" Catalinas and Bonnevilles were winning on America's stock car tracks and drag strips, and the brand had become a sales leader in the GM lineup. The newly discovered youth market of the 1960s moved the Pontiac Division into third place nationwide and doubled sales from 372,000 units in 1961 to 687,000 in 1964. All this occurred under the directorship of Estes, who took Knudsen's place as head of Pontiac in 1961 when the latter became general manager of the flagship Chevrolet Division.

Pete Estes was forty-five years old at the time. A large, loose-limbed man, he was gaining a reputation as a consummate corporate politician. He was a classic GM superstar: conservative in dress and style, a good family man, a white Anglo-Saxon blessed with that special brand of midwestern folksiness that injected levity, faint self-mockery and first-name banter into the weightiest of conversations. He was a man bred in the General Motors system, a "good guy executive" who had superficially shed the aloofness of the Sloan dynasty. Had he not been a major force in the world's largest industrial entity, he would have fit perfectly behind the counter of the corner drugstore in his southern Michigan home town.

Estes moved up toward the Fourteenth Floor executive suite in the General Motors Building in 1965 when he took Knudsen's place as general manager at Chevrolet. The more rebellious DeLorean in turn moved into the top slot at Pontiac, where he pushed hard with the division's GTO muscle car and its teenage street-racer image. It was during this period that DeLorean sanctioned the racing antics on Woodward Avenue with the clear understanding that sales in the car-crazed 1960s were based on marketing audacity.

In January 1968, Bunky Knudsen resigned, a rare act among the corporation's six thousand executive-level loyalists. Knudsen then had a brief flirtation with the mercurial Henry Ford II as president of the Ford Motor Company, but lost out to the master salesman from Chester, Pennsylvania, Lee Iacocca.

Knudsen's downfall at General Motors could be traced to his progressive business posture and his individuality, which contrasted too sharply with the Politburo atmosphere of the GM executive suite. Not so with good soldier Pete Estes, who took his place on the Fourteenth Floor almost a year to the day after Knudsen's departure. With thirty-five of his fifty-three years devoted to unbending service to the Corporation, Pete Estes had made it, even though critics note that he left behind a Chevrolet Division with sagging profits, a diminishing share of the market, lower quality levels and reduced dealer profits. His new job was to oversee the Car and Truck Group, a manufacturing responsibility with a direct line to the presidency. DeLorean once again followed him up the ladder, leaving the Pontiac general managership to take Estes's job at Chevrolet, which was DeLorean's next-to-last post before he resigned from General Motors after a rough political squabble.

Individualist Knudsen had been elbowed out, but Pete Estes had made it comfortably to the Fourteenth Floor. His future was confirmed in October 1972, when he was elevated to the executive vice presidency in charge of the key Operations Staff. From that base camp it was only a short climb to the summit. The system seemed to be working. The transitions were taking place in perfect harmony, although outside the great fortress there were signs of rebellion. The passions and frustrations of the Vietnam War were shredding the nation's social fabric. The federal government was harassing the industry with new demands for safety and exhaust emission improvements. The imports were nibbling at a 20 percent share of the domestic market, but nobody seemed to be paying much attention.

The Fourteenth Floor was operating in monkish isolation, with the perpetual committee meetings broken only by trips to New York for corporate board sessions, lavish conferences at exclusive resorts, small weekend dinners and golf games, and near-sacred hunting trips to northern Michigan, where vast preserves like the Turtle Lake Club cater almost almost exclusively to auto industry princes.

Estes survived the crises coolly and less than two years later it all paid off. In September 1974 he was elected president and chief operating officer of the Corporation he had served with unshakable loyalty, if not with sheer brilliance, for forty years. Although he had been a powerful executive for much of his adult life, Pete Estes had developed few of the social graces generally associated with rank. The cuff links got bigger, the suits more expensive, but they still clothed the shambling small-towner from Mendon, Michigan.

He was a practitioner of the tough-talk interview, where folksy chatter laced with light profanity was intended to be equated with sincerity. Hardly a devotee of the King's English, he easily meandered into mixed metaphors and nonsequiturs. During an interview with *Car and Driver* in 1976, which the editors had the bad form to print verbatim, Estes said about the oil embargo: "By December, we couldn't sell a big car to save our ass from first base."

Two months after Pete Estes became president of GM, Thomas Aquinas Murphy, known to all as "Tom," ascended to the chairmanship. A month older than Estes, Murphy had been with the Corporation since his graduation from the University of Illinois in 1938. His appointment followed a tradition which insisted that the presidency was to be held by a manufacturing expert while the chairman was to be a man with a strong financial background. Tom Murphy was an authority in financial analysis.

Though he and Estes implemented the General Motors decision to downsize its lineup following the 1973 oil embargo, and are therefore unjustly credited with being industrial visionaries, Murphy maintained the standard industry bias about big versus small. Big "family-size" vehicles were sensible machines for right-thinking Americans, while little cars were at best stopgap oddities designed for the underbelly of the market.

During a 1976 question-and-answer session at the Detroit Economic Club, Tom Murphy discussed the then-new Chevette from that ingrained perspective: "We think the subcompacts are a good value for people who are interested in that type of product... I think the Chevette is a fine automobile. It has the best gas mileage of any car built in America today... I'm not satisfied with our business in that area... All I can say is, if you haven't driven one, try it, because it's a helluva value."

Murphy had artfully steered around the reality that the Chevette was an ordinary small car, rushed into production with parts scavenged from the German Opel Kadett and various Brazilian GM sources. It had been thrown onto the American market within 18 months in reaction to the oil embargo. The Chevette was a legitimate, if retroactive, small car, but it contained no sparkling technology. There were those inside the Corporation who smiled at its entry on the market, along with the much-heralded "small" Cadillac, the

Seville. This car, hastily patched together from a Chevrolet Nova substructure, was Cadillac's tardy entry into the battle with Mercedes-Benz.

Several imprudent young men had informed the moguls during this period that over 75 percent of the cars being produced in the world were *smaller* than a Nova and that by the mid-80s a majority of the cars on the road would be the size of the Chevette. "They were laughed out of the boardroom," recalls a corporate informant. But General Motors did reverse its field more quickly than either Ford or Chrysler and was able to build a case, however tenuous, that it was responding to the demands of the market, even if the public was not overjoyed with its new products.

Tom Murphy quickly gained a reputation for tough talk. At one point he remarked that he would not be satisfied until General Motors "sold every car that was sold," thereby thumbing his nose at the Justice Department and its veiled threats of bringing anti-trust proceedings against GM if its market share seriously exceeded sixty percent. In fact, as the two GM executives, good old Pete and Tom, celebrated their sixtieth birthdays (Murphy turned sixty in December 1975; Estes in January 1976) they openly espoused a "60-60-60" formula which Murphy described as "an internal slogan type of thing—a motivator." It referred to the goal of boosting GM's sagging common stock price to $60 per share, while regaining a 60 percent share of the domestic market during the executives' sixtieth year. Despite Murphy's oft-repeated contention that, "if you're in a competitive business, then you ought to be out there trying for every sale," 1976 passed without either goal becoming a reality.

Pete and Tom retired in 1981 and were replaced by "Jim and Roger." Francis James "Jim" McDonald had trailed Estes and the fallen DeLorean through the general managerships of both Pontiac and Chevrolet. Roger B. Smith had followed Murphy through the Corporation's financial hierarchy before reaching the chairmanship.

Like Estes, Jim McDonald was a Michigan native (Saginaw) and had been a member of the GM team from the time he entered the General Motors Institute in 1940. Smith had been at GM since 1949, when he was awarded an MBA from the University of Michigan.

Both men were branded with the GM "Mark of Excellence" early in their careers. Smith soon gained a reputation as an expert accountant and mathematician. His early career is still remembered for his furious output of information blitzes. Shortly after he was hired, he is said to have deluged his bosses with a hundred-page report on the German Opel subsidiary. Smith used this technique and the clear lessons of unstinting team play to reach his $800,000 a year payoff.

Now in power, McDonald and Smith, with hearty midwestern optimism, insist that there is an infusion of fresh thought in General Motors. But there is little evidence of change. Early in 1981, when the automobile business was in its greatest sales slump since the 1930s, Smith appeared on a national television news program to announce a major campaign to lift General Motors out of its doldrums. On the air Smith enthusiastically described his revelation: *a sweepstakes.*

Industry observers sat slack-jawed as the chairman of the world's largest automobile manufacturer articulated a recovery scheme that involved a soggy sales gimmick as innovative as a "going out of business" sale. Yet he seemed heartened by the notion, convinced that he was announcing a revolutionary idea to a public long since stupefied by the circus of industry rebates and related price slashing.

Compared to Chairman Roger Smith, President Jim McDonald was a public relations dream. The chairman increasingly fell victim to more gaffes. It was in early 1982 that Smith announced that he was cutting his half-million dollar a year income by $135 a week as a personal sacrifice in the face of declining sales. Then, in a sad moment in GM history, Smith and his colleagues voted themselves increased bonuses just hours after the Corporation had extracted $2.5 billion in long term wage concessions from the Union. UAW chief Douglas Fraser was prompted suggest that "a zipper be placed on Roger Smith's lip."

/////

The Detroit Mind of Estes, McDonald, Murphy and Smith is wedded to the solid traditions and values of the American Midwest.

In many ways these values are admirable, but unfortunately they are not sufficient for survival in the competitive technological world. In the midst of an automotive recession and the possible collapse of large segments of the American car industry, Detroit public relations men still trumpet the strong family instincts and basic goodness of their new leaders. "These guys are family men. They work like hell all over the country, but if there's any way, they'll be home with their families at night," says a senior GM public relations man. "I can't begin to count the times that I've ridden all night on company planes with Jim and Pete, just so they could get home to their own beds."

General Motors spokesmen even brag about the fact that Roger Smith has on occasion flown home simply to deliver his twelve-year old to his job at the McDonald's in Bloomfield Hills. Jim McDonald, the ex-newsboy, fraternity president, and submarine officer, once told an interviewer, "Letting the public know and see what kind of people run General Motors—just *ordinary* people, and that's a big revelation to a lot of people—is vitally important."

Both Smith and McDonald had middle class fathers, one a banker, the other a dentist who was wiped out in the Great Depression. Their beginnings were humble but decent, the environment that made America great. They are no more like the robber barons in striped pants than is the corner grocer. The problem is that they are part of an industry tied to the old WASP traditions of business with an overlay of a newer midwestern ethic of good fellowship and social conformity. Smith and McDonald are victims of their own small town upbringing and the premium placed on the *work ethic* rather than the *creative ethic*. In the market they once dominated, their narrow tastes and their personal needs could be sold to an unknowing public. Once this world was open to the competition of new ideas, the provincial Detroit Mind could not comprehend, let alone meet, the challenge.

A younger breed of managers at General Motors may be aware of this shift in national and international sensibilities. Robert Stempel, the youngish general manager of Chevrolet and a serious candidate for the presidency, says: "The kids who grew up in the 1960s and 70s grew up with hi-tech. It's part of their lives. It's no big deal. They simply expect it to be part of everything, including their automobiles."

Stempel is correct in his analysis of the new automotive consumer, but he, like all his colleagues, insists on defending Detroit's record. Stempel and others argue that much of the engineering funding and expertise of the industry was consumed in the 1970s by meeting the requirements of a paper storm of government emissions-control and safety edicts. This may be partially true but it ignores two realities: the abject failure of earlier Detroit leaders to recognize major shifts in consumer attitude and the fact that many smaller European and Japanese carmakers met the US government standards without complaint while producing generally superior products.

Can things be changed? Is the American automobile industry finished as the world leader and permanently relegated to secondary status?

Perhaps. If this is not to happen, Detroit must undergo an internal revolution, one that encourages the more daring, more sophisticated, more ethnically and culturally diverse executive who understands that Detroit and its splendid suburbs are not the epicenter of western civilization. Most important, they must realize that the Detroit Mind can no longer be the philosophical model for American industrial society.

CHAPTER III

The Small Car War: Are Detroit's Wounds Self-Inflicted?

"DON'T CALL 'EM IMPORTS. Call 'em foreign. That makes 'em mad," remarked Chrysler Corporation vice president R. K. Brown over lunch at Detroit's Little Harry's restaurant. It was 1968, a time when it was safe, almost requisite, to laugh about small foreign cars. The imports were rising out of the dismal sales pit that had left them with only 4.89 percent of the American market six years earlier, but their share was still hovering at less than 10 percent. Their combined American sales were under a million units, half a million less than Chrysler alone and minuscule in comparison to that year's model of one brand, the Chevrolet, which would be bought by over 2 million Americans.

But the "foreigners" would not go away. They had captured 10 percent of the domestic market once before, in 1959-60, but they had been repelled by Detroit's three-pronged offensive against the imported small cars: Chevrolet's Corvair, Ford's Falcon and Chrysler's Valiant. But these "compacts," as Detroit euphemistically termed them, soon followed the inevitable American pattern. They almost magically grew in size and price, allowing the imports to squeeze back through the crevices in the market and into the affections of that seemingly mad coterie of American eccentrics, the small car lovers. Now, nearing the 1970s, foreign car sales were on the rise again, especially in bellwether California, where nearly one car in four sold was made outside the United States.

A few months prior to Brown's dismissal of the import problem, General Motors board chairman James M. Roche had dedicated the new GM Building, in its modern marble Italianate splendor, at Fifth Avenue and Fifty-ninth Street in New York. He surprised the press with an announcement. GM, he confided, was reentering the small car war. The General Motors entry would be code-named XP887. It would be introduced in 1971 as the Chevrolet Vega and would permit the Corporation to be competitive at the bottom of the automobile market where size, economy, and low price seemed to be the attraction.

Ford was quick to follow the American leader. It too announced that it would resume the small car competition. The trade press was alive with rumors that a subcompact called the Ford Pinto would reach the showrooms at the same time as the GM entry. Chrysler, which was now being run by a phalanx of CPAs, decided there was little potential profit in such minuscule vehicles. They shelved earlier plans for the "25-car," the factory code name for the Chrysler subcompact model. At the time Chrysler was importing both the Cricket, a shabbily built sedan manufactured by its English subsidiary, the Rootes Group, and the 1204 Simca, a spindly, oddly styled, front-wheel-drive car from France. Discussions had begun with Mitsubishi Heavy Industries to import and sell a lineup of Japanese-built cars in 1971. There seemed to be little pressure to tool up to satisfy this unprofitable underbelly of the domestic car market.

The smallest of the four domestic carmakers, American Motors, had developed a corporate policy that was professionally two-faced. They would try to carve their few percentage points out of the conventional American market while simultaneously representing themselves as the standard bearer of the small car. The AMC Gremlin was produced for this market, but it proved to be a blunderbuss, created by sawing twelve inches off the tail of the Hornet, which they had introduced two years earlier. The Gremlin was not only heavier than its competitors, but thirstier as well. It offered mileage only in the 20-22 mpg range for normal driving, hardly impressive for a small automobile.

This showdown with the imports was set for late in 1970. It was almost ten years to the day after the 1960 campaign and, ironically, the enemy would be the same imported car—the wheezy, underpowered machine from Germany that had remained virtually unchanged in design for nearly forty years and was now suddenly achieving a cultlike following among certain Americans. It was the ubiquitous "Beetle," the famed Volkswagen which had been designed by German engineering genius Dr. Ferdinand Porsche.

The car had briefly intrigued Adolf Hitler, who envisioned it as a universal worker's vehicle, but due to the war effort and Nazi party bungling, it was never produced in quantity. Its production facilities were finally destroyed by Allied bombing. After the war the Volkswagen was rejected for purchase by a number of established American and European carmakers, including Ford, who saw little future for the toylike auto. When it began to appear in appreciable quantities on American shores late in 1953, it seemed little more than a leftover touch of whimsy from the now defunct Third Reich.

This tiny, bubble-shaped machine with barely enough power to operate the air conditioning unit of America's largest automobiles was initially a source of amusement in Detroit. But, miraculously, it sold. It was generating the kind of cocktail party chatter that can initiate unstoppable marketing campaigns. By 1956, 50,000 of the Beetles had been imported from Germany and bought by drivers who were willing to forgo the luxury of automatic transmissions, efficient heat, and pavement-ripping acceleration for the payoff of negligible operating costs, high mileage, technical originality that optimized simplicity, and anvil-like toughness. One colleague who owned a "Volks" roared into a curve on a country road with his 1956 VW, lost control, and rolled it over on its roof. He climbed out, unhurt, flopped the car back on its wheels and drove off while a farmer sat on his tractor in open-mouthed amazement.

This tiny machine, which was gaining the same status as the sturdy Ford Model T of thirty years earlier, was transforming the national consciousness about automobiles. The idea that something smaller in autos might be preferable to something larger was gaining credibility. The new small cars from Ford and Chevrolet, the Pinto and Vega, now had a target: the strange machine shaped like a beetle but which had the resiliency and near-immortality of a cockroach.

General Motors had already tried to close the small car gap by importing the Opel Kadett from its German subsidiary for sale through its Buick dealers. But the Kadett was a mediocre machine, and it was being sold by big car advocates who were condescending in their attitude toward potential buyers. The Buick dealer's sales pitch for an Opel was usually demeaning. It went like this: "If you can't afford one of our *real* Buicks, let me show you one of our *little* German Opels." Condemned to second-rate status by dealers whose profit margins were considerably higher on the large cars, the technologically nondescript Opel Kadett was clearly inadequate to the challenge. The Kadett was never intended to be a serious competitor, and it failed to even slow the foreign invasion. Like Detroit's other entries into the small car field, the Opel stole sales from other GM brands, but was unable to sway the loyalty of the growing body of imported car enthusiasts.

By the end of the 1960s, the Japanese—particularly Toyota and Datsun—had also become a factor in the imported car field. But Detroit still regarded small cars as cheap alternatives to regular cars, and was slowly, but inexorably, losing any chance to gain credibility in the small car segment of the market. Ford too made a stab at the market with the Maverick, an amalgam of the old Mustang and a Falcon, but it too was obviously a halfhearted attempt. Now a new, full-scale assault would have to be mounted against the pesky, persistent foreigners.

Ford decided to tread an ultraconservative path. Their new 1971 Pinto was a small, front-engine subcompact with no distinguishing engineering features. It carried an engine imported from Ford's British subsidiary and proved to be a rather noisy, modestly powered car slightly larger and more cumbersome than the Volkswagen, Toyota, Opel, Datsun and Fiat models that now dominated the import market. Originally the Pinto was not unsuccessful in the marketplace; critics described it as the "car nobody loved but everybody bought."

But the Pinto was a slave to its fastback styling. It had limited rear seat space, positioned shorter drivers at chin level with the window wells, and provided only a tiny storage trunk. The ride generated by its rudimentary suspension was choppy and abrupt, and early tests revealed a general flabbiness in its fabrication, a tendency toward rust and rattles, and relatively high road noise.

The General Motors entry, the Vega, was touted as an import killer of lethal dimensions. An ambitious pre-announcement ad campaign hinted: "Coming Soon: The little car that does everything well." It also boasted that "Our little car's engine will use hypereutectic alloys and other delights." Despite such hyperbole, the car behind the ad campaign proved to be rather ordinary. The only important technological advance in the Vega was its all-aluminum, four-cylinder engine, another brainchild of Ed Cole, the engineer who had become the president of GM.

The Vega carried all the trappings Detroiters had discovered were necessary to be taken seriously in the small car world: optional four-speed, floor-mounted shift (a component they insisted for years Americans would and could not use), front disc brakes, and an overhead camshaft engine, albeit a bulky, low-revving version. Although well-sized and reasonably styled, the Vega—like the Pinto—tended to err on the side of conservatism. It was, on paper, a solid contender in the second offensive against the imports which by this time had already captured 15 percent of sales nationwide and nearly twice that in California.

But on the road the Vega displayed major flaws. Cole's aluminum engine proved to be noisy, underpowered, and prone to leaks and overheating, all the while vibrating like a diesel. Despite the much-publicized shift to robotics at the new Lordstown, Ohio, assembly plant, constant labor strife only added to the monumentally bad workmanship. The car was blighted by infuriating oil leaks, warped cylinder heads, rusted bodies and rattles as well as a harsh ride, heavy steering and cramped interior space. The Vega also came to market with a price tag several hundred dollars higher than the competition and at 250-300 pounds over its designated weight.

In 1971, the Vega and Pinto were helped by the Nixon administration decision to let the dollar float against foreign currency, which revalued the Deutschemark and the yen upward and gave the domestic products a small pricing advantage. But this advantage was temporary. The harsh verities of the marketplace could not be denied. Compared to the constantly improving Japanese competition—and even the aged but indomitable Beetle—the Vega and Pinto were second-rate machines.

Ford and GM had entered a market that was unbelievably volatile and churning with creativity. The milestone Honda Civic was only a few months away and a revolutionary new Volkswagen replacement for the Beetle, the Rabbit, was on the drawing board. But both American giants had entered the competition with old-fashioned, overweight, underpowered automobiles that only served to confirm the suspicion among buyers that Detroit was incapable of building anything but chromed land arks.

The whole American small car effort came to a dramatic climax when the Ford Motor Company was charged with reckless homicide in a criminal trial in Winamac, Indiana, in 1980. The case stemmed from a crash in 1978 in which three girls in a Pinto had burned to death. The prosecution contended that Ford knew there was a flaw in the fuel filler necks of pre-1976 Pintos that could cause the car to burst into flames in the event of a rear-end collision, but that the company did nothing to correct the problem. The charge was not sustained, but the trial destroyed what little credibility was left for the hapless machines. The Pinto disappeared from the market shortly thereafter, but it had outlived GM's Vega by three years. Of the two it proved the more successful product.

Before his recent misadventures, John DeLorean claimed that his Chevrolet Division engineering staff had created a superior version of the Vega, but that it was rejected in favor of the design developed by the Corporate Design Staff as part of GM's move toward centralization.

/////

The Vega and the Pinto were heavily promoted, but the messages that reached the American public from Detroit's executive suites were ambiguous, even confusing. While publicly extolling small car virtues and congratulating themselves for their prescience in entering the new market, most of Detroit's traditionalists were hoping this dalliance with the midgets would soon end. Only then could the industry's divinely mandated role of building large cars for real Americans be resumed, full scale.

Big cars were not only the American way but they represented big, immediate quarterly profits and dividends as well. The actual cost of building an automobile in Detroit is as carefully guarded a secret as the Coca-Cola formula, but the trade is well aware that a large Chevrolet Caprice—loaded down with thousands of dollars' worth of high-profit options—can be built for only hundreds of dollars more than a stripped Vega. It was inevitable that the men who were then running Detroit, elbow-deep in ledger sheets and intent on increasing short-time profits, wanted to see the Vega and the Pinto operate like hired assassins: to eradicate the nuisance imports, then disappear from the automotive scene as quickly as possible.

In Detroit, the subcompacts and the imported interlopers were viewed as an abstruse, anti-American phenomenon rather than the bellwether of a major market shift. But outsiders were more realistic in their judgments, warning that this could be the making of a future American industrial Waterloo. *Car and Driver* magazine, as a prelude to its unenthusiastic reviews of the new Pinto and Vega, told its readers: "Now Detroit is making its last stand. Ford and General Motors have anted up not millions, but hundreds of millions of dollars to tool the Pinto and the Vega 2300 and no excuses or copouts are being made. Neither is a half-hearted, cut-down intermediate with 'broad appeal'; instead they are the best, most import-beating subcompacts American technology knows how to build. If VW and other small-car intruders survive this attack they'll be assumed invincible."

The intruders did survive. While the Vega and Pinto sold creditably, they did little to impress the buyer who had already been subtly seduced by foreign styling and technology. Instead, the American compacts found their market among Chevrolet and Ford loyalists looking for second cars or economy. The hoped-for conquest sales were not there. Detroit was not whittling away at import strength, and by 1973 sales of German and Japanese units had edged to 1.7

million. That grand joke, the Beetle, now in its design dotage, was still a dominant force in the market, but newer products from both Toyota and Datsun were about to signal its demise.

All of this churning was, from Detroit's point of view, at the undesirable bottom of the market. It promoted little more than superficial alarm on the Fourteenth Floor. After all, in 1973 GM had produced 8.6 million cars, trucks and buses worldwide and had generated a net income of $2.3 billion. No one was ready to overreact to the nagging presence of the Japanese and their little automobiles. "Down-size" was a new trend to be reckoned with, but corporate enthusiasm was hardly strong.

That Detroit had failed to understand the trend toward small cars is deplorable. But that they understood and had consciously tried to subvert the trend is even worse. There are those who believe that Detroit's failure has been self-inflicted, that in attempting to stem the movement toward small autos in the sixties and seventies they *purposely* made their economy cars a cheap imitation of their standard-sized models. The motive was simple: to sell the public the specious idea that *small* is *poor*.

I recall the remarks of a senior marketing expert, sitting in the walnut-walled sanctity of Detroit's Caucus Club talking about the just-introduced small-sized Chevrolet Vega. "I've got to believe that the car is a conscious second-rate effort that's intended to turn as many people off as it does on," he told me. "If the Vega is a major success, it'll threaten the big cars, and that can't happen. The Vega is not viewed as a mainstream automobile, but simply as an import fighter in the low-cost segment of the market."

Several years later this sentiment was echoed by an engineer from Ford. "The Pinto could have been a better automobile in many ways, but to have made it better might have permitted it to intrude into areas of the market where it wasn't supposed to be."

This philosophical bias, in which small cars were not regarded as real cars, was the genesis of Detroit's demise as the world leader. Had their best effort been put forth in automobiles like the Vega and the Pinto—or even in the later J-car—the position of the so-called compacts would have been altered. Detroit's small cars, which were inevitably to be their future, would not only have been seen as quality products within the industry, but they would have impressed the buying public with the same idea. As it was, small cars were regarded by Detroit as substandard products that would—when the world returned to spin in its accustomed orbit—be quickly supplanted by larger, more profitable, more normal automobiles.

/////

To comprehend why such a fatal mistake in long-range planning was made, and why small cars (or any different cars) were not taken seriously, it is important to realize that Detroit has been influenced by only two success stories in its long history. The first was Henry Ford and his Model T, which revolutionized society and laid the foundations for the mass production system.

The second was the rise of General Motors. This megacorporation displaced Ford as the financial and philosophical engine that was to set the patterns by which automobiles were built and sold for fifty years. The secret to General Motors' success was simple: offer more—at least the illusion of more—than the competition. In the beginning, the competition was a single make of automobile, the venerated Model T of Henry Ford.

The Ford Model T, the "Tin Lizzie," which was first produced in 1908, practically reoriented the socioeconomic structure of the nation. It was a basic car, designed for economical transportation. Although little attention was given to styling or comfort, over a nineteen year span *fifteen million* of them (most in basic black and with simplest, most rugged mechanical components imaginable) were sold in the United States and Europe. By 1920 *one* in every *two* automobiles in the world was a Model T.

The creation of the first assembly line at Ford's Highland Park plant in 1914 permitted him to steadily increase production while reducing the price. The Model T was introduced in 1908 with a price of $850; by 1916 its price had dropped to $360 while its numbers had increased *one hundredfold*, from about 6000 to nearly 600,000. When pressure from his son, Edsel, his harried executive staff, and the marketplace finally caused him to angrily stop production of the "T" in 1927, Ford's retail price for the car was only $290. The assembly lines stayed idle for over a year while a replacement, the Model A, was readied by frantic designers.

While Ford was launching the Model T, William Crapo "Billy" Durant was forming General Motors. A spell-binding salesman and speculator, Durant took the financially-troubled Buick Company and linked it with several other of Ford's struggling competitors. One was the Cadillac Motor Company, which had been created by engineering perfectionist Henry Leland, who also invented the electric hair clipper. Another was the Oakland Company, later to become Pontiac. Durant then brought in Oldsmobile and several smaller makes including Carter, Elmore and Welch to form General Motors. It was during this period that Alfred P. Sloan, Jr., a young MIT graduate and president of the Hyatt Roller Bearing Company in New Jersey, became involved in the car business when he began to supply precision bearings for Leland's Cadillacs—which from the onset had a reputation for superb quality.

Billy Durant's financial acrobatics with General Motors put the young company on the brink of bankruptcy in 1910. He was finally eased out. Undeterred, Durant immediately joined up with a garrulous Swiss racing driver and former Buick engineer, Louis Chevrolet, and they began manufacturing cars under the name of the Chevrolet Motor Company. Their hope was to challenge the Ford Model T at the bottom side of the market, but they caused barely a ripple. But Durant was irrepressible. With General Motors still in the doldrums, he created a scheme in which he would trade Chevrolet stock for GM's.

This financially adroit move caught the attention of the DuPont family, who considered General Motors a fire-sale property with enormous potential. They financed Durant and he was soon back in control of his wobbly automotive empire. Durant immediately went on a corporate buying spree. He purchased a majority position in Fisher Body, then took over the small Guardian refrigerator company, which he promptly renamed Frigidaire. He then acquired Hyatt and persuaded Alfred P. Sloan, Jr. to join his burgeoning empire.

But by 1920 Durant had again lost control of the board room. General Motors stock plunged from nearly $400 a share to $12, and his sponsors in Wilmington, the powerful DuPont family, pulled the plug. "Fabulous Billy," who with Henry Ford was the last of the great automotive entrepreneurs, was out on the street. He tried again with Durant Motors, but that ended in failure with the Great Depression. Before he died in 1947, Durant was operating a supermarket and a group of bowling alleys in New Jersey.

Billy Durant had been removed by a combine of DuPont and J. P. Morgan capital, which installed Pierre DuPont as president of General Motors and Sloan as executive vice president and chief operating officer. This marked the beginning of the competitive showdown between Ford, the rural backyard genius, and Sloan, the aloof analytical college man backed by the Eastern establishment who took over the presidency from Pierre DuPont in 1923 and made General Motors into a perfectly-lubricated machine that would dominate Detroit.

Henry Ford was refusing to accept the fact that new management techniques, new sales philosophies and new customer sophistication were boring into his empire. The fact that the Model T was basically a small, spartan, cheap car that was perfectly suited to proletarian aspirations was Ford's Achilles heel. It was this that Sloan took advantage of. Several of those around Ford saw the threat. His patient lieutenant Charles E. Sorensen, and Ford's own son, Edsel, a tragic man of Shakespearian magnitude who finally gave everything, including his life, to his father, knew that Ford had to change but they could not force Henry to make any significant shift in his styling or marketing stance.

Meanwhile Sloan convinced William S. Knudsen to leave Ford in 1921 and join Chevrolet. Two years later, Knudsen became Chevrolet's general manager. He attacked Ford and his basic Model T on a multitude of fronts, giving eager customers a bright, well-styled selection of automobiles in all price ranges instead of Ford's simple Model T. As the car buyer moved up from a Chevrolet to a Buick or even a Cadillac, he was simultaneously purchasing immediate social status with his larger, more expensive automobile.

Ford tried to fight back with the acquisition of Lincoln from Henry Leland in 1922 (Leland created both Cadillac and Lincoln during his brilliant career) but it was hopeless. He was being blitzed by a new force which employed modern financial planning and analysis, advanced engineering, and powerful marketing techniques. Most important, General Motors gave consumers a carefully choreographed annual model change every autumn. Under Sloan, General Motors also strengthened its franchised dealer body, encouraged used-car trade-ins and installment buying through its own financing arm, the General Motors Acceptance Corporation.

These were revolutionary changes within an industry that had been controlled by Henry Ford's sodbuster mentality for nearly twenty years. When Sloan took over, the net sales of GM totalled $698 million a year. By the end of the decade GM annual sales had jumped to $1.5 billion and Chevrolet had far outdistanced Ford as the number one seller in the world. Reflecting on this surge, Sloan said, "Mr. Ford failed to realize it was necessary for new cars to do more than meet the need for basic transportation. Middle income buyers created the demand for progress in new cars, for comfort, convenience, power and style. This was the actual trend of American life, and those who adapted to it prospered."

In recognizing this, Sloan displaced Ford as the single most powerful individual in the automobile industry and not only relegated Ford to a permanent second place in the market, but established selling patterns that became Detroit's counterpart to Joseph Smith's Golden Tablets.

/////

Yet Henry I and the 15 million Model Ts he produced and sold had left an indelible impression on the American psyche. As the car buyers of the thirties, forties and fifties yielded to their cravings for chrome and status as defined by GM's best, they were still tinged with guilt for abandoning Ford's verities of functionalism and Calvinist simplicity. Portions of the market still dreamt of a return to the honest days of the Model T, when automobiles served a basic purpose and were not crude symbols of upward mobility.

Some manufacturers attempted to exploit this nostalgia, but few survived the Great Depression of the 1930s. To the amazement of a vast body of academics and populists, the Depression only solidified the market position of the status-laden auto, while scything away dozens of Model T pretenders, including an important one from Ford itself.

In 1936 Ford developed its Model 92A, one of the first small cars designed to be mass-produced by a major automaker. It was a smaller version of the mainline V-8 Ford set to be introduced a year later. Accountants discovered that the 92A, though 600 pounds lighter and a technical success, could be produced for only $36 less than the full-size model. In a market where GM's "full-line" strategy had placed a premium on size and luxury, the 92A would be an anachronistic failure. It was cancelled.

The paradox of the 1930s was that the social ferment, the bread lines, the labor riots, sit-ins and lockouts that carried the nation to the point of near revolution only confirmed the mammoth Cadillac as the ultimate status symbol. With the Sloan system working flawlessly, America was on a big car binge. It was interrupted for five years while Detroit was being recast as the "Arsenal of Democracy," but the automakers immediately resumed their highly profitable ways at the end of the conflict.

World War II had a staggering impact on the automobile business and on America's automotive consciousness. It opened the way to new technology and spawned a generation of consumers anxious to drive vehicles more glamorous than the boxy prewar sedans. Nearly five years of pent-up demand greeted Detroit at the close of the war and the industry eagerly turned to supplying a car-hungry American public.

But there were problems. Former GM president William Knudsen died in 1948, his health severely impaired by his efforts as a coordinator of war production. Henry Ford had retreated into senility. By 1945 Ford had fired his most trusted aide, Charles Sorensen, with cruel abruptness. The company drifted out of control in the hands of the thuggish strikebreaker Harry Bennett, who had gained Rasputin-like control over the eighty year old auto mogul. Young Henry Ford II, the son of the old man's late, brilliant son, Edsel, was released from the navy in 1943 to assume command but it took two years for him to wrestle the presidency away from his now-incoherent grandfather. It was an almost Olympian power struggle that left the company in ruinous shape.

But new men were arriving on the scene, shucking army khaki or spartan wartime offices for the executive suites of Detroit. Charles E. Wilson took over as president of General Motors, only the fourth man to hold that post in the company's forty year history. He would be remembered as "Engine Charlie," who would later serve as Secretary of Defense under Eisenhower and would outrage many with his aphorism: "What is good for the country is good for General Motors and vice versa." Regardless of the remark, Wilson was an energetic leader who kept GM operating full-throttle during the postwar transition.

It was not as easy for young Henry Ford II, who discovered that once the war contracts ended his company was losing nearly $10 million per month, with chaos rampant in every corporate department. Ford hired a brilliant administrator, Ernest R. Breech, away from the presidency of North American Aviation as his executive vice president and brought in a group of ten young Air Force officers, who would become known as "the Whiz Kids." Specialists in financial management, their nominal leader was Charles "Tex" Thornton, who lasted little more than a year before heading west to create his own electronics empire, Litton Industries. The best known of the group was Robert S. McNamara, who would rise to the presidency of Ford before assuming the post of Secretary of Defense in the Kennedy and Johnson administrations.

With the "Whiz Kids" came another historic shift in the Detroit mentality. These were numbers men, human calculators whose strength lay in analyzing data. They had little interest in, or knowledge of, the automobile as a mechanical device. To them it was simply a product composed of steel, rubber, and glass that had to be manufactured, marketed and distributed in large quantities on a worldwide basis. McNamara would have devoted the same intellectual and analytic intensity to his mission at the Ford Motor Company if the commodity had been fountain pens or ladies ready-to-wear. The equation happened to involve automobiles, and McNamara and his associates helped to put Ford back on an even financial keel.

Robert S. McNamara was the first of a new breed of accountants,

MBAs, and financial technicians rising to power in Detroit. (Eventually, General Motors, Ford and Chrysler would all be controlled by men with financial rather than automotive backgrounds.) But as McNamara rose through the ranks of Ford, the flaw in his temperament became evident: He was a slave to data. His faith in polling, market research and statistical analysis was absolute. It was this fixation with numbers that led McNamara and his associates at Ford to build the Edsel, the monumental disaster created for tomorrow's market based on yesterday's statistical inputs.

The late 1940s and 1950s also witnessed a massive explosion of technological and design energy in the American car business. The finest products of the era were the 1948-49 Cadillacs, which in two model years set the patterns of the industry for nearly twenty years. The Cadillac has now become a symbol of bourgeois excess, but in 1948 it held a well-deserved reputation as a superb luxury automobile. Such devices as the self-starter and the first production V-16 engine had already been introduced on earlier models.

It was in the Cadillac Division that General Motors introduced its revolutionary overhead valve V-8 engine, a lightweight, highly efficient, high-compression unit designed by engineers Edward Cole and Jack Gordon, both of whom would rise to the presidency of the Corporation. Generating 160 horsepower yet over 200 pounds lighter than the chunky in-line eight cylinder car it replaced, the 1949 Cadillac was, with its sister car, the Oldsmobile, the progenitor of the large, overpowered automobiles that dominated the industry in the prosperous, postwar 1950s.

Within six years every major manufacturer—including the doomed carmakers, Hudson, Studebaker, Packard, Willys-Overland and Nash—would enter the "horsepower race" with giant chrome-laden cars powered by enormous V-8 engines in the Cadillac-Oldsmobile mold. In fact, by 1955 the top twelve makes were rated at an average of 203.6 horsepower, almost *double* the power output of cars of a decade before. And the cars had grown considerably larger. The Automobile Manufacturers Association revealed that the average car produced in 1955 was six inches longer than its immediate postwar counterpart.

Some minor players were resisting this trend toward power and bigness. In 1954, Nash made the first serious postwar attempt to market a small car. It was an unfortunate venture: the miniature Metropolitan, an English-built two-seater that resembled a four-wheeled mailing tube and was powered by a wheezy, 42 horsepower Austin A40 four-cylinder engine. Nash had just merged with the tottering Hudson Motor Company to create American Motors, and the absurd Metropolitan was to become the lead in an implausible lineup.

During the same year that the "Metro" arrived, another small car of dubious performance and quality, the "Henry J," was brought to market. A relatively small, stubby, poorly finished, easily rusted fastback with ludicrous nubs of tail fins, it disappeared after a dismal four-year performance, leaving small cars with a tainted reputation for quality. This machine, the namesake of California industrialist Henry J. Kaiser, was one of his last entries in an eight year campaign to survive in the automobile business. Like the managers at the other threatened automakers, Kaiser was discovering that the economic power of the Big Three was overwhelming.

That year—1954—was an ironic turning point in auto history. While the poorly crafted, down-sized Metropolitans, Henry J's, Willys Aero-Larks and Studebaker Champion Sixes were being laughed at, a seemingly even more absurd machine with a weird little air-cooled engine hung on behind the back wheels—the *Volkswagen*, or People's Car—was gaining its foothold.

But little cars posed no threat, Detroit was convinced. Not only had all the recent attempts failed, but the industry graveyard was littered with hood ornaments carrying the names of such obscurities as Crosley, Jetmobile, Crue-Cut, Muntz, Astro-Gnome, King Midget, Cushman, and scores of others who had wasted millions in the naive belief that Americans wanted small, economical, functional automobiles.

America was in the midst of its big car romance and "power" was the aphrodisiac. In that same year, 1954, Chevrolet revolutionized the bottom of the market with its brilliantly conceived 165 horsepower, 265 cubic inch V-8 that would be the basis of all General Motors V-8 and V-6 engines even twenty years later. It was not all a frivolous waste of energy. This extra power was necessary simply to move the cars after they had been loaded down with Detroit's ingenious new gadgetry. The automatic transmission had ceased to be a novelty and now was being offered on a majority of automobiles. Power windows, power seats, power steering and power brakes conferred instant status on their owners. Air conditioning was no longer a whirring, unreliable nightmare that dripped water on your feet. In Detroit's mechanical hands it became the efficient servant of a controlled environment.

Lurid hues, including flaming pinks and Caribbean turquoises, were now coloring car bodies that Henry Ford once believed could only be decently covered in funereal black. It was act one in a postwar extravaganza, a national celebration that the fifteen year nightmare of depression and bloodshed had truly ended. Ike and Mamie were in the White House, or close by on the golf links of Burning Tree, and the great machines of industry were happily stamping out the curiosa of the new American good life with gleeful abandon.

If there was a head cheerleader for that good life, it was Harlow J. "Red" Curtice, the president of General Motors during the 1953-58 glory years. A native of Eaton Rapids, a small town in southern Michigan, Red Curtice was the one who fully exploited the American yearnings for overblown, chromed cars and thus codified the Detroit method for the next two decades.

Curtice broke two major management molds at GM. As a midwesterner who started with the Corporation as a junior bookkeeper in the AC Spark Plug Division, he had advanced to the general managership of the ailing Buick Division in the mid-1930s. He was to assume a corporate role that had been reserved only for "product men," the cigar-chomping ex-mechanics and engineers who were the master brewers of the car business. These tough, direct men had a simple aim: to build the strongest, fastest, most reliable automobile they could with the money that was given them, then to let the less gifted sell the cars.

But Red Curtice was a salesman. His lack of knowledge of stamping presses was balanced by an uncanny intuitive understanding of the status drives of the American bourgeoisie. It was Curtice who took the Buick, mired in a marketing swamp as a numbingly dull "doctor's car" and, through a series of design and label changes, fashioned the Special, the Century and the Roadmaster, transforming the car into an openly ostentatious alternative to the higher-priced Cadillac. It was Red Curtice who put the famed portholes (called Ventiports by GM) on the 1949 Buicks, a useless styling gimmick that became the division's trademark and survives in mutant form on some Buick models to this day. In the midst of the Depression Curtice had openly boasted in his advertising that Buicks would run 100 mph in stock trim. It was true, but it was a fact that contemporary auto executives would be less likely to discuss in public than their extramarital sexual adventures.

Red Curtice was a commercial freebooter in the classic American mold. He understood the Main Street urge for instant status as embodied in long-hooded, fast cars better than did Chairman Sloan and his eastern establishment cronies. By the time Curtice took over, most of the aging auto Brahmins were in semiretirement and the power center of the industry had shifted from GM's Manhattan headquarters to West Grand Boulevard in Detroit.

/////

When Red Curtice assumed the presidency of GM, the domestic car market was splitting into two divergent segments. The imports were on the move, albeit in erratic directions no one could get a handle on. Car sales hit a record 7.9 million in 1955. An overwhelming majority were option-laden monsters of the Curtice genre. Yet the machines being produced by a revived European economy—the Beetles, the Renaults, the Hillmans, Simcas, DKWs, Borgwards, Singers—were establishing themselves in the small economy sedan market, still an infant sales arena. The more substantial (but still relatively small-sized) MG, Jaguar, Triumph, Alfa Romeo, AC, and Aston Martin were creating a new awareness in the upper end of the market. Their sleek styling, high efficiency engines, brakes, steering, and suspensions seemed to coordinate with life on Long Island's exclusive North Shore and in Fairfield County, Connecticut, early enclaves of foreign car enthusiasm.

In 1955, automoguls reassured themselves that the small car

market segment was too thin to worry about. Unless a car model could be produced in bulk lots of 200,000, the economics of modern mass production would not make it profitable. Aside from George Romney of American Motors, who had become a prophet of smallness complaining about the "dinosaurs in the driveway," the industry's attitude toward small imports was summarized in one oft-repeated statement: "America has all the low-cost transportation it needs. We call them *used cars.*"

Yet George Romney, his Mormon moralizing aside, seemed to have a point. While Curtice was preparing the 1957 lineup of GM cars and Ford was prepping the introduction of the Edsel, the imports were gaining strength. They were capturing the upscale, college educated segment of the market. Curtice was baffled by data that showed that two out of three Volkswagen buyers had incomes almost *twice* as large as the average Detroit customer. Since the data seemed to belie the low-cost "used car" motivation, the corporate line shifted. People attracted to foreign crackerboxes were not real Americans, but a coterie of sophisticates, eggheads, and urban snobs who drank French wine, read *The New Republic*, and possibly voted for Adlai Stevenson. This minute band of cultural renegades offered no reason to change strategy. The folks from Eaton Rapids, Red Curtice was convinced, would always unload much of their life savings on six passenger, full-power movable palaces that could be produced in only one environment: Detroit.

This assumption was suddenly challenged by the first real postwar recession. Domestic car sales softened, then plunged in 1958 to 4.2 million units, a *40 percent* drop from the record year of 1955. Yet the imports kept gnawing at the market. By 1958 they had won 8 percent of the domestic car sales. Volkswagen led the way with an astounding 78,000 units. Romney's American Motors, because of its new line of small Ramblers, was stretching toward its first profit in four years. Sales would approach 400,000 units. Even lame Studebaker had developed a hastily modified, lower-line Lark that would move the comatose corporation into its first profitable period in six years.

As owning an import became faddish, entrepreneurs purchased dealerships for any one of the nearly fifty small-sized European brands hoping to penetrate the lucrative American market—Lloyd, Simca, Deutsch-Bonnet, Dyna Panhard, AC Bristol, Isetta, Lagonda, Jowett Javelin, Borgward, Skoda, Gutbrod, Goliath, Delahaye, Allard, Austin, HRG, Morgan, Humber, Lancia, Siata, and dozens other similarly obscure, even bizarre, trademarks.

"Every car dealer in the country who didn't have a Volkswagen franchise wanted some kind of an import," recalls Robert J. Sinclair, now the president of the highly profitable Saab-Scania of America, importers of the excellent Saab 900 coupes and sedans. In those days, Sinclair roamed the eastern United States, setting up franchises for Saab. The dealer investment involved no more than the purchase of a small sign, a few hundred dollars' worth of spare parts, and perhaps two new cars. "I can remember running through upstate New York and spotting some funny-looking little sedans sitting in front of a gas station. I stopped and asked the dealer what they were. 'Wartburgs,' he said. I inquired where they were made. 'Eisenach,' he answered. 'Where's that?' I asked. 'I think it's in Germany,' he replied."

The importation of many of these foreign cars proved to be premature. Several of the automobiles were inferior, most were unsuited for American driving conditions, and they were generally backed by inept parts and service organizations. Widespread customer discontent was inevitable. "Except for Volkswagen and some of the higher-priced English and German sports cars and sedans, the entire imported car boom of the late 1950s was a case of the wrong dealers selling the wrong cars to the wrong people," says Sinclair.

But amid the confusion, a segment of the American car-buying public was being exposed to an entirely new automotive experience: one that involved mechanical sophistication, efficient use of interior space, and, when things were operating properly, genuine *fun* in driving.

Although Detroit did not feel threatened, the loss of over 10 percent of their business to small domestics and imports demanded some response. By the end of the disastrous sales year of 1958, the major automakers once again decided to enter the small car market. Chrysler, having been stung by several previous forays into the small car field, was cautious. Its Valiant would be a conventional four-door sedan and wagon with a rather powerful "slant-six" engine that would prove to be the most enduring component of the entire campaign. With the Plymouth Valiants, Chrysler would continue the policy it had followed since the death, in 1940, of its leader, Walter P. Chrysler: stoically accepting the number three slot and carefully driving in the tire tracks left by Ford and General Motors.

At Ford, Robert S. McNamara saw the shift to smaller cars as an opportunity to expound his vision of utility. The Ford small car entry, the Falcon, was a mediocre economy sedan that appealed to his humorless, somewhat Spartan personal predilections. In his book *The Best and the Brightest* David Halberstam describes McNamara as convinced that "man seeks the highest form of efficiency without grace and without psychological feelings at all." A fellow Ford man noted that if McNamara had not joined Ford, he would have ended up teaching at the Harvard Business School, driving a stick shift Volkswagen and snickering at large Detroit cars with automatic transmissions.

If the Plymouth Valiant and Ford Falcon were ambitious exercises in the mundane, General Motors' entrance into the compact market was a burst of engineering audacity. Their small car, the Chevrolet Corvair, was to make it clear that the world's automotive leader would pay homage to no one in car technology. It was imperative that the new GM compact be a brilliant, original design. If American know-how had thwarted German technology in the war fifteen years earlier, it certainly could do as well when challenged by such a silly automobile as the Volkswagen Beetle.

General Motors had already made a move toward the small car business. Immediately following World War II Chevrolet pressed ahead with plans to market a modest-sized (108 inch wheelbase, 2200 lb.) economy car with fully independent suspension and a price tag of $1000. Labeled the Cadet, the vehicle was designed to fill a gap at the bottom of the GM lineup. Chairman Charles Wilson cogently argued that the war had proven that people could make do with aged automobiles. Many would simply stay out of the market if prices soared beyond their reach. However a number of problems, including postwar expansion, delays in factory construction, and strong opposition from the big car lobby within the Corporation—with Red

Curtice in the vanguard—doomed the Cadet to remain as airbrush drawings on the GM styling studio walls.

Now, a decade later, the driving force behind the Chevrolet Corvair was Ed Cole, who had risen to the general managership of the Chevrolet Division. A brusque, highly intelligent engineer, Cole was fascinated with air-cooled engines. He had worked with them at Cadillac during the war, as chief design engineer on light tank and combat vehicle research. Later, as chief engineer at Cadillac, he had worked briefly on a stillborn rear-engine prototype. He was convinced that Chevrolet's new compact ought to carry an air-cooled engine mounted in the rear, the same arrangement that had proved so successful in the Volkswagen.

This time Red Curtice, the man of the portholes, flight-deck hoods, dorsal fins and monster motors, did not resist. Jack Gordon, who had teamed up with Cole to create the Cadillac V-8 in the late 1940s, fought the Corvair concept to the end. But Red Curtice agreed to go ahead: His only stipulation was that at least one version of the new car be priced below $2000. This would make it competitive with the Volkswagen while providing more room (six passengers *vs.* four), more power (80 hp *vs.* 30 hp) and more amenities, including an optional automatic transmission *vs.* the Volkswagen's four-speed manual.

By choosing essentially the same layout as the VW, with the engine hung out over the back wheels in the place where a conventional trunk would go, Chevrolet engineers created a very sensitive weight distribution in the Corvair. While normal front engine cars carried about 60 percent of their weight over the front wheels, the situation was exactly reversed in both the Corvair and the VW. This made both vehicles vulnerable to what engineers call "oversteer," a tendency for the rear wheels to slide more quickly than the front ones. Chevrolet perpetuated the inherent oversteer capability in the Corvair by using the same swing axle rear suspension system that Dr. Porsche had designed for the Volkswagen in the early 1930s. It made both automobiles handle differently, and sometimes with less stability, than normal front-engine machines.

When the first 1960 Corvairs were shown to the motoring press in the summer of 1959, the quirky handling was quickly noted, but not viewed with alarm. Writing in *Sports Cars Illustrated,* the respected, MIT-educated journalist Karl E. Ludvigsen noted, "Let us be honest as usual; the Corvair is a fundamentally profound oversteerer. With 62 percent of its weight on the back wheels it could only be otherwise if very ingenious suspension techniques had been called into play. This was not the case." But after test driving the car, Ludvigsen observed, "For a moderately skilled driver the Corvair is a ball to drive, it being possible to hustle hard into tight corners and bring the tail around with just a twitch of the wheel, counter-steering until the slide stops and the time for acceleration begins. This is not, of course, everybody's way of driving."

Ludvigsen instantly recognized that the car's propensity for oversteer could have been corrected with the installation of an anti-roll bar or sway bar on the rear suspension. "For all its novelty, the Corvair is surprisingly naive in this respect," he noted. Cole and his engineers also understood the need for such a component, but it had been thrown out in a cost-cutting program mandated by the new board chairman, the New York-based financial wizard, Frederic Donner. A Sloan man, his only interest in automobiles lay in their profitability. He adhered to his patron's maxim that "General Motors is not in the business of making automobiles; it is in the business of making money." In accordance with this philosophy, Donner and his new president, Jack Gordon, the ex-Cadillac man who was convinced that small cars were cheap cars, sought maximum profit from each Corvair.

The sway bar was discarded for a reputed savings of $15 per car. A somewhat larger wheel and tire combination was also rejected even though the engineers felt it was necessary. The lack of the proper tires and sway bar, coupled with an engine that turned out to be about a hundred pounds heavier than designed, produced more oversteer than was necessary. The automobile had other major flaws as well: an engine that leaked oil from its various seams and joints, fan belts that snapped like rubber bands and a general looseness in the car's fabrication that soon had the body rattling like a can of walnuts.

Initially the Corvair and its competitors, the Ford Falcon and Plymouth Valiant, were sufficiently well received to repel the imported car invasion. But the cars simply did not perform in the market as expected. The Falcon, an automotive bottom-feeder of the worst kind, became a success only after McNamara left the industry to become Secretary of Defense and the tough-talking, crafty young man from Pennsylvania, Lee Iacocca, took over as Ford division manager. He rejected McNamara's reveries about proletarian transportation as nonsense. He jazzed the Falcon up with hardtops, fancy trim, sporty suspensions, and larger engines. General Motors took the same route with the Corvair. By 1962 a sporty Monza coupe, complete with bucket seats, had become the largest seller in the lineup.

The Corvair failed, but had Donner and Gordon been able to shed their aged prejudices about small cars being cheap cars back in 1960, the entire course of the American automobile business might have proved radically different. This much we can be sure of: Had an extra hundred dollars been expended on the original Corvairs for the proper suspension components, tires and quality, a world of agony would have been avoided by General Motors, and perhaps the entire auto industry.

There would have been no lawsuits charging that the Corvair's rear-engine swing-axle setup, and the resulting dreaded "tuck-under" of the rear wheels during cornering, had sent the car twirling off the road like a pinwheel. The company's response to the first action against the Corvair proved to be a tactical mistake. GM chose to settle out of court for $70,000 after proving that the accident had been caused by an apprentice mechanic who had improperly set the tire pressure. This decision underscored the fact that the Corvair was sensitive to tire pressures, which was considered a flaw by the mechanically unaware average American driver. The hapless Corvair was essentially a European-type automobile: The traditional European driver considered constant maintenance a normal part of the automotive experience, while the American driver did not.

The out-of-court settlement opened the floodgates. Suddenly the nation's courts were overflowing with litigants charging that they had been grievously wounded by their Corvairs. General Motors won the two major lawsuits involving the Corvair, and a subsequent report by the Department of Transportation exonerated the car for its alleged treacherous handling. But the damage was done. In its early price-pinched configuration, the Corvair led to Ralph Nader's *Unsafe at Any Speed*, which used the car as the centerpiece of its indictment that the major American automakers were manufacturing cars designed to kill their customers.

In 1966 an aroused Congress passed the National Traffic and Motor Vehicle Safety Act, which put bureaucracy into the car business in a big way. Detroiters predictably reacted with outrage. Had they been more willing to adapt to the brickload of regulation that fell on them, their later nemesis, the National Highway Traffic Safety Agency (NHTSA), might never have been come into being.

Ironically, the Corvair improved in direct proportion to its failure in the marketplace. The car was completely revamped in 1965, receiving a new rear suspension that corrected the old tendency for oversteer. Unfortunately, it arrived on the market just as the earlier version with its steering problem was being featured on the front page of every newspaper in the nation. The Corvair died and its demise seriously impaired America's chances of competing technologically with the Europeans in the small car field. While Ford and Chrysler were content to produce conservative compacts, GM had taken an engineering gamble with the Corvair during an era when finances and corporate confidence were strong—but they compromised on quality by cutting costs. And they failed.

/////

During these early years of the 1960s, Detroit turned its attention to the "youth market," the result of the postwar baby boom that brought millions of affluent youngsters into the marketplace. An estimated 20 percent of all automobiles were owned and operated by teenagers. Acting on market research data, which was considered minor gospel in Detroit, the automakers turned ravenously toward this group. Ford was the first to "Think Young" in its advertising, pandering to teenagers with such gimmicks as the "Ford Caravan Folk Jazz Wing Ding," rod and custom exhibits, teen fairs, and a massive advertising campaign built around the "Lively Ones."

The youth binge was creatively exploited by former Ford district

sales manager Lee Iacocca who, as Ford Division manager, introduced the Mustang in the spring of 1964. Prior to that sales triumph
Ford had in 1962 canceled its "Cardinal" project, a truly original
small car with front-wheel drive that would have marked a quantum
leap for the American industry. It was not until twenty years later
that it would reappear as the popular Escort. But a market that was
shifting toward faster, larger cars prompted Ford to back out of the
plan to build the Cardinal (which was instead manufactured by Ford
of Germany under the Taunus label) and take a more conventional,
and as it turned out, more lucrative, course.

By looting the existing Falcon and Fairlane parts bins, Iacocca's
designers and engineers created the Mustang, a rakish little sport-
ster that, despite its mechanical banality, was one of the styling
milestones in automobile history and an inspiration for many later
Japanese small car designs. Iacocca's three option-laden models, a
hardtop, a convertible and a fastback, all base-priced in the $2500
range, were instant sensations. Between their introduction in April
1964 and the end of the year nearly 700,000 Mustangs were sold.
Ford analysts estimated that during those feverish nine months
demand exceeded supply by fifteen to one.

The Mustang was initially perceived by the industry as a second
car to supplement the larger family vehicle. But in reality, it was an
early forerunner of the small, nimble urban vehicles that were fun to
drive and that were later to dominate the market. But even the most
creative thinkers in the industry missed the point that tastes were
changing. Looking ahead to the 1980s and beyond, they could see
various outcomes, but none included the scenario in which Detroit
would be displaced as the world leader in automotive production and
sales. That was beyond their comprehension.

In 1970, John DeLorean told me, "The Japanese can only go so
far. Their factories, which were new after the war, are going to need
major capital investments soon. And their workers are going to
demand wage scales similar to ours. Both those factors will seriously
reduce their advantage over us." Moreover, DeLorean cited one
trump card in the American deck: "Americans are the best managers
in the world. Our managerial class will make the difference." Yet not
long after he made these predictions, that same managerial class

levered DeLorean out of the GM executive suite.

Another casualty was Robert Anderson, the general manager of Chrysler-Plymouth. Shortly after DeLorean's ouster from GM, a frustrated Anderson left the auto industry to become the president of Rockwell International. It is noteworthy that without Anderson and another progressive, Dodge General Manager Robert McCurry, Chrysler shelved plans for a Pinto/Vega counterpart in the early '70s and instead offered the public an entire new line of leviathans just as the 1973 oil embargo hit the nation. It was one of the management decisions which would propel Chrysler first towards bankruptcy, then to government charity.

While the Pinto and Vega briefly helped to stabilize imported car penetration at about 15 percent, the booming overall car business lifted sales of the hated "furrin" cars to nearly 1.5 million in 1971. Again, conquest sales were a problem. Chevrolet and Ford dealers had little trouble selling existing customers the new subcompacts, but imported car loyalists remained skeptical. The Vega and Pinto had failed to repel that invasion. In fact, they may have aided it. By creating awareness of the practicality, even pleasure, that is inherent in driving a small automobile—and then marketing mediocre Vegas and Pintos—Ford and General Motors were generating increased potential sales for Volkswagen, Toyota, and Datsun.

/////

Many industry analysts have blamed the government for Detroit's failure to become competitive in the small car field. By keeping oil prices artificially low, they reason, the government not only maintained American dependence on imported oil, but stimulated the market for the gas-guzzlers. Cheap gas stunted any desire Detroit may have had to build smaller cars. This thesis is not without merit. By way of confirmation, small car sales dipped badly in 1974-75 and again in 1976-77 when the availability of gas and a rising economy resulted in a resurgence of the American love of big cars.

In the 1970s, no one in Detroit knew what was going on in the auto market, which was being whipsawed as various administrations tried to hold the lid on the pump price of gasoline. In fact, the foreign car makers, who have been credited with such universal wisdom, were witless spectators in the various petroleum shortages and gluts, panics and panaceas from 1973 to 1979.

Both Volkswagen and Toyota were so ill prepared for the 1973 OPEC oil embargo that their inventory was rapidly swept away in a small-car buying frenzy. On the other hand, managers of American Motors, which had been staggering under the load of unsold compacts, were suddenly hailed as latter-day Solomons. One day the Middle Eastern status quo would change and small cars would be on six-months backorder. The next day a Washington politico would pledge his honor that gasoline prices would not rise a farthing and every monster sedan in the nation would be sold out. For auto marketing men it was a time of madness.

GM product planners could only discern a trend toward smaller cars, especially in 1976 after the government mandated that the CAFE (Corporate Average Fuel Efficiency) be increased for all manufacturers to 20 miles per gallon in 1980 and to 27.5 mpg in 1985. The standard "full-size" American automobile was simply too heavy to accommodate such numbers. The same basic machines had been guzzling as much as a gallon every ten miles in the halcyon days of cheap gasoline. Now a fuel efficiency of more than double that was being required by law.

During the crucial 1970s Detroit underwent a series of economic shocks, each of which accelerated the demand for smaller cars. The worst shock came as a result of the 1979 Iranian revolution and the subsequent petroleum squeeze, which doubled the price of gasoline between January 1979 and June 1980. By then the domestic carmakers clearly saw the inevitability of smallness; General Motors was already deeply involved in its much-acclaimed "down-sizing" program which had begun in 1974.

Corporate historians chronicle GM's portentous decision to make smaller cars as orderly and clear-eyed. But, in truth, General Motors was dragged, thrashing and shouting, into the program. According to a General Motors executive who was present at several Executive Committee sessions on the subject, the impetus to downsize did not come from within the Corporation. Its champion was one of the "outside" members of the GM board of directors who had traveled extensively in Europe. "He kept harping on the fact that the automobiles in virtually every country of the world were smaller and more efficient than ours," says this GM manager. "But nobody listened until he finally got the ear of Dick Gerstenberg [GM board chairman 1972-1974] and it was he who pushed the whole idea. Ed Cole and most of the Executive Committee fought like hell. They wanted to increase fuel mileage simply by using lightweight materials and keeping the traditional, big-sized cars. Believe me, there was plenty of desk pounding and cursing before Gerstenberg got his way."

The OPEC embargo energized GM, Ford, and Chrysler to seek short term solutions to the fuel consumption problem. Chevrolet went abroad and brought home the Chevette, a version of its "T-car" being produced in Germany and Brazil as the Kadett, and introduced it in 1976. Ford came into the market a year later with its Fiesta, which was being built by its European divisions for sale in the United States until a new domestic small car could be designed. Unlike the Chevette, a conventional front-engine, rear-wheel-drive car, the Fiesta was a contemporary front-wheel-drive vehicle. Both cars were small, were relatively well-built, provided excellent gas mileage, and were competitive in price with all but the cheapest imports.

American automakers believed they would stop the imports with these entrants, but once again they failed. Detroit and its dealer body had spent so many years indoctrinating their customers with the notion that small cars were silly, even un-American, that they could not sell effectively to anyone seriously interested in a small-size import. This was Chrysler's experience with Mitsubishi, the Japanese giant whose cars were sold from 1974 onward under the Plymouth Sapporo and Champ nameplates, along with the Dodge Colt and Challenger labels. They were excellent examples of contemporary Japanese carmaking, but they never made a serious dent in the market.

The failure was partially traceable to Chrysler's marketing and dealer organization, which never understood how to sell imports, especially after their product planners had "Americanized" the

Japanese-made cars with softer springs, vinyl roofs, whitewall tires and other optional items. These automobiles prove that the problems of the American industry go deeper than even cost and product. In the case of the Chrysler-Mitsubishi arrangement, the product already existed, at a competitive price. It was the old-line domestic sales mentality which made dealers unable to sell against the entrenched foreign competition.

Chrysler's Dodge Omni and Plymouth Horizon, the first authentic front-wheel-drive compacts to be produced by an American manufacturer on these shores, were handicapped in the same way. Introduced as 1978 models, these were essentially copies of the Volkswagen Rabbit with French Simca front-wheel drive units. The early versions even used modified VW four-cylinder engines. Although poor workmanship marred the early models, Chrysler had soundly beat both Ford and General Motors to market with small, roomy, high-mileage automobiles in the imported idiom. But it was unable to exploit the advantage. The public was responding to a total image of quality, reliability, fit and finish, and an aware dealer organization—a combination only the imports seemed to offer.

A dramatic example of this sales problem—of American automakers selling foreign-made, or foreign-inspired small cars—exists in the uncomfortable alliance of the ailing American Motors and France's state-owned Regie Nationale des Usines Renault. Since 1979 Renault has controlled nearly fifty percent of the American firm, which is itself an amalgam of failed automakers. Efforts to sell the Renault R-5, frivolously named "Le Car" in the United States, and the larger, more costly 18i, both as a sedan and as an attractive but underpowered Fuego sports coupe, have produced disappointing results. A major impediment is that the AMC sales organization has not been able to adjust to the challenge of selling French automobiles.

The entry of the French into the AMC fold was met with dismay and endless backbiting. "Everybody calls 'em 'the Frogs'—behind their backs, of course," confides one company insider. The Renaults were creditable, high-mileage automobiles of the type that industry observers claimed America was begging for, yet they sold sluggishly in the hands of the AMC dealers. The new Alliance, a French-designed, American built sedan tailored for the domestic market, is doing somewhat better, but such a true turnabout is not likely until the marketing prejudices that infest Detroit and its traditionalist dealerships have been purged.

Many experts attribute the serious collapse of another domesticated foreign car, the Volkswagen, to their failure to replace the aged, over-priced Rabbit. But some speculate that the recent transformation of the "Volks" into an American-built car has exacted an enormous penalty. "The old German image is gone now," says Steve Smith, a veteran automotive writer and columnist. "Since they've touted themselves as being built here, you've got to wonder if people think they've got the same shabby craftsmanship they associate with Detroit."

Image remains a critical factor in the car selling business. But its ingredients have changed radically in the past few years. Detroit still believes that the old Sloan ideal of "more" in terms of glitter is most important. But the rise of the imports has given prominence to a different image: one of quality, workmanship, engineering creativity, and durability, as well as low operating costs.

Detroit still does not understand. There is still more profit in large automobiles, and as long as that theorem continues to dominate the Detroit Mind, the industry is headed toward doom. The American-made import fighters were designed simply to plug a hole in the market and not to create the serious shift in buying habits that Detroit feared would cut their profits. It is a myopia has made Detroit's defeat more self-inflicted than externally caused.

/////

The long-awaited shift in Detroit finally came in 1981, which the trade press described as "the year of the small car." During a 12-month period Detroit played its aces. General Motors came in with its ill-fated J-car, overweight, over-frilled and overpriced. Eight months earlier, in the autumn of 1980, Ford produced a winner with its Escort. A thoroughly European front-wheel-drive sedan, it was a legitimate "World Car" (code named "Erika") that was also marketed by Lincoln-Mercury under the Lynx nameplate. Ford's

Escort/Lynx quickly soared to the top of the sales charts and by 1982 had become the number one seller in the United States.

Chrysler brought itself back from oblivion with its K-cars: front-wheel-drive sedans that featured an excellent new four-cylinder, overhead camshaft engine mated to mediocre workmanship and classically garish Hollywood styling designed to make the smaller car magically appear to be larger and more luxurious. No matter, the K-cars saved Chrysler. Despite a slow early start when over-optioned, high priced versions frightened away customers, the success of the K-car has solidified the federal government's resolve to guarantee the loans that salvaged the Chrysler Corporation.

Nine months after the J-car was brought to market, General Motors board chairman Roger Smith introduced the 1982 cars by touting GM's newest line of down-sized vehicles. "We decided you're not going to get a guy out of a Toyota by giving him a Toyota," he said. "You've got to give him something better than a Toyota. Our game plan is to get out ahead of the imports and stay ahead of them."

Smith's game plan sounded promising, but it resulted in the new General Motors A-cars, a peapod collection of sedans and coupes marketed simultaneously as the Chevrolet Celebrity, Pontiac J-6000, Buick Century and Oldsmobile Ciera. The A-car is part of a semi-frantic effort by Detroit to catch up with the rest of the world, particularly with German engineering and styling. Both General Motors and Chrysler are producing a group of American-made vehicles which have been dubbed "Eurosedans," and Ford is contemplating a similar move.

They are offspring of the companies' new front-wheel-drive intermediates, gussied up (or more accurately, designed down) to resemble continental-style touring sedans. The target vehicle is the excellent Audi 5000S, a five passenger, four-door car that is less than 109 inches in overall length and rides on a wheelbase of 105 inches. The American Eurosedans follow the German and Swedish tradition and employ firmer springs and shock absorbers than is usual on domestic-made cars and a quicker steering ratio to provide more precise handling and control—an attempt to solve the common complaint that American cars float.

The General Motors A-cars were cloned from the highly-successful, if mechanically-plagued, front-wheel-drive X-cars of 1979 by reskinning and elongating the body and making some technical changes. Most of the A-cars are only superficial copies of European cars and carry lumpy, generally underpowered engines with none of the performance and handling characteristics of the Audis, BMWs, Volvos, Saabs, or even the top-of-the-line Toyota Cressidas and Datsun Maximas they were designed to "stay ahead of." The A-car that comes closest to European performance is the Pontiac 6000STE, part of that GM Division's attempt to create a technically-progressive image. The car is Audi-sized and has a relatively powerful 135 horsepower V-6 engine. But with typical GM oversight, the car is still not available with a five speed manual transmission.

Chrysler's new Eurosedans are among the best fabricated cars that the company has produced in years, a great improvement over the crackerbox bodies they have been selling. Lee Iacocca has also copied the Audi and other European sedans, and his new Dodge 600ES, which is a slightly stretched variation of the K-car, has a general tightness and road holding capability that is a high-water mark for the company. Its precise steering gives it more the feel of a European car than any other American product. The ES does have a five speed manual gearbox, but it is equipped with a rather crude shift linkage. Like its competitor, the A-car, the Dodge 600ES is underpowered, but Dodge hopes to correct that condition soon by the addition of a turbocharger. It has a good interior capacity with room for four—or even five—passengers, as well as a large trunk.

The new Eurosedans are not unattractive, but unfortunately, the Detroit product planners cannot break their linkage to their Hollywood past no matter how hard they try. The new Dodge includes a garish instrument panel and an innovation in Detroit gimmickry: an infuriating *computerized human voice* that nags the driver to fasten seatbelts, release the parking brake, fill the windshield washer reservoir, and other tasks. This sophomoric brand of hi-tech, which is also to be found on some Japanese cars, is exactly the kind of frivolity that new American automobiles—seeking to establish themselves in the more serious, upscale segments of the market—do not need. In fact, initial customer reaction was so hostile that

Chrysler quickly equipped later models with switches to cut off the voice.

Neither the A-cars nor the Chrysler "E" series are equal to the genuine European article in terms of their lack of full instrumentation, four-wheel independent suspension and a general feel of purposeful function. However, the Dodge 600ES, the Pontiac 6000STE, as well as similar cars from Buick, Oldsmobile, Chevrolet and those coming from Ford, are a step in the proper direction. They act as harbingers of the day when the American industry may be able to offer complete lines of nimble useful, mid-size, five-passenger sedans that rival anything in the world.

Meanwhile, the introduction of the A-cars produced one of the great yawns in modern automobile history. They were reasonably utilitarian automobiles, but they fell between two marketing stools. "We're loaded for bear," General Motors president F. James McDonald told a Los Angeles audience of automotive writers weeks before the cars were introduced. "Dollar for dollar, or gallon for gallon, we're selling more value, more utility, more comfort, and yes, more style than anybody." Within six months of that statement, he and his cohorts were reporting the worst month of June sales since 1958. While the import sales were down slightly, they had captured a record 30.61 percent of the American market.

Despite their unit construction and front-wheel-drive, the new As failed to create a strong demand. What had happened was that consumers quickly realized that other GM cars which bracketed the A-cars in size, price and performance—the X-cars on the down side and the only slightly larger and better-performing Chevrolet Malibus, Pontiac LeMans, Oldsmobile Cutlasses and Buick Regals on the up side—were all better deals. By mid-1982 the four "A" models had sold only 158,461 collectively, a total that was exceeded by such single domestic brands as the Ford Escort and the aged Chevette. Older X-cars like the Buick Skylarks and the Chevy Citation outsold their newer brothers by twice, and even the new Camaro and Firebird—specialty cars intended for a minor segment of the market —produced 153,000 sales, nearly equal to the four A-cars together.

General Motors was left with a pair of losers within less than a year, and most significantly, without a stellar model with which to face the future. The strength of the old Malibus, Monte Carlos, Grand Prixs, Cutlasses, Regals—already five years old—lay in their surprising parity with their replacements. Only four inches longer overall, and with essentially the same amount of interior room, the old machines were somewhat less fuel efficient than the A-cars but they produced substantially better performance with their base engines at a price that was from $500 to $1000 less, depending on options. The "old" cars were one of few bright spots on the GM horizon.

/////

Once again the hopeful forecasts that had been made for 1982, ranging from 10 to 10.5 million total domestic sales, turned out to be over-optimistic. For the third consecutive year, industry analysts offered excuses for the failure: high interest rates, the price advantage of Japanese imports, stable gasoline prices which blunted the demand for fuel-efficient new models, and an economic recession.

They chose not to mention several windfalls: a new, more liberalized industry-wide contract with the United Auto Workers; voluntary import curbs of 1.68 million cars per year that had been self-imposed by the Japanese industry; inflationary pressures on the yen and Deutschemark which steadily forced imported car prices upward; the decision by both Honda and Datsun to manufacture cars and light trucks in the United States, which also pressured Toyota to consider doing the same; a rising tide of advocacy in Congress for a local content law demanding that ninety percent of any car sold in America be made in this country. If nothing else the threat of the law encouraged further restraint on the part of the Japanese. All of these developments presumably would have helped the bewildered Motor City.

If the sickness of the economy and the egregious interest rates were the sole cause of malaise, import sales should have suffered equally with the domestics. That was not the case. Instead, while domestic sales plummeted, imported car sales moved upward, capturing nearly 30 percent of the market nationwide, and half of the market in California.

In the past decade, Detroit has invested some $80 billion in retooling and revamping its model lineup to meet the import challenge. But it has steadily lost ground. The roots of the debacle are in the past, but the problem has grown more serious in the present. In its backhanded battle to discredit the small car Detroit managed only to discredit itself.

By deluding itself and trying to delude its customers into thinking that *small* meant *bad*, Detroit succeeded instead in convincing many Americans that all their cars were outmoded and inefficient. Had the industry system been modified so that the building of smaller, more contemporary automobiles could generate profits, as it did for European and Japanese car manufacturers, many of today's dilemmas could have been avoided.

Detroit has now found religion and is struggling to compete in the small car market. As it piously attempts to join the believers, the age-old philosophical conundrum continues to nag: Can the Heathen be converted quickly enough to be Saved?

Germany and Japan: World War II Rewritten

THE TEST TRACK behind the headquarters of Daimler-Benz AG, manufacturers of the legendary Mercedes-Benz, in the Stuttgart suburb of Untertürkheim, is small by American industry standards. Its entire acreage could easily be lost in the woods bordering the main entry gate of the General Motors Proving Ground in Milford, Michigan. Confined by a local building boom and elements of the U.S. Seventh Army on the perimeters of their property, the Mercedes people have made ingenious use of a small wedge of space.

There, in a stand of leafy hardwoods, they have erected a tight, vertically-banked turn that sends cars hurtling around it at almost a ninety degree angle to the ground, as if they were hung on the side of a building. In this spectacular fashion the company's test engineers, all of whom are expert drivers, can sustain high speeds for long distances in a relatively small space. For the men who design the cars of Daimler-Benz AG, speed is not a teenage ego-booster or a vague abstraction prattled about by the advertising department, but an integral aspect of every automobile they build, something to be as routinely included as an efficient heater.

Speed lives in southern Germany, where it is viewed with typical

Teutonic intensity at Daimler-Benz AG and at Dr. Ing H.C.F. Porsche AG in nearby Zuffenhausen and at the Bayerische Motorenwerke AG (BMW) in Munich, about 90 miles to the southeast. Here the Autobahns are wide and flat and clearly marked. On most open sections there is a 130 kilometer per hour (approximately 80 mph) "recommended" speed limit that is, by the standards of most American highway patrols, not seriously enforced. The drivers of Bavaria, Baden-Württemberg and most other German states have repeatedly repelled government attempts to impose further restraints on a network of extraordinary highways that once enjoyed no speed limits at all. In fact, the advocates of reduced speed limits on the American model have even been accused of trying to return to the rigid civil controls of Hitler's Third Reich.

But the question of speed is essentially apolitical on the Autobahns, which are amazingly safe. Although speed is always cited in America as a major factor in accidents, the rapidly traveled Autobahns have an accident rate about equal to that of the American Interstate system, even though speeds of 100 miles per hour are not uncommon in Germany.

I have traveled thousands of miles on the Autobahn system at speeds that would have been rewarded with a stay in the county jail in my homeland. I recall a night trip from Salzburg, Austria, to Baden-Baden in a 450SEL Mercedes-Benz. It was clear and warm and the big sedan whispered along the smooth four-lane at 100 mph while my wife slept beside me and another couple dozed in the backseat. The powerful quartz-halogen headlights seared down the road for half a mile, uncovering potential hazards in their clean, white light. The drivers of slower cars, generally better trained than American drivers, stayed in the right lane as the quicker traffic slipped past. The Mercedes was as steady as Mt. Rushmore as it flew across Bavaria.

Driving the 450SEL at 100 mph was effortless. The steering was precise, with none of the wander or play one often finds in a comparable American car. The wind noise was minimal, thanks to the endless hours devoted to high-speed aerodynamics by Mercedes-Benz engineers. The suspension, taut but resilient like a great steel feline, kept the automobile bonded to the highway. I knew that if trouble arose ahead, the car's four-wheel disc brakes would bring it to a rapid stop as if it had run into a sandbank.

I spotted a set of lights behind me quickly closing the intervening distance. Until then I had been driving about as swiftly as anyone on the highway, although I had sighted several BMW's and smaller Mercedes cruising at over the 100 mph mark. But now the headlights in my rear view mirror were growing larger and I eased into the right lane to let what was obviously a faster vehicle past. Blocking traffic in Germany by loafing in the fast lane of the Autobahn is considered a mortal sin, as is passing on the right. The faster machine drew even, then burst into the night. It was a Porsche 930 Turbo coupe, pressing along, with two men on board, at perhaps 120 mph. This was not a race or a macho exhibition of speed, but merely a routine night drive on the Autobahn by a very fast automobile in the hands of an expert driver. In a few moments the taillights were pinpricks of red in the darkness and the Porsche was gone. I continued along at 100 mph, musing about the level of usefulness of the German-made automobile.

My thoughts drifted back to the Mercedes-Benz test track at Untertürkheim, where cars like the one I was driving had been fashioned to be capable of great speed while embodying the most advanced safety components. For years Mercedes-Benz had stressed "evasive capability" in its automobiles: proper steering, suspension, and braking to permit a driver to maneuver his way out of an *in extremis* situation.

Mercedes-Benz, along with other European manufacturers, has been in the forefront of building cars with "crashworthiness." This engineering philosophy involves designing automobiles with sufficient front-end "crush" to absorb energy in collisions; with rigid passenger compartments that will not collapse in rollovers; with vaultlike door latches that will not fly open on impact; with sufficiently padded instrument panels, collapsible steering columns, and shatter proof glass to protect passengers. These, combined with carefully trained drivers who might not be fully licensed until a two year probationary period, plus an immaculately marked and maintained road system, has created the most advanced driving environment on earth.

For years European automobiles, in general, have exemplified superior handling and braking. American cars, by contrast, have traditionally emphasized soft, wallowing, mattresslike rides, which from an engineering standpoint are dangerously imprecise. European automobiles have been in the vanguard of development in brakes, suspension systems, engines and steering gear that place a premium on nimbleness and the ability to operate at the upper limits of performance.

The French Citroën CX2400 is a classic example of the advanced car generated by the European driving environment. Not imported into the USA, the CX 2400 is a four-door, radically streamlined sedan capable of carrying four adults on sustained, smooth, and silent trips along the four-lane Autoroutes of France at 100 mph. Because of its advanced shape and engineering, the CX 2400 exhibits this extraordinary performance although its engine is no larger than a Ford Pinto's. It is hardly an experimental design: the CX2400 has been on French roads for over a decade.

In creating automobiles like the CX 2400, the Europeans have pioneered most of the engineering components we now take for granted. These components were largely ignored by American manufacturers, who abandoned serious new engineering developments after they perfected the three-speed automatic transmission and the large-displacement overhead valve short-stroke V-8 engine in the mid-1950s. Since then, American manufacturers have made a few laudable efforts in the area of hi-tech—the General Motors aluminum V-8 of the early 1960s, the Chrysler slant-6 engine of the same period, the high-revving Chevrolet V-8's, and nonpareil air conditioning. But in the main, Detroit spent the sixties and the seventies immersed in an inane preoccupation with gadgetry.

Meanwhile, the Europeans continued to move ahead with fuel injection, disc brakes, rack and pinion steering, radial tires, quartz headlights, stalk-mounted windshield wiper and dimmer controls, ergonomically adjustable bucket seats, five-speed manual transmissions, high-efficiency overhead camshaft engines, independently sprung suspensions, advanced shock absorbers, and strict crashworthiness standards.

Not all their efforts were praiseworthy. Europeans did, and still do, produce some notably bad automobiles. Many Italian cars were prone to rust and rattles and bedeviled by erratic electrical systems. Both Swedish cars, the Volvo and the Saab, suffered through a decade plagued by endless niggling ailments. Many French cars appeared to have been built entirely of plastic. Sadly the once-proud British automobile industry collapsed after its archaic industrial system could do no better than produce obsolete, badly fabricated, ambulatory jokes. We also tend to forget that European stylists aped Detroit until the early 1970s, adorning their cars with dollops of chrome, vinyl roofs, and dual headlights in the American grand manner. Even the Mercedes-Benz sprouted vestigial tail fins and some models retained them until 1968.

But a basic split in automotive philosophy between Europe and America arose about thirty years ago, a schism which has become most obvious over the last half dozen years. From the fifties on, the Americans concentrated on building large mechanically stagnant automobiles while certain elements of the European industry aggressively explored the technological frontiers.

/////

If there is a center for the European search for excellence, it is the tight-looped Mercedes test track at Untertürkheim. Advancement is achieved there through a curious combination of adventurousness and caution. Mercedes-Benz pioneered in diesel power for passenger cars, fuel injection, supercharging, turbocharging, and dozens of other engineering advances. But Untertürkheim has hardly been a font of automotive inventiveness. Instead it has become a kind of vehicular think tank where practical but technically aggressive men take risks in the laboratory but remain ultra-conservative when modifying the lineup of production machinery.

Mercedes-Benz is always inclined to take the long view, to empirically consider what will be needed a decade ahead and to plan methodically for it. There are no quick fixes; an alteration of the lineup is never made to seize an opportunity for sales. Proven Mercedes-Benz components are seldom changed. For example, the ergonomics of the driving position—instruments, pedals, steering wheel, seat—are essentially the same on a contemporary Mercedes-Benz as they were twenty years ago. The fully independent suspension has been improved and updated over three decades, but it remains thematically linked to enduring M-B practices. The same is true of Mercedes-Benz power plants, which have been proven through millions of miles of testing and real-world driving.

Critics have sometimes complained that Mercedes cars are overcomplicated. Six different bolt sizes may be used where a single one might have sufficed with slight compromises, as is the American and Japanese practice. But few compromises are permitted at Mercedes-Benz. As a result one of its modest-sized sedans can cost as much as six Chevrolet Citations or Ford Escorts. There is nothing revolutionary about a Mercedes-Benz, unless it involves technological trivia in the form of a bearing, gasket, seal, valve, bracket, connecting rod bolt, piston ring, door latch, or fuel line.

But there is more to a Mercedes-Benz than a collection of thoughtfully engineered bits and pieces. As they are being brought together to create a new model—a process that can consume nearly a decade—each component is severely tested in the laboratory and on the test track. A Mercedes-Benz is designed to be *driven*, not to meander around the suburbs or be taken down an American Interstate at 55 miles an hour. The top engineers flog their test vehicles with a zeal normally witnessed only on major auto race tracks. Engines are expected to run at top rpms for hours on end. Transmissions are designed to upshift and downshift perfectly without slippage. Brakes must not fade and pull after miles of Alpine hairpins and switchbacks. The Mercedes-Benz is intended to operate at top speed—not in short show-off bursts, but over long passenger-carrying trips.

The men who set these precise requirements are a cadre of experts who not only understand the theories of high-level automotive engineering but who can, if necessary, drive the wheels off the fastest cars in the world. Perhaps the greatest of these test driver/engineers was Rudolf Uhlenhaut, who retired in 1972 as the head of design and development at Daimler-Benz. The son of an English-woman and a German bank director, he was born in London but returned to the Continent as a boy. He graduated from the University of Munich as a mechanical engineer in 1931 and immediately joined Daimler-Benz. By 1937, when barely thirty years old, he was selected to run the Mercedes-Benz Grand Prix motor racing effort, a sports propaganda campaign underwritten by the Third Reich to show off German technology.

The young Uhlenhaut decided that he had to learn the racing business from the cockpit up. The setting was the celebrated Nurburgring race track, a monstrous, fourteen-mile circuit with 174 major curves in the Eifel Mountains, to which Uhlenhaut brought a team of mechanics and two 600 horsepower Mercedes-Benz single seater Grand Prix cars. "I made my first circuit of the course at a speed slower than I would have driven a passenger car," he recalled years later. "Then I drove both machines hard until they broke." After 200 miles of personal testing, Uhlenhaut returned to his drawing board with a firm notion of what was required to handle a powerful, treacherous racing automobile.

One American journalist remembers a ride from Reno to Lake Tahoe with Mr. and Mrs. Uhlenhaut in the early 1970s. "There were no speed limits in Nevada in those days and Uhlenhaut drove most of the way with the speedometer riding between 100 and 110 mph. It was all very relaxed and neither he nor the car were anywhere near their limits, but as soon as he entered a speed zone, he immediately slowed to the legal limit and puttered along without complaint," the engineer recalls. An open, pleasant man with a perfect command of English, German and French, Uhlenhaut later returned to America with his wife to receive an award in Las Vegas. It was his intention to drive a Mercedes-Benz back to the East Coast in order that his wife might see "a bit of the country." "Uhlenhaut left Las Vegas on Sunday morning and arrived in Jacksonville on Tuesday," relates his American colleague. "One wonders how much sightseeing Mrs. Uhlenhaut did at 120 mph."

Uhlenhaut sought for perfection in his automobiles both on his test track and on his endless long-distance journeys across Europe and America. He was brutal in his evaluations; seldom, if ever, did he find a competitor's product capable of withstanding his brand of punishment. He theorized that automobiles had to be designed for peak loads, to have reserves of power that would permit them to be driven at maximum speed and tension without endangering the passengers.

Uhlenhaut's automobiles were somewhat meager in gadgetry. Styling was a minor function of the engineering department at Mercedes-Benz, the necessary annoyance of cloaking the mechanical innards with a safe, weatherproof, body, which might coincidentally be attractive. The traditional grille with the crosshatch design was retained as a matter of tradition rather than for serious aesthetic reasons. The bodies were stodgy and square looking compared to the swooping lines of the competitive Cadillacs, Lincolns, or Jaguars. In 1974 William Mitchell, the flamboyant styling chief of General Motors, openly derided the "boxy" lines and "old fashioned" grille treatment of the Mercedes-Benz. Within five years, his corporation and most major domestic automakers would be aping those prosaic, even antiquated, themes.

The emphasis on mechanical design made Mercedes a laggard in providing creature comforts in the luxury car field. In the temperate German climate a highly efficient air-conditioning system was ignored until the mid-1970s. Mercedes-Benz cars had no power seats or automatic headlight dimmers or lighted vanity mirrors. Velour and tufted leather upholsteries were noticeably absent. The dash panels were covered with readable instruments devoid of chrome bezels.

Customers making the transition from luxury-laden Cadillacs often found the more expensive Mercedes-Benz spartan, even harsh, by comparison. The German car did not coddle its driver on mushy springs, nor lull him into a false euphoria with chimes and multispeaker stereos. The car demanded to be driven as Uhlenhaut and his associates had created it.

Market research has a low priority at Mercedes-Benz. It has become habit in Detroit to sniff out the marketplace for new trends, then tailor automobiles to suit. Such fads and features as hardtops, vinyl roofs, convertibles, dual headlights, fake wire wheels, designer interiors, limited editions, personal cars, hood scoops, ad infinitum were developed in this fashion. Mercedes-Benz and most German manufacturers—with the exception of Volkswagen which, since moving to America, has fallen into the same trendy trap—have clung to their original concept of valid design, ignoring the vagaries of a fickle marketplace.

Only in the technical sphere are the Mercedes people adventure-some. Both Mercedes-Benz and Audi have produced sedans pow-ered by highly efficient five-cylinder turbocharged engines. Porsche's 928 coupe is a cornucopia of sophisticated engineering, as are some of BMW's more advanced designs. Yet when Porsche's new intermediate-sized 528 series was introduced in 1981, its styling innovations were so subtly different from the previous model that the uninitiated could barely tell them apart.

/////

Much of the German engineering success in automobiles is related to their pre-war and World War II tradition of technology. Dr. Ferdinand Porsche, the Austrian genius who created such memorable machines as the Volkswagen and the Wehrmacht Tiger Tank of World War II, believed in air-cooled, rear-mounted engines in automobiles. After the war was over and while he was interned by the French, Porsche perfected the Renault 4CV. (The company's founder, Louis Renault, had died in prison as an accused Nazi collaborator.)

Porsche's first Volkswagen prototypes—designed by him in 1931 and 1932 for the Zundapp motorcycle firm but never produced—contained all the essential technical ingredients of the immortal Beetle that remained in production for 44 years and eventually numbered over 19 million units. Prior to his death in 1951, while working with his son, Ferry, Porsche created the sports car that bears his name. It incorporated the same design elements as the Volkswagen, and to this day the Porsche 911S remains an extension of the tenets laid down by Dr. Porsche in the 1930s and 1940s. In fact, after Porsche's company was integrated into the Volkwagen consortium and new models were planned that carried conventional water-cooled engines mounted on the front of the chassis, old-line members of the Porsche family and company staff viewed the changes as heresy.

BMW, which started in 1916 as the manufacturer of the aircraft engines which powered the "Flying Circus" of Manfred von Richt-hofen, the "Red Baron," in World War I aerial combat, has also maintained its links with the past. Its smooth twin-cylinder, shaft-driven motorcycles were first produced in 1923 and remain concep-tually unchanged. Like the rival Mercedes-Benz, BMW can trace part of its engineering heritage back to World War II, when both firms produced powerful aircraft engines. The Daimler-Benz DB-601 series engines were manufactured for, among others, the Messerschmitt ME-109 fighters. At BMW the 801 series radial engines were built for the Focke-Wulf Fw190's. BMW also devel-oped the first production jet engines for the Luftwaffe.

The company's Munich works were shattered by Allied bombing and its Eisenach factory seized by the East Germans, but BMW struggled back. At first it manufactured cooking pots and baker's utensils out of old engine cylinders, then made motorcycles. BMW had produced a series of distinguished high-performance sports cars in the 1930s and resumed automobile production in the 1950s, when it tried to penetrate both ends of the market simultaneously with a luxury sedan and a tiny, two-passenger urban economy car. But not until the 2002 sports sedan was introduced did the BMW marque really fire the imagination of foreign car buyers. Nimble but housed in a rather incongruously boxy body, the 2002 was the progenitor of a series of sedans and coupes that electrified the automotive world in the 1970s. All were conservatively styled, powered by extraordinar-ily advanced in-line engines, and most of them boasted quality that rivaled the best in the world.

Like Mercedes-Benz and Porsche, BMW makes no effort to conceal its role in World War II as a potent military arm of the Third Reich. This is an acknowledged fact; indeed, it is sometimes una-shamedly offered as evidence of the company's dedication to techni-cal excellence. Although Porsche himself was apparently quite apolitical and never aligned himself with the party, Mercedes-Benz's management had a number of fanatical Hitler supporters within its ranks. All *der Fuehrer's* personal cars bore the three-pointed star of M-B.

The major survivors of German postwar auto competition (and there have been numerous casualties: Borgward, Champion, DKW,

Goliath, Gutbrod, Lloyd, NSU, and even Messerschmitt) share this obsession with technical excellence. It can lead to frustrating conservatism, as with Mercedes-Benz' refusal to design anything except conventional, front-engine, rear-wheel-drive automobiles, or Porsche's long-standing love affair with air cooling, or BMW's evolutionary creep forward in styling.

This conservative German auto idiom has created the finest automobiles on earth. Other nations produce some excellent cars, but in a collective sense the machines of Germany are without peer. They sometimes err on the side of utility with their monotonous gray interiors and stark flanks, but beneath the prosaic trimmings are tucked the best brakes, the most supple suspensions, the highest-efficiency engines, the most efficient gearboxes, and safest bodies on earth. The Americans, Swedes, the French, the Japanese, have all made major contributions to the art of the automobile. But the Germans, with their refusal to compromise to short-term market trends, are the world's leaders.

/////

Surprisingly the German auto industry is more closely linked to the American than one would think. Not only is there cross-pollination through Ford, GM and Volkswagen but also through men such as Peter Schutz, the managing director of Porsche, who is an American citizen, and Porsche's chief designer, Tony Lapine, who was trained at General Motors. They are not industry freaks. Most accomplished German engineers will acknowledge that Detroit has as much raw information and sophisticated understanding of automobile design as any place on earth. Privately it puzzles the Germans why that intelligence is not more often applied to the product.

Several years ago a small group of American journalists was standing on the edge of the Untertürkheim test track. One of the automobiles circulating the course, at modest speed, was a Cadillac Seville. As it passed, a Mercedez-Benz engineer said, "The car is sprung so softly that it bottoms out during fast driving and the brakes fade badly after a few laps. It simply won't hold up." One of the Americans noted that General Motors had mountains of unused knowledge that would permit it to build a better Seville. The Mercedes engineer nodded in agreement, then a bewildered look spread across his face. Why, he was obviously wondering, would GM build such an expensive car and not use that knowledge? *Why,* indeed?

While Detroit frittered away the 1960s by trying to coat the highways with overpowered, chromed cars, major European and Japanese manufacturers were singlemindedly attacking certain segments of the market. Mercedes-Benz was quietly influencing the Cadillac and Lincoln audience.

It has hardly been a blitzkrieg for Daimler-Benz in America. Because Stuttgart had been an important manufacturing center during World War II, most of its factories had been leveled during Allied raids in September, 1944. By the time the war ended, over 75 percent of the company's four major plants had been destroyed, prompting the board of directors to remark, "Daimler-Benz had ceased to exist in 1945." Yet by 1946 the company was producing a modest 38 horsepower, four-cylinder prewar sedan and beginning to rebuild amidst the rubble. Five years passed before serious manufacture of a new line began and Mercedes-Benz could restore its historical continuity.

By 1952 Rudi Uhlenhaut was back in business, introducing the famed 300 SL "gull-wing" sports car and winning a string of major victories, including the prestigious Le Mans twenty-four hour endurance race. In 1954 and 1955 the factory took up the ultimate motor sport, Grand Prix racing, and carried the great Argentinean driver, Juan Manuel Fangio, to two world championships. After the 1955 season Mercedes-Benz discontinued major racing competition and has not returned to it.

While not officially involved, Mercedes-Benz still feels strongly about the value of motor sport. "The experience gained in motor racing, and the use made of it for the improvement of the normal type of vehicle, is of supreme importance to the automobile engineer, who above all is called upon to meet the demand for safety," the company states.

Despite its relatively quick recovery in Europe, Mercedes-Benz lagged behind in the American market. In the mid-1950s the crumbling Studebaker-Packard Corporation aligned itself with aircraft manufacturer Curtiss-Wright and received the distribution rights for Mercedes-Benz in America. Owing to Studebaker's precipitous decline, the Mercedes cars were never properly marketed. When Studebaker-Packard finally collapsed in 1963, Mercedes-Benz set out to create its own North American sales and distribution system. They implemented lessons learned from Volkswagen, whose customers appeared to willingly fall under the control of white-coated service managers, all of whom behaved like ex-Wehrmacht artillery officers. Rigid customer-relations and service policies were adopted and dealerships took on the antiseptic appearance of a surgical theater.

A Mercedes-Benz advertising campaign created by Ogilvy & Mather violated all the tenets of American luxury car "image" advertising. The automobile was presented in full-page detail-laden, text-heavy black and white newspaper ads, not the usual four-color magazine display of a luxury vehicle parked in the driveway of a fashionable country club. Sales turned around, and Mercedes-Benz began an ascent that within fifteen years would make it America's most popular prestige car.

Its milestone auto was the 250 series, introduced to America in 1966. Smallish by American standards, it had a wheelbase over twenty inches shorter than contemporary Cadillacs and weighed a thousand pounds less. But it featured technical details unknown on standard American cars: fuel injection, four-speed automatic transmissions, advanced unit body construction and four-wheel disc brakes, which GM engineers wrongly contended would not work as well as the conventional drum units. The automobile cost over $7000, about 25 percent more than a Cadillac, and featured no vivid styling variations. Yet it was a potent force in the establishment of the imports in the American market as more than cheap economy cars.

The Mercedes and the Volkswagen, which made up much of the import market in the mid-1960s, were linked thematically if not in price. While Detroit analysts deluded themselves that foreign cars were being purchased primarily by those who wanted fuel economy above all else, it was actually the beginnings of a mutiny against

American cars by important opinion-makers. Young executives, college students, academics, professionals, and media members were buying the Volkswagen, drawn by its outrageous styling, its unique mechanics, and its strongbox simplicity.

Perhaps the most important attraction of the Volkswagen was that it was a visual and philosophic repudiation of the bourgeois extravagances of big Detroit machinery. Detroit, to its eventual sorrow, mistook the Volkswagen movement as the bizarre ritual of a clique of eccentrics, when in fact they were dealing with the nation's trend-setters.

In the context of the Detroit theorem, the Volkswagen made no sense. So underpowered as to border on the unsafe, so cramped and ugly that its monumentally successful ad campaign focused on its peculiar appearance, the Volkswagen was an automotive bumblebee —it should not have worked. Cursed with a vulnerability to cross-winds, a heating system that somehow seemed to promote rather than inhibit frostbite, a feeble engine with an appetite for its own fanbelts, and a suspension capable of evil spates in the hands of novices, the Beetle nevertheless raised the American consciousness toward functional automobiles.

As no-nonsense German automobiles, the Volkswagen and the Mercedes-Benz established a powerful link between both ends of the market. The third year law student or the medical resident, wobbling along in their ratty VWs with 120,000 miles on the odometer, aspired to, and eventually achieved, ownership not of a destroyer-sized Cadillac, but a 250 or 280 Mercedes-Benz.

Volkswagen prospered throughout the sixties, creating hundreds of millionaires among its American dealer body and building a legend of marketing brilliance. However, as Daimler-Benz gained awesome power, Volkswagen faltered. Bad management decisions, including the failure to replace the Beetle with a desireable alternative, coupled with an increase in the value of the Mark, made VWs more vulnerable to growing Japanese competition.

The 1975 introduction of the Rabbit, a contemporary front-wheel-drive sedan, temporarily corrected the problem, as did the opening of an American production facility in an abandoned Chrysler assembly plant in Pennsylvania. But the company was increasingly pinched in the marketplace by the Japanese with their cheaper, and often better, small cars. By 1982, the Volkswagen Rabbit was becoming antiquated by comparison with new Japanese models. There is little doubt that Mercedes-Benz, Porsche, and BMW will continue to dominate substantial portions of the over-$20,000 market, but VW will have to pull another Rabbit out of its hat to survive.

As Mercedes-Benz prospers a number of misconceptions remain. Americans imagine German cars being painstakingly sculptured out of solid billets of high-tensile steel by leather-clad German workers who have devoted their lives to the quest for mechanical perfection. This is not exactly the case. During the West German industrial boom of the 1960s and 70s, skilled domestic labor became extremely scarce, and substantial numbers of foreigners—Greeks, Turks, Italians and Slavs—were imported to work in the German automobile factories. Far from being Swabian perfectionists, these newcomers were nonetheless integrated into the system, and quality seldom faltered. The conclusion is clear: If management can create the proper working environment, high standards can be maintained, regardless of the composition of the labor force.

While most German cars have developed a reputation for high quality, it has not been deserved in every case. A number of Audi models, most specifically the 100LS and Fox sedans, were riddled with rats-nests of mechanical ailments. Earlier German-built Opels, sold through GM's Buick dealers, were utterly undistinguished vehicles. The first Lincoln-Mercury Capris (1971-78) manufactured by Ford of Germany provoked widespread complaints of body deterioration and V-6 engine trouble.

No nationality has an exclusive franchise on quality or on low levels of manufacturing skill. If given the proper tools and directed by good managers, any reasonably motivated work force will produce a well-made product. Even the redoubtable Japanese acknowledge that management policies (often formulated by observing, then improving, archaic practices in England and America) are the key. The Germans are an industrious people, but probably no more so than other Europeans or North Americans.

/////

The power of both the work ethic and good management is particularly evident in Japan. The domestic auto industry likes to explain the success of the Japanese in the U.S. market solely as a factor of lower price. A Toyota or a Datsun car theoretically contains $1500 worth of *free* features when compared to the price of an American automobile. While essentially correct, the argument avoids one vital issue: Market price is a component of function. If Japanese cars did not perform, they could not be given away. Early Japanese imports were weak, uninspired copies of outmoded English designs, and while cheap, they did not sell well. As soon as they were upgraded to fill the needs of the American market, the Japanese car "miracle" began.

The Japanese had no serious automobile industry until the 1960s. The first car was built in Japan in 1902, but there was no significant auto manufacturing activity until the mid-1920s when Ford, Chevrolet and Chrysler built small assembly plants there. A modest domestic industry was created in the 1930s as the economy mobilized for war, but it concentrated on the production of trucks and commercial vehicles.

It is remarkable that the Japanese car business got started as soon as it did. There were few good roads outside the major cities and the 1923 earthquake had destroyed much of the country's industrial base. Toyota manufactured automatic looms for the textile industry until 1935. Datsun had begun building cars on a small scale as early as 1911, but did not become a sizable business until 1933, when it was reorganized under Nissan Motor Company, Ltd., and sought technical assistance from the American Graham-Paige Company, which was absorbed into the abortive Kaiser-Frazer Corporation following World War II.

During this period of worldwide depression, jingoistic zeal in Japan powered a rapid industrialization. Most of the effort was directed toward rearmament but there were some Japanese, like a young rebel named Soichiro Honda—in some ways the Henry Ford of Japan—who remained fascinated with the technology of the passenger automobile. The son of a small-town blacksmith, Honda spent the thirties as a wild amateur car racer and founder of a firm which intended to manufacture piston rings. An impulsive man who scorned formal education, Honda belatedly discovered that his product was hopelessly brittle. He had been unaware of the crucial need for silicon in his metallurgy. He pressed ahead, corrected the problem, and managed to succeed.

Like the rest of his country, Honda's business was ravaged by the war. His small factory was first hit by American bombs, then leveled by an earthquake shortly after the war ended. Japanese industrial strength, from the Mitsubishi giants to the struggling Honda, was reduced to zero in 1945.

Yet the economic miracle of the 1950s was born, and with it came a new Japanese automobile industry. In the beginning it was source of amusement to Westerners rather than a perceived threat. In 1953, Nissan began the production of the British Austin A-40 sedan under license. Hino made a similar arrangement with Renault to manufacture the tiny 4-CV, and Isuzu contracted with the English Rootes Group to make the Hillman. This fit the Japanese stereotype: an industrious but essentially uncreative people. It was part of Western industrial lore that the Japanese were simple innovators, copying everything they could—even the iron replacement patches on the boilers of early British battleships. This smug dismissal of Japanese talent left Europe and America vulnerable.

By 1950 Soichiro Honda had teamed up with another young industrialist, Takero Fujisawa, and created the prototype of the "Dream Type D" motorcycle. Within 15 years, the machine would dominate the world market and destroy the British motorcycle industry which had been the imperious leader since the mid 1920s.

The antithesis of the stereotyped Japanese automaton, Honda propelled his little company to the top by creating the most technically advanced motorcycles in the world. In the 1930s he had attended the High School of Technology in Hamamatsu, a city on the south coast of Honshu, in the same region where Sakichi Toyoda, the founder of Toyota, and Torakusu Yamaha, the motorcycle and piano manufacturer, were raised. Honda attended school for only two years, refusing to study German or to take military training, and left without a diploma. "A diploma is worth less than a theater ticket," he told the school's administrators. "The ticket guarantees that you can get into the theater, but the diploma can't guarantee you that you'll make a living." Honda displayed the same cynicism about teachers: "If a theory leads you to an invention, all schoolteachers will become inventors."

Honda's former partner, Fujisawa, once ruminated about their unconventional backgrounds. "Just imagine what would have happened if either Honda or I had entered one of the existing large enterprises," he said. "We did not have any educational background, and so we would have probably remained lowest ranked for the rest of our lives. But both of us acted with purpose, and cultivated technology and experience."

In explaining current Japanese industrial power, much has been said about how the Japanese enjoyed the advantage of having their old industrial complexes destroyed in World War II, then rebuilt as modern plants with American capital. This avoids the main issue. The Japanese could have moved into their new factories and resumed the simple-minded copying of European cars, locomotives, ships, radios, and toys that they had engaged in before the war. But they did not. The Russians picked up little in the way of industrial sophistication from the war. The French and Italians hardly revolutionized their systems, and the English built new industrial complexes in Coventry, Birmingham and the Midlands but immediately reverted to manufacturing things as they had in 1939.

The Japanese emerged from World War II with renewed vigor, but they faced enormous handicaps. The label "Made in Japan" was synonymous with the shoddy and the tasteless. They were saddled with a language that defied straightforward translation of technical terminology, few natural resources, a rudimentary road network, and a population that was ignorant of, and often unsympathetic to, Western industrial civilization.

But they did enjoy some significant advantages. Despite the war, Japan remained a homogeneous society with powerful family loyalties and a strong tradition of working for the common good. Education, built around the work ethic, was of uniformly high quality. The labor force was imbued with a sense of team play. Management seemed less inclined to isolate itself from the workers than was common in the West. Moreover, the major Japanese banks considered it their national mission to underwrite long-term Japanese industrial recovery.

The banks created a symbiotic relationship with many basic industries, including automakers. It is normal for a car company's major banking connections to hold 3-4 percent of the voting stock and to have a seat on the board of directors. This permits the financiers to become deeply involved in both short-term financial management and long-range planning. Added to these advantages is a relatively stable political climate and a government openly sympathetic to the needs of big business. The government-business partnership called Japan, Inc. came into being at the same time that some in the American media were fulminating against General Motors president Charles Wilson's remark that what was good for the United States was good for GM, and vice versa.

The Japanese auto industry blundered ahead during the 1950s in relative obscurity. In 1955, when Detroit pumped out a record 9.2 million cars and trucks, the entire Japanese industry produced 68,932 vehicles, of which only 20,000 were passenger cars. It was during 1958 that the "miracle" began, but on a miniature scale. Datsun and Toyota placed small allotments of their L-210 and Toyopet Crown four-door sedans on freighters to begin the slow, ten-day sea voyage to California. Their arrival was barely noticed. After all, over fifty brands of imported cars were fighting for less than five percent of the American market. The Big Three had, within the decade, driven Kaiser-Frazer into oblivion, forced Willys-Overland, Hudson, and Nash to merge, and had Studebaker-Packard propped up for the final blow. No foreign manufacturer, much less the Japanese, seemed to pose a serious threat.

But 1958 brought the first serious postwar recession and with it a spurt in small-car sales. For two years, until the Big Three countered with their compacts, the imports, led by Volkswagen and Renault, snatched 10 percent of the market. The Japanese were still nonplayers. Datsun sold 83 cars in the U.S. in 1958; a similar number of Toyotas were bought. At the time there was little prestige for a Japanese executive in being sent into the export market. The most promising talent was kept at home; it was the dissidents and adventurers who were sent to Southern California to carve out an empire among the heathen.

Such a man was Yutaka Katayama, a sales specialist who arrived in America in early 1960 to join his engineering associate, Soichi Kawazoe, in the hope of creating a Datsun sales network. With the help of American dealers who were looking for *any* imported car franchise to capitalize on the small sedan boom, Datsun sales jumped to 1300 units in 1959. But when the Americans retaliated with with the Falcon, Corvair and Valiant, the tide seemed to be turning against the imports. How could the Japanese, with their out-dated cartoons on wheels, expect to make major inroads?

Kawazoe was an American-educated engineer, with a B.S. from M.I.T., but Katayama knew only a few words of English. Yet it was his job, with a tiny cadre of salesmen with the same linguistic handicap, to set up a national dealer network for a car Americans had never heard of. Simultaneously other Japanese, uniformly dressed in neat dark suits and white shirts and generally shouldering single-lens reflex cameras, were on similar pilgrimages to the Occident in the name of Toyota, Sony, Honda motorcycles, Nikon, Canon, Matsushita Electronics, and Yamaha pianos and motorcycles.

The Japanese automobiles were met with tolerant smiles by the motoring press. A 1958 edition of *Road & Track* described the performance of the first Datsun as "melancholy," while noting that it was still better than most small imported British cars. Several years later, *Car and Driver* said that the Toyota Tiara sedan was "utterly lacking in technical novelty." It dismissed the Datsun P-410-U sedan as a repeat of an old English design. Yet the magazine lauded the Toyota's fit and finish as "better than might be expected" and praised the Datsun for having the "very reassuring quality of stoutness about it."

Despite such cautious praise, the Japanese entries were still something of a joke to the automobile cognoscenti. Observed *Car and Driver* in a 1965 discussion of the Japanese automobile industry, "If you want to understand [the business] go see a samurai movie. Japanese life can make the *Mikado* seem like a documentary. No one stops. [An automobile factory] has the frantic jumpiness of hand-cranked movies of a 1912 food riot."

Most American buffs remained loyal to the German and British brands that then dominated the import market. Japanese motorcycles were beginning to sell impressively, up from 6300 in 1959 to 148,000 in four years, but the traditional British brands, Triumph, BSA, Norton, were still leading the field. Even the Americans who worked for the Japanese told endless jokes about the formality of their employers, their oppressive "squareness" and their hilarious butchery of the English language.

But the Japanese were hardly to be laughed off. Like the Germans, these people worked. The results of their labors were being felt in every civilized nation. They could be ridiculed and ostracized, but they could not be ignored. Their products were now too good. One telling incident, which converted a group of skeptical Americans en masse, illustrates the quality of many postwar Japanese products.

During the early 1960s a New York State Datsun dealer folded, a not uncommon occurrence in those days, and a large auto finance firm was left with a stock of unwanted, presumably unsalable cars. The firm decided to let their salesmen drive the leftovers. Accustomed to plush Impalas and Bonnevilles, the salesmen despised the narrow, midget "Jap" cars and did everything they could to destroy them. They refused to lubricate the bearings, they rode the clutches, over-revved the engines, jammed the gears and left them to rust in the bleak winters. But the ugly duckling Datsuns refused to die. They plugged ahead under the awesome abuses, generating a grudging, if confused, respect among men who had grown up with the idea of "tinny" Jap goods embedded in their brains.

/////

The revolution in the quality of Japanese products was being accomplished by men like Soichiro Honda, who was obsessed with high quality motorcycles. His interest in automotive technology began while Honda was recovering from serious injuries sustained when his Ford-powered racing car had flipped over while leading the

"All-Japan Speed Rally" on the banks of Tokyo's Tama River. Once in the motorcycle business, he decided he had to win the most prestigious motorcycle race in the world, a gruelling event which was run over winding lanes on the Isle of Man in the Irish Sea.

In 1951 he came to the Isle of Man knowing that the motorcycles he was producing at home were too hopelessly underpowered to race against the German NSU's and Italian Gileras. He ignored the racial slurs and the outright rudeness. Honda lost, but he returned home determined to create a machine that would win. Eight years later he came back to the island with a Honda racer that produced twice the horsepower of its nearest European rival. Two years after that his motorcycles took the first five finishing places on the Isle of Man, and were overwhelming the English, German, Italian and American motorcycles in the salesrooms of every consumer market on earth.

Unlike the hulking Harley-Davidsons and Indians, the Hondas were tiny, lightweight urban transportation vehicles. They more resembled girls' step-through bicycles than the bloated Harley "hogs." With marketing built around the ad slogan, "You meet the nicest people on a Honda," the company probed the up-scale segments of the population, people who would normally no more consider the purchase of a motorcycle than a black leather jacket. As Honda and his rival Yamaha began to import higher-performance motorcycles into the country, it was soon discovered that they could outrun the heavier domestic products with engines half as large. It is probable that much of America's awareness of Japanese automobiles was created by entry-level customers who had discovered a whole new dimension of riding on Honda motor bikes.

Although the Japanese and the Germans, particularly visionaries like Honda and Uhlenhaut, set the new standards, they cleverly made use of American talent in penetrating the U.S. market. German and Japanese occupied the top jobs, but most of the upper-echelon operations positions in sales and distribution were held by Americans. "We're kind of a forgotten breed," says an expatriate from Oldsmobile. "But without the Americans who went to work for the imports, they'd barely have gotten their cars off the docks." By contrast with the Germans and Japanese, the French, Italian and English carmakers could not put aside their national loyalties and attempted to staff their American operations with their own countrymen, most of whom had no idea how cars were sold in the United States.

Like many inventive geniuses, Honda was not infallible. After entering the car business in Japan in 1963 with a small minitruck and sports car designed for the domestic market, he became fascinated with International Grand Prix motor racing. From this came his interest in air-cooled engines and his absurd N360 minicar. It was hopelessly underpowered and noisy and only imported into the United States in small quantities. Finally, he yielded to his partner, Takero Fujisawa, and his senior staff, and the company went on to design the conventionally water-cooled Civic, surely the most brilliant small car in automotive history. Meanwhile, the intensely competitive Honda kept his independently owned Honda Research and Development firm involved in international motor sports.

Even as he edged toward old age Honda maintained a firm, if erratic, grasp on the company's creativity. In response to the Clean Air Act of 1970, Honda introduced his "CVCC" engine, a power plant with a revolutionary cylinder head that combined ample performance with low exhaust emissions. He accomplished this while the major American manufacturers were complaining in unison that the Federal standards were impossible to meet, and were heading to court to prove it.

Honda was not the silent, stoical Japanese who operated in an ethereal Buddhist state beyond the comprehension of the Western mind. He was a passionate man of almost Latin propensities who would rap uncomprehending young engineers over the head with a wrench—what he called his "thundering method" of education. Honda had no tolerance for corporate moguls who remained isolated from their workers. "It is wrong for executives to act like feudal lords and not know what is going on below them," he once said.

Honda learned from empirical evidence of all kinds, including a hunger strike staged by his work force during the 1957 recession. He noted that the dissident workers complained about working conditions and low wages, but still played baseball on the company fields with zest. "In collective bargaining, they complain that they work too hard. But when it comes to playing baseball, they do it until they become completely exhausted, even though baseball does not bring a penny to them," he stated. "I must recognize that man achieves his highest degree of efficiency when he plays. If someone says he works out of loyalty to his company, he is a damn liar. Everybody must work for himself. Even I work because I like working. I must create a workshop where everybody enjoys working."

Always the rebel, Honda argued against employing only the conforming worker. He never ceased to remind his managers, "If you hire only those people you understand, the company will never get people better than you. Don't try to hire people just because you like them. Always remember that you often find outstanding persons among those you don't particularly like."

From this environment came the two great automobiles of the 1970s: the tiny, space-efficient Honda Civic of 1973 and the stunning Accord of 1976, the first modest-sized automobile to offer the interior room, comfort, craftsmanship, and performance usually associated with more expensive European models.

Having started his company in impromptu fashion, Honda departed with much the same suddenness. In 1973, at age sixty-six, he retired along with his partner, Fujisawa, and left the company in the hands of younger men. Honda appointed as his successor forty-five year old Kiyoshi Kawashima, who was both an engineer and the former manager of the company's racing program. As he grew older, Honda never lost his enthusiasm for radical change. Many of his senior managers are men in their early thirties who share his enthusiasm for egalitarian teamwork. His executives and line workers, all of whom wear the same white Honda coveralls, fight for the same parking places and eat together in the same cafeteria.

It was Honda who defied conventional Japanese thinking and built the first factory on American soil in Marysville, Ohio. His associates believed that the American laborer, embroiled in union politics and handicapped by a sloppy work ethic, could not meet Japanese standards of quality. Honda thought otherwise. At first, the Marysville factory manufactured motorcycles on a limited basis. But the results were so encouraging that production was raised to 60,000 units a year and some models were even exported.

Honda was prompted to expand the facility to produce automo-

biles, and, following some skirmishes with the UAW, the operation
proceeded smoothly. Honda's results with American workers inspired Nissan to proceed with plans for its pickup truck plant in
Tennessee, removing some of the political pressure against Japanese imports.

Now in his mid-70s, Honda is still an active adviser for his
company. The Accord is now in its second generation and costs more
than twice as much as its 1976 introductory price of $3995. Yet it
remains a benchmark for small-size automobiles. The Accord more
than any other Japanese car endowed that nation's automobile
industry with an aura of invincibility. The car has been openly
praised by other manufacturers and used as the model for several
other successes, including the Nissan Stanza, and such failures as
the General Motors J-car.

Yet like other cars produced by the presumed wonder workers of
Japan, it had some serious failings, including the penchant for
blowing head gaskets and rusting around the front fenders. Much of
the Japanese reputation for infallible automobiles is undeserved,
perhaps as traceable to the defensive bleatings of the American auto
industry as the actual quality of Japanese cars. We tend to forget the
ill-fated Mazda RX2's, 3's and 4's, whose Wankel engines were
unreliable gas-eaters. The Datsun F-10, a small front-wheel-drive
model, was markedly inferior to all other vehicles of its kind. Several
Toyota, Subaru and Datsun models can be faulted for chintzy
interiors, choppy rides, bad seats, engine problems, and bizarre
styling.

Myths abound about the Japanese. In reality, their manufacturing techniques possess few of the magical qualities envisioned by
those who have never toured a working Japanese factory. One
imagines surgically clean chambers filled with hissing robots tended
by short, lean Orientals in coveralls. Coursing through the great
halls are automated assembly lines filled with perfect little automobiles, each more flawlessly detailed than the last.

The fact is that Japanese automobile factories look and function
much like American, German, French, Swedish, or Italian ones.
They are large, open buildings packed to the ceiling with clanking
columns of partially assembled cars, all being tended by knots of

workers. There is little significant difference between the physical layout or the manufacturing techniques at the Honda plant at Hamamatsu, the Mercedes-Benz factory at Sindelfingen, or the General Motors Assembly facility at Lordstown, Ohio. The Japanese workers are uniformed in their company overalls and one is usually impressed by such odd details as flower vases on tables in the employee rest areas. But in stark terms of fitting together an automobile out of raw bits of steel, rubber and plastic, there is precious little difference.

It is true that in immense Toyota City, where the consistently high-quality Toyotas are produced, there is an aura of communal energy unknown outside Japan. Stacks of worker housing surround the factory, and a 30,000 seat stadium, plus acres of recreation grounds, dominate the landscape. The workers, like their colleagues at Nissan, Honda, Subaru, Toyo Kogyo, are loyal, men and women involved in a cradle-to-grave relationship with their company. They proudly wear the company uniform and, much to the bafflement of Westerners, they sing the company song after a round of pre-work calisthenics.

But the illusion of high efficiency obscures the fact that Japan's labor situation is hardly as harmonious as one might assume. During the 1970s, the gestation period of the Japanese superworker myth, more man-days of labor were lost to illness, absenteeism, and strikes than in either Germany or Scandinavia. Moreover, mediocre labor relations at the Japan National Railways have resulted in both poor service and fiscal deficits.

The harmony that permeates the steel, electronics and automobile industries did not exist much before the 1960s and was the simple outgrowth of necessity. Japan was devastated by World War II, perhaps more so than Germany. The Japanese were forced to create a manufacturing system that could compete in world markets on a small island containing but one valuable resource—a highly motivated, well-educated labor pool. To offset the costs of importing raw materials and shipping their products over vast expanses of ocean, manufacturing had to be accomplished according to the leanest, most efficient patterns known to man.

It is ironic that while this economic miracle was underway, the

American automobile industry was losing its competitive edge. Business was so good that it was easier to pay off, essentially in the form of industrial blackmail, a work force more interested in creating an opposing power structure than in joining a campaign to increase efficiency.

It took the Japanese about fifteen years to perfect their system. Because transportation was relatively slow on the crowded mountainous island of Honshu, satellite suppliers gravitated to locations around the primary manufacturing plants. From the clustering of Japanese suppliers developed the legendary "just-in-time" or *kanban* system of inventory control. Because of the proximity of the suppliers, parts and components can be delivered to a Toyota or Nissan factory on a daily basis, and in some cases within hours of the time they are needed on the assembly lines.

This gives the Japanese an advantage over American automakers whose farflung supply network makes it necessary for assembly plants to carry huge inventories of engines, axles, and sheet metal, sometimes totaling over a month's supply. General Motors has estimated that it annually spends $3 billion simply to maintain its inventory of parts.

The Japanese have also developed a more centralized management system in which a single team can handle a number of geographically separated operations. This compares with the American system of redundant executive groups being responsible for each individual operation. Perhaps the greatest advantage of the Japanese system is the enhancement of worker responsibility. It is not uncommon for a Japanese assembly line worker to be able to shut down the entire operation if he spots a flaw.

In contrast, the American system dates back to the origins of the industrial revolution when the worker was considered no more than a semihuman component of the manufacturing process. In America, the worker has no more control over the movement of the assembly line than he would over a runaway freight train. The Japanese system confers two benefits. First, an error is immediately sighted and corrected. Second, the notion that an individual worker has some control over his work environment boosts his morale and level of loyalty.

Japanese automobile manufacturers involve their workers in what is generally referred to as "quality circles," small groups of individuals who gather to discuss how to improve their collective performance. This is slowly being integrated into the American experience, but the tradition of the omnipotent boss lording it over the cipherlike worker whose only ally is a pugnacious shop steward mindlessly blocking increased production, will die hard in the UAW-dominated American factories. Economic adversity has produced new levels of cooperation between American labor and management, but a general sense of distrust still exists. Any increase in the economy could produce a lapse back to the old, self-destructive ways.

The Japanese new wave philosophy leaves old line American managers shaking their heads in awe. That the Honda work force annually provides over a million suggestions is difficult to comprehend for managers accustomed to massive absenteeism on Mondays and Fridays by workers whose average pay is over $20,000 per year. American managers can deal with the advanced applications of robotics, much of which was developed in the United States, in the manufacture of Japanese cars. But the notion that Honda company picnics trigger thousands of worker-inspired inventions unnerves them.

Americans are inclined to dismiss the Japanese successes on the simplistic basis of a homogeneous work force that is paid about half as much as the average American, and privileged to work in the latest high technology factories. This thesis has several flaws. The presumed $1500 price advantage each Japanese car has over its American counterpart involves only $500 in labor costs. Over two-thirds of the cost differential can be traced to higher productivity levels. Neither is this efficiency the result of space age technology. The main Toyota engine plant is over fifteen years older than several American counterparts.

/////

Behind the German and Japanese "miracles" and the American failure is one disheartening fact: Men such as Rudolf Uhlenhaut and

Soichiro Honda would never have survived in Detroit. As an obsessive performance enthusiast, Uhlenhaut might have ended up designing rear suspensions for Corvettes. Honda, with no college degree, would never have been hired.

The present trends in automobile design have been molded by the Germans and the Japanese. German high technology has been transformed by the Japanese into a mass sales device. This symbiotic relationship between the German and Japanese automobile industries has been more rewarding than their ill-fated World War II alliance, and together they have gone a long way toward dominating the world market. In 1980 the two nations produced almost twice as many cars and trucks as the United States (13.8 million vs. 8 million) and almost monopolized the field of technological advance.

This is an inexcusable situation for the United States, a nation that mobilized the most awesome industrial enterprise in history during the Second World War. In the current cliche, a nation capable of putting men on the moon should be able to produce a competitive automobile.

Germany and Japan will continue to lead in automotive technology as long as their flexible industrial environments invite the participation of men like Honda and Uhlenhaut, and Detroit encourages the rise of its unimaginative "team players." Unless the American automobile industry finds the will to match its competitors and responds in kind, our position as a secondary automobile—even industrial—power is assured.

CHAPTER V

Detroit Styling:
A Lost Hollywood Dream

BY THE TIME THE CRUEL WINDS of January 1982 eddied around the stony facade of the General Motors Building, the failure of the J-car introduction of nine months earlier had been privately accepted. A few heads had rolled or were anxiously awaiting the coup de grace, but otherwise it seemed to be business as usual. Only the usual confident tone was muted. Three years earlier, when Chevrolet Division sold 2.3 million cars and the Corporation dominated the domestic industry with 5.2 million total sales (excluding trucks), a breakfast for the press had featured champagne and eggs Benedict. But as 1982 dawned with Chevrolet sales down nearly 700,000, the breakfast had been downgraded to coffee and Danish pastry.

The occasion for the celebration, no matter how modest, was the introduction of yet another series of all-new automobiles. They would include the long-awaited "F-cars," the new Camaro and Firebirds from Pontiac, and "A-bodies," the series of slightly larger, more opulent alternatives to the ill-fated J-cars. The Camaro and Firebird were splendid vehicles; low and aerodynamic, with truly vivid styling that was distinctively American, yet embodying all the panache of the best European sports cars. Like so many of GM's offerings, they were somewhat overweight, but they coupled excellent performance (in a market where power is a premium) with world-class handling qualities.

But the A-cars were a different story. Built on the Corporation's first front-wheel-drive platform which had formed the basis for the hot-selling but mechanically-troubled X-cars in 1979, the new autos were nearly a foot longer and 200 pounds heavier, while sharing exactly the same wheelbase and essentially the same engine and transmission components. Most important, perhaps, they were $2000-$3000 more expensive. It was a differential that could be attributed to a single but terribly important element of the Detroit system—styling.

While the X-cars had reached the market in April 1979 looking like conventional chromed GM automobiles that had had their hoods and trunks chopped off in an accidental encounter with a hydraulic press, the new A-cars seemed, dare it be said, *European*. They had the look of German-styled vehicles, but with a Detroit accent that ruined their authenticity. Just as the J-car had been designed to compete with the Honda, Toyota and Datsun, the A-car was targeted for customers who were now buying an Audi, Volkswagen, Volvo, Saab, or BMW. But once more the American product was a weak imitation of the style-leading European cars. Neither truly American nor fully European in look, and lacking originality, the pseudo-Teutonic A-car failed to make a true styling statement.

The chrome was gone, replaced by expanses of single-tone paint and flat-black trim. The lines were sharp and disciplined, with none of the organic bulges and vestigial fins that had become trademarks of Detroit. The interiors were in muted shades of cloth and vinyl. And, miracle of miracles, the tires were blackwall, in the tradition of Mercedes-Benz, BMW and the powerful marques that ruled the Autobahns and autostradas of the continent. "The Road Kings have a new rival, now the excitement *really* begins!" trumpeted the Pontiac advertising for the J-6000. It was an oblique admission that the "excitement" that had presumably begun with the J-2000 J-car had never materialized.

"The A-car is pleasant, but lacking in individuality," says an outspoken officer who has been frozen in an upper-middle management post. "You could line up twenty of 'em from all four divisions on a street and not tell one from the other."

And they were copies. For an industry which had served as the leader in worldwide automotive styling tastes for forty years to be obediently tagging along in the tracks of a smallish Bavarian manufacturer was an indication of how far the mighty had plunged. Barely seven years earlier, GM design vice president William Mitchell had hooted at the Mercedes-Benz styling and now every car division in America was stealing touches (or perhaps more important, the subtle *absence* of styling touches) from the German carmaker. Detroit had suddenly discoverd the aesthetics of simplicity.

Of the 1983 American cars, only the Ford Thunderbird displayed a new shape, made up of dramatically rounded lines and compounded curves designed to cheat the wind. With its low coefficient of drag (the measurement of wind resistance), the car is a milestone in domestic styling. The same is true of the full-size Ford LTD which was introduced as a 1983 model. For the first time in recent memory Ford was marketing automobiles with original lines, models that did not appear to be old General Motors rejects or bad copies of European and Japanese cars.

Much of the earlier Ford design was the work of Eugene Bordinet, the company's longtime chief of design, whose fascination with long hoods, low rooflines, high noses and gobs of brightwork was keyed to the tastes of Henry Ford II and his associates. "You take our EXP and LN-7s," states a Ford insider. "We can't give 'em away because they're so ugly. Their high headlights and raised ass end turn people off, although they're pretty good little cars. They are good examples of Bordinet's work, just like the square and boxy Lincolns and Fords of recent years. How did he get away with it? Simple: Bordinet had power with the Fords."

When Eugene Bordinet retired in 1980 with full corporate honors, his place was taken by John "Jack" Telnack, a veteran of the Ford design wars. "We had the T-Bird and LTD ready to go," relates a Ford design staffer. "They were Bordinet cars, boxy and square. Ugly dogs, if you want to know the truth. They had been approved by the various corporate committees and the tooling was in the works. But Petersen put a stop to that."

Donald E. Petersen, president of Ford and considered an automotive progressive, realized that their cars were rehashes of the same look that had caused Ford to lose a large percentage of its domestic market share since 1974, and demanded a late-hour change. There was little choice but to turn to the in-house work of Telnack and his associates, who had been working on advanced aerodynamic designs. In a sense, their new Thunderbird and LTD creations won by default. "The committees who usually stick their noses in at this point were shut out of the projects, and they are infinitely better looking for it," says a Ford designer.

/////

In car styling the simplest method of expression has been the classic "three-box" look that appears as if packing crates had been stacked together to create a space for the engine, the passengers and their luggage. This is essentially the look that carried the American industry into the 1930s before being rejected for what General Motors' patriarch Alfred P. Sloan, Jr. liked to call "Hollywood Styling." That school made billions for Detroit in the decades of the 1950s, '60s and '70s before bankrupting itself in an orgy of self-parody—the automotive equivalent to a Busby Berkeley dance routine.

As American stylists veered off in a hyperbolic display of gimmickry, the Europeans, particularly the Germans, continued with the stark functionalism of the three-box notion. By the late 1970s, thanks to the social cachet enjoyed by the Mercedes-Benz and its imitators, the look of clean utility was back in fashion. Suddenly Detroit, which had prided itself on being the styling center of the automotive world, was an outcast.

Over the years Detroit styling has involved periodic bouts with the tasteless, the grotesque, the bizarre and, surprisingly, on more than one occasion, the beautiful. For every frog-lipped Edsel or bustle-backed Seville or flying-buttressed Buick or giant-finned Plymouth, we can find sparkling examples of the coachmaker's art.

The 1930s will be remembered for a number of clean-lined classics from Cadillac, Packard, and Duesenberg as well as the daring, perfectly proportioned "coffin-nose" 810 Cords of 1936-37 and the first of the Lincoln Continentals, with their trunk-mounted spare tires, which appeared on the eve of World War II. Even during the 1950s, when finned, snaggletoothed dinosaurs with three-tone pastel skins ruled the road, Detroit stunned its critics with such triumphs as the sylphlike Studebaker Starliner of 1953, the first Chrysler 300 hardtop of 1955, and the two-seater Thunderbird of a year later.

When most American automobiles seemed to be afflicted with elephantiasis during the 1960s, Detroit confounded the skeptics by producing such masterpieces as the 1961 four-door Lincoln Continental convertible, the 1963-64 surgically sculpted Buick Riviera, and the broad-shouldered, dead-simple Pontiac GTO. Even the first Mustang, while not a perfect harmony of space and line, was a courageous effort to bend sheet metal into a pleasing shape. The 1970s gave us little of styling excellence except perhaps the Chevrolet Camaro and Pontiac Firebird sport coupes.

These were exceptions in a thirty-five year binge of generally tasteless Detroit products. The old mastadons have mainly been buried by the demands for efficiency in fuel, aerodynamics, and weight, but the Detroit brand of design seems fixed. For every clean flash of excellence created by their styling studios, the American industry seems cursed with an abundance of cars loaded down with glistening gewgaws, vinyl and chrome.

A classic current example of the Detroit syndrome is Chrysler's much-ballyhooed K-car, a Big-Little car of the American school of design. It was fashioned at a time when aerodynamics were first being widely recognized as a key component of driving efficiency: At 55 mph, over 60 percent of the fuel consumed is used simply to plow through molecules of air. Since the K-car was created as a tall, squared-off shape intended to deceive the eye that it was larger than it actually was, it was oblivious to the need for aerodynamic design. Chrysler bragged loudly about how it would carry six passengers, although research data indicates that less than 5 percent of all driving involves that many occupants in a vehicle. It was the old big-car-family-vacation-to Upper-Michigan-instinct at work again. The result is a smallish car with a rather sophisticated drivetrain and a badly outdated body shape.

Ironically both Ford and GM have always been able to create superb-looking cars for their overseas markets. Two examples of the aesthetic gap that exists within both companies are the Ford Granada and the Opel Senator. The Granada is built by both Ford of Great Britain and Ford of Germany and has, since its introduction in the early 1970s, been an excellent example of a low, clean-surfaced, four-passenger sedan in the modern idiom, with spacious interior room.

Then came the American version of the Granada in 1975. It had been transformed into a heavy, lumpily-styled, over-chromed, mushily suspended travesty. Ford later embellished the Granada joke by witlessly attempting to sell it as a bogus Mercedes-Benz. Its EES model was a styling masquerade that poorly copied the German car's appearance, and did nothing to imitate its performance. "When I saw what the styling department in Dearborn had done to a perfectly good automobile, I was appalled," recalls a former Ford of England executive. "It was obvious that they simply did not understand that American attitudes about cars were becoming more worldly."

How could this happen? How could the same company produce two automobiles on essentially the same theme and have one look so good and one so bad? "It's the committee system," confides a Ford stylist, who, like many of his colleagues at GM and Chrysler, is a man of personal taste. "The sales types still have this idea that chrome sells. They think it adds a look of value to the car. So we put together a really nice shape, and then the big shots are in the studio telling us to add an accent stripe here and a hood scoop there. Pretty soon the car looks terrible, or it looks as if a dozen different guys who never talked to each other designed the car. You take a look at our '76 Mustang. It looks like three different committees worked on the front, the middle and the back without ever talking to each other, which is almost what happened.

"It's really frustrating. The Ford Escorts we sell in Great Britain and Germany are nice, clean shapes. We've got the same body here, but it's got too much stuff hung on it. Don't blame that on the designers. It's the sales guys and the big shots. They think they know what Americans want. The trouble is, they're ten years behind the times."

The Opel Senator—and its English sister, the Vauxhall Royale Saloon—built and sold by General Motors in Germany has been a source of bafflement to industry observers for years. It is a truly splendid looking automobile with a low, rounded hood, sloping windshield and aerodynamically clean sides with large windows. Built on a 105 inch wheelbase, with a modest 189 inch overall length, the Senator, as well as its less expensive sister, the Commodore, is a brilliantly-conceived five-passenger sedan that would, in the minds of many experts, have been a perfect GM entry for the American market. To be sure, special American standards would have required changes, but no more so than when the Chevette was created from the German Kadett, or when Ford modified its Fiesta subcompact from existing European designs.

The Senator is a conventional front-engine rear-wheel-drive car with fully independent suspension, excellent brakes and steering that would give GM a competitor against the upscale Volvo, Saab, BMW, and even Mercedes-Benz. But it is not being imported into America. Why? "Not suited to American driving conditions" is the standard GM answer. "It's a helluva car in Germany, but a little too stiff and sporty for our market," sniffed a senior Chevrolet engineer.

Too stiff? Too sporty? Stiffer than a Mercedes-Benz? Sportier than a BMW 320i? Not likely.

A more plausible answer: Not invented here. Although the Senator was designed by Americans on the GM staff, it is viewed by the Corporation as a German automobile for the German market. Somehow they have managed to ignore the reality that the Germans and Swedes have seized a sizable portion of the American status market by importing cars—fast, compact, stiffly sprung, very *sporty* automobiles—designed specifically for Europeans.

"The Senator and our Granada *look* too European for the big shots," remarks a Ford designer. "They still think cars should have long hoods and lots of chrome. They basically hate the new front-wheel-drive cars we're making now, because all the old glitter is gone. Every day some sales guy is down here saying, 'Can't you make it look *bigger*?'"

An American businessman recalls seeing the Senator on display in the lobby a hotel in Frankfurt, Germany. "The car was smashing," he recounts. "It was surrounded by people who were fascinated by its good looks. Most of them were Americans. They couldn't believe it was a General Motors car. They kept asking, 'For God's sake, why don't they sell a car like that in the United States? I'd buy one in a minute if they did.'"

Why not, indeed?

To answer requires a look back into the origins of the automobile, one that reveals how styling and its later perversions came to dominate, and ultimately help corrupt, the American automobile industry.

/////

In the beginning it was pure function. The early automobiles were simply motorized carriages. As the ancient ash and fabric frames gave way to all-steel bodies and enclosed cabinwork in the teens and early twenties, "style" was largely limited to distinctive radiator shells and art nouveau figureheads on the radiator caps.In some cases, as on the exotic Pierce-Arrow, such devices as swooping headlights integrally mounted to the front fenders made certain marques stand out. But for the most part, the cars were tall, angular black boxes with few distinguishing external characteristics.

The primary considerations were maximum interior space with proper head clearance for behatted ladies and gentlemen, and sufficient room to hide the engine and other running gear. Beyond that, appearance was of little concern. Too much energy was required to make needed mechanical improvements such as self-starters, interior heating, electric lights, improved gearboxes and suspensions, and better ignition systems, to be distracted by the idea of styling.

It was Alfred P. Sloan, Jr. and his new associate, Lawrence Fisher—the youngest of four brothers whose body-building business had been acquired by GM in 1926—who took the responsibility for the shape and color of automobiles away from pragmatic engineers and placed it in the hands of a new breed of "stylists."

The first, and perhaps the greatest of these, was Harley J. Earl, whom Fisher discovered during the same year his company was integrated into General Motors. Earl was working for Don Lee, a Los Angeles Cadillac dealer who was a favorite of the nouveaux riches of the booming movie industry. In keeping with the ostentatious taste of his clientele, Don Lee was heavily engaged in the car customizing business. Wild paint schemes, new fenders, wheels and in some cases entire new bodies were being applied to the Cadillacs of film stars and moguls. Earl's flashy aesthetics impressed Fisher, who hired him as a design consultant. Earl moved to Detroit and did a quick cosmetic fix on the 1927 Cadillacs and LaSalles, adding vivid accents of paint trim and subtly modifying the body panels so that they assumed a more uniform shape.

Chairman Sloan was delighted. He was convinced that technical advances should be deemphasized in favor of styling, sales, and marketing. Earl, with his exciting automotive shapes, was the perfect man to advance that cause. Sloan imperiously brushed aside the opposition of his various division managers—who then jealously guarded the independence of their lines—hired Earl as the head of the new "Art and Color Section," assigning him the job of creating long-range styling themes for the entire General Motors lineup.

This move was pivotal for three reasons. For one, it began the centralization of GM, a concentration of authority that by the 1970s had transferred almost all decision-making from the once-independent divisions to the Corporation. Secondly, Earl's hiring gave substance to the concept of an annual model change, based mainly on styling. Before that most "new" cars ambled onto the market in haphazard fashion, changed in appearance only because the chief engineer was suddenly inspired to alter a fender line or modify a bumper. Now a master customizer, a man who cared little about mechanics, would become the major arbiter of change, an annual event beautifully orchestrated each fall by Detroit.

Thirdly, Harley Earl's California-show business background injected a whole new element into the Detroit equation. California was becoming the embodiment of the American dream. Within its dazzling Hollywood fantasies there was a place for big, whopping automobiles with daring lines and California sunshine colors. The California materialist ethos was being translated into rolling dreamboats by Earl, and through his daring eyes General Motors was tapping the hunger for status among the rising middle class. Alfred P. Sloan, Jr. never hesitated to credit GM's success to Earl's "Hollywood styling."

It was clearly cheaper to stamp out a new sheet metal skin each year than to continually tool up new engines, transmissions or suspensions. As manufacturing became more complex, Earl's stylists supplanted the old engineers as the prime movers in selling automobiles, and to this day his successors and most important, his philosophy, remain intact.

Although the first traces of superfluous bodywork in the form of front-end streamlining, swooping fenders, enclosed trunks, drooping running boards, began with Harley Earl at GM, his efforts were hardly ignored by the remainder of the industry. Henry Ford first concerned himself with styling in his 1928 Model A, adding such garnishes as a reddish-tinted steering wheel and the now-famous Ford blue and white, scripted radiator emblem. But the Ford Motor Company only seriously entered the design competition with their 1933 models, which featured a sloping, shield-shaped radiator and a leaner, lower body profile.

The styling race stumbled to a halt in 1934. That year, Chrysler made the error of pushing too far ahead of public taste when it introduced its Airflow models, which were in some ways the embodiment of advanced car design. The car's headlights were tucked into the bodywork beside a bulging radiator shell that protruded from the nose of the car like a misplaced bicep. The windows were little more than slits in the steel side panels and the rear wheels were covered with skirts, like several popular fighter planes of the day.

Regardless of its controversial styling, the Airflow was a legitimate engineering effort. It carried an overdrive transmission; its engine was mounted farther forward than usual to enhance interior room; and its steel-hooped body structure was stronger and more rigid than most cars. The typical autos of the day were such blunderbussess in terms of cutting the wind that one engineer discovered they were more efficient running in reverse. But the Airflow was about 40 percent more aerodynamically efficient than its rivals. No matter; it was a stunning failure in the marketplace.

The experiment succeeded in imprinting a message on the brains of Sloan and Earl: (1) high technology could not compensate for externals the public did not appreciate and (2) slow, evolutionary advances were better than single, shocking leaps forward. Only today has the Airflow been given its due. It has become a minor classic among antique car buffs.

When World War II intervened, the early patterns of the hyperbolic styling of the 1950s were already being developed. A few years before the war, Cadillac's beautiful 1938 "60 Special" appeared without running boards and assured the future of Earl's protege, William Mitchell. This automobile forced both Lincoln and Packard to respond with increasingly buttery shapes that gave the impression they were melting before the viewer's eyes. Unfortunately they were also the forerunners of the finned and spinner-festooned fifties.

Totally committed to Earl's concept of "dynamic obsolescence," General Motors raced out of the war and into the showrooms with a collection of redesigned cars that were devastating weapons against the smaller, weaker carmakers who could not compete with the new styles and the collective marketing power of the Big Three. The once-proud competition—Hudson, Packard, Willys, Nash as well as such postwar upstarts as Kaiser-Frazer—could not generate the capital to annually revamp their lineups.

Postwar styling had an unusual inspiration. The Cadillac styling team, headed by Harley J. Earl and his protege, William L. Mitchell, had become fascinated with the rakish, organic lines of the twin engine, twin fuselage, Lockheed P-38 fighter plane, the most dramatic-looking combat aircraft of World War II. They set out to create a new generation of automobiles featuring such aerodynamically inspired fillips as pointed noses, long sweeping pontoon fenders, curved windshields, and a generally elongated length that was inspired by airborne, not land-based, transportation.

In 1948, the new Cadillac first unveiled what has become the historic symbol of Detroit's obsession with frivolous glitter, the tail fin. "From a design standpoint, the fins gave definition to the rear of the car for the first time," Mitchell said. "They made the back as interesting as the front, and established a long-standing Cadillac styling hallmark." Although modest little protrusions by comparison with the knife-edged, metallic slabs that adorned some cars by the end of the tail fin craze, the 1948 Cadillac was regarded as daring by a public which discussed this styling innovation with an enthusiasm generally reserved for show biz scandals.

The race toward excess was underway. Studebaker countered in 1950 with what it hailed as "the next look in cars." It was a revolutionary-looking vehicle designed by Raymond Loewy, with a glassed-in passenger compartment which looked almost the same from the front or back. Its grille was a pointy-nosed curiosity capped by a chrome knob inspired by an airplane propeller spinner. Ford produced a similar—if more conservative—version of the same theme.

The Studebaker was an ill-destined attempt at original design, but other manufacturers came up with milestones of kitsch. Particularly vivid examples were the Nash's '49-'51 "Airflytes" that looked like inverted bathtubs; the lugubrious 1954 Buicks, Cadillacs, and Oldsmobiles that featured Earl's latest triumph, the so-called panoramic windshield, which did nothing to increase visibility; and virtually every 1957-58 befinned chrome-gobbed "Forward Look" "Airborne" "Triple-Turbine Turboglide," "Swept-Line" "Firesweep" "Turnpike Cruiser," "Swept-Wing" "Starfire Golden Rocket," "Golden Commando," "Wide-Track" abomination that hit the road.

They were loaded with gadgetry: Buick's canted headlights, Cadillac's "Autotronic Eye" light control, DeSoto's "Hiway Hi-Fi" built-in record player, Dodge's "Pushbutton Powerflite" transmission, Edsel's revolving speedometer, and Oldsmobile's "Dual Range Power Heater." Collectively, they came to typify what discerning people around the world referred to as "Detroit Iron." The American cars of the era were the embodiment of the tasteless exploitation of style at the expense of functional vitality.

The mid-1950s had also seen practically every major brand introduce their version of the lightweight, powerful overhead valve V-8 that had first been introduced by Cadillac and Oldsmobile in 1949 and set the patterns for the industry for the next *thirty* years. These new, efficient V-8's—the "Rockets," "Firedomes," "Torque-Flos," "Red Rams," "Interceptors"—were a boon to the stylists.

They were a foot shorter than the old in-line eight-and six-cylinder engines they replaced, which meant there was even more room for the passengers. The extra space also permitted the voluminous draping of sheet metal within the wheelbases to be stretched out to 125 inches.

Moreover, these new engines were producing enormous horse-power (the 1946 Fleetline Chevrolet put out 90 hp; the 1956 Bel Air as much as *225 hp*) which not only made for flashy road performance but also allowed quantities of extra-cost options and gadgetry to be added on. The old wheezy six-cylinder produced barely enough power to propel the car, but the new V-8s produced sufficient surplus energy to run all the generators and hydraulic pumps necessary for such power-robbing components as automatic transmissions and power-assisted steering, windows, seats, door locks, trunk lids, and air conditioning.

The stylists and engineers were becoming little more than gadget builders, slaving compulsively over such problems as the creation of opera lights or automatic headlight dimmers while the essentials of the automobile—the brakes, suspension, steering—were left virtually unimproved.

Only Chrysler Corporation waged a program of engineering progress, a legacy of its crusty old former president, K. T. Keller, who was a devotee of the stodgy "three-box" body style. "Cars should accommodate *people* rather than the dreams of far-out designers," he had grumbled prior to his retirement in 1954. Keller was responsible for the Chrysler Corporation's reputation as a leader in engineering, one that persists, with little justification, to this day. However during the 1950-60 decade, Chrysler was truly in the engineering vanguard, developing such significant devices as the hemispherical combustion chamber, the famed "Hemi head" (1951); hydraulic shock absorbers (1952); the superb Torqueflite three-speed automatic transmission (1956), which is considered by many to be the finest automatic ever built and is still widely used today; torsion bar suspension (1957); and welded unit body construction (1960).

But it was not K. T. Keller and his engineering department who made the major impact on Chrysler sales. That credit belongs to a lean-framed stylist named Virgil Exner, who had left Studebaker to join Chrysler in 1949. It was Exner—with the blessings of Chrysler's new president, Lester Lum "Tex" Colbert, a management whiz and former protege of founder Walter Chrysler—who was to enter his company into the flash and chrome wars with what became known as the "Forward Look." By 1958 the Chrysler, Dodge, and even the lowly Plymouth, had fins so outlandish that they appeared to have been stolen directly from the drawing boards of Boeing Aircraft.

A sign of the trend in which the frivolous became more important than the functional had turned up in 1953, when Buick engineers produced a paper for the Society of Automotive Engineers. In it, they boasted how they had developed a special vertically mounted valve layout for their new 322 cubic inch V-8s specifically to conform to the restricted engine bay space allotted to them by the stylists. This marked a complete reversal of the traditional role of the engineers, who had always been in charge of design essentials. If they chose to build a car with an engine six feet long and four feet high, it was up to the body-makers to accommodate these ungainly dimensions. But with the arrival of Harley J. Earl and his Art and Color Section, all that changed. From then on, the men in the styling studios (soon to be upgraded to "design studios") were in command.

William Mitchell had succeeded Earl as GM's chief stylist in 1954. That same year, the new Cadillac appeared with its panoramic windshield and a pair of airplane-type prop spinners on its front bumper that immediately became known as "Dagmars," after a bosomy television personality of the day. Mitchell was as flamboyant as his mentor; he believed in dramatic assaults on the eye as a selling tool. "A perfectly proportioned design can be easily forgotten," he later stated. "Every great shape has something that jars the eye—something that makes it stick in your mind."

With Mitchell and Earl in control at GM, Exner at Chrysler, and the equally flashy George Walker at Ford, the industry was on the road to styling Babylon at the expense of engineering. Said Walker during the midst of it: "The ultimate in elegance is to be dressed in a white suit, driving a white Thunderbird with white upholstery with a white Afghan dog beside you." Exner contributed three-tone paint Chrysler products, many of which featured the pastel pinks, purples, and greens that were the fashion of the day. Any part of the car that was not garishly painted was coated either in white vinyl or chrome.

/////

This episode of excess was probably inevitable. In the 1950s the nation was preoccupied with forgetting the agonies of the past twenty years and seeking material diversions on a scale never before seen. The automobile had been the ultimate middle class status symbol since the Roaring Twenties, and now, with prosperity pervading the nation and big engine technology making wild gadgetry possible, the public was determined to enjoy the chrome-plated fantasy.

With that fantasy came the proliferation of styles, a trend that continues to this day. In 1947 the ten principle car companies produced 182 different models. In 1982, when that number of carmakers had been reduced to four (excluding Volkswagen of America, which makes only the Rabbit on these shores), the American manufacturers were producing *307* different models. While that was a small reduction from the all-time high of 325 in 1975, the fascination with model proliferation is unchanged. Ford Division alone offers forty-one different models under its label; Chevrolet has thirty-four. "There are so many different models out there that nobody—the production people, the marketing people, or the salesmen—can tell one from another," a GM management veteran complains. "And those idiots on the Fourteenth floor still think that the American public doesn't know that about half of 'em are the same goddam car!"

The "same car" phenomenon was at one time a sales triumph for the industry. That triumph has now turned model proliferation into a babel of confusion. Today four of the GM divisions sell the same X-cars and A-cars, and all five divisions are peddling slightly modified versions of the same J-car. Chrysler sells identical K-cars under the Dodge and Plymouth label, and Ford and Lincoln-Mercury are doing the same.

The damage done to the integrity of the industry can be seen in the change in the Chevrolet. It first displaced the Ford as America's number one seller, then went on to become GM's flagship in the sixties and seventies only to serve as a prime example of the Corporation's failings in the eighties.

The 1946 Chevrolet was a modest device, carrying a six-cylinder engine and available in three different models and ten body styles. Ten years later the Chevy had roughly the same overall dimensions and was still available in three basic models: the 150, the 210, and the top of the line, the hot-selling Bel Air. The 1946 and 1956 Chevrolets both weighed about 3100 pounds, and aside from the addition of the V-8, the undistinguished but popular Powerglide automatic transmission, and the exciting new "hardtop" body styles, the two automobiles were, in a broad sense, sisters.

Then another decade passed, and the 1966 Chevrolet had blossomed into more than just an automobile. Now it was a four-wheeled conglomerate of its own, controlling nearly 30 percent of the entire car market through no less than thirteen different models including the Corvette and the Corvair (not to mention a number of trucks) encompassing 72 different styles and eight engines, ranging from the now-antique six to a 409 hp V-8 ("She's real fine, my 409" sang the Beach Boys). Moreover, the mainline Impala, which had replaced the Bel Air at the top of the lineup in 1959, had added three inches to its wheelbase, nearly a foot to its overall length, and 400 pounds to its bulk in the intervening decade.

Yet, despite the masses of options, body styles and overt gadgetry, the basic automobile, with its "Jet-Smooth-Ride," mushy all-coil spring suspension, antiquated solid rear axles, old fashioned rail frame chassis, two-speed automatic transmission, slow, imprecise steering, and pre-World War II technology had become a collection of mediocrities. The high performance V-8 engine excepted—which was, and is, a milestone—there was almost nothing significant to distinguish the "longer, lower, wider" 1966 Chevrolet from its decade-old ancestor or from a dozen other full-size American automobiles.

But the styles! Hardtop coupes and sedans, convertibles, coupes, four-doors, in every possible shape and color. If there was one Detroit technical development in the first twenty postwar years to stand alongside the V-8 high compression engine and the efficient automatic transmission, it was the refinement of mass-production through computerization. This process made it possible for manufacturers to create inventories of high-profit accessories and options and thus allow a customer to virtually "build" his own model from the parts catalogue. It was a logical extension of Henry Ford's idea of an everyman's vehicle. But now, through the magic of computer-controlled assembly lines, "everyman" could make his Chevrolet or Ford as luxurious as his boss's Cadillac.

In the case of the luxurious Chevrolet Caprice, it was the bosses themselves who first sought this gratification. Prior to the 1966 model year, it was standard practice for senior GM management men in all car divisions to drive Cadillacs. That car was, after all, the ultimate expression of having scored a middle-class touchdown. Thanks to GM corporate discount structures, it could be driven by executives for several years and traded in for almost no out-of-pocket cost.

Then came a corporate edict which required that personnel working for Chevrolet will drive Chevrolets, Pontiac men will drive Pontiacs, and so on. Cadillacs would be driven *only* by executives working for Cadillac. The pronouncement sent shock waves through the Chevrolet management. Did this mean that they would actually have to drive a Chevrolet Impala—the same menial machine being wheeled into the parking lots by their foremen and junior accountants? At least the Buick guys had their Electra 225; the Olds 98 was a fair copy of the Caddy.

Enter the Caprice. It was nothing more than an Impala gussied up with cut-pile carpeting, brocaded upholstery, a flashier overlay of chrome trim, some extra wads of sound-deadening insulation and a few extra gadgets. But it was Chevrolet's executive-brand pseudo-Cadillac and it was marketed as much for the benefit of a small cadre of Detroit and Flint executives as for the general public. These were big car glory days for GM. Despite the flap over the Corvair and the bombardments from Washington, such luxuries could be afforded. The Caprice was a hot seller (180,00 in its first year) and went on to become one of the favored icons in the Chevrolet temple of excess.

Regardless of such internally inspired oddities as the Caprice, a great shift toward centralization was beginning to take place in the entire industry during the 1960s. It had begun with the so-called "intermediates" in 1961. These neatly sized and styled cars—the Buick Skylark, Oldsmobile F-85 and the Pontiac Tempest—all shared the same basic Fisher-built body shell and marked the onset of a trend that, for reasons of cost, would force all of the major carmakers to build three, four and sometimes five different brands from the same basic interior "platform."

With this steadily increasing slide toward centralization came more power for designers such as GM's William Mitchell, Ford's Eugene Bordinet, and Chrysler's Elwood P. Engel. It was their job to create pleasing and salable basic body shapes upon which the individual car division stylist could "skin" his own sheet metal to make a Ford appear different from a Mercury, set a Buick apart from an Oldsmobile and separate a Plymouth from a Dodge.

Now, a flawed roofline or a badly raked hood could wreck the sales of not just a single car division, but an entire Corporation. With so much at stake, the 1960s saw automotive styling retreat somewhat from the strident 1950s philosophy of Harley Earl, which proclaimed, "go as far as you can, then pull back." Some of his disciples had gone too far, and even the American public had been repelled by the fins and chrome gobs of the 1958-59 models.

By the middle 1960s the absurd jet-plane fashion had given way to a cleaner, more precise look and Mitchell was establishing himself as a brilliant, if somewhat erratic, world leader in styling. "Ford and Chrysler remain one full design cycle behind Mitchell and General Motors," declared *Car and Driver* editor David E. Davis, Jr., "And the Europeans are still farther behind than that," he added.

At the time it was true. While GM cars were hardly getting smaller, they were gaining a grace of line and proportion that made them, collectively, the best-styled automobiles in the world in the late 1960s and early 1970s. The acclaimed Italian school, led by the great coach-builders Pininfarina, Bertone, Ghia (whose company had been bought by Ford), Scaglietti, and soon to be joined by the young genius and ex-Bertone apprentice Giorgetto Giugiaro, were still involved in designing custom bodies for such exotic brands as Ferrari, Maserati, and Lamborghini, and their ideas were not in the automotive mainstream.

The average Italian Fiats were ordinary three-box sedans with no distinctive features. All French cars tended to look as if they had been lifted from the panels of an old Flash Gordon comic strip and the few English cars left on the market, except for the Jaguar, had an aged look. The Germans built characterless boxes and were the object of Mitchell's open derision.

"Mercedes-Benz has only one guy working on styling," he hooted in 1974 while assaulting what he called "boxcar" styling. Within three years of that comment every stylist in Detroit, including Mitchell himself, would be tacking barefaced copies of the fine-mesh, gracefully shaped Mercedes-Benz radiator grille on everything from luxury cars to economy sedans. And during this same period the Japanese were slavishly, even comically, copying every tasteless American styling gimmick, including quad headlights, chrome spears, vinyl roofs, hardtops and lumpy, nose-heavy grille treatments.

With such inept competition, Mitchell and General Motors chose never to consider the day when things might change. The big car's market share was slipping away, but was being replaced by highly profitable intermediates like the Chevrolet Chevelle and cleverly restyled "personal luxury" models like the Monte Carlo and Pontiac Grand Prix and the more expensive Rivieras, Toronados, and Cadillac Eldorados. Admittedly, some of these Mitchell shapes were superb. His 1971 Chevrolet Camaro/Pontiac Firebird cars are considered by many to be among the all-time classics. But others, like his 1971-76 Buick Riviera, with its boat-tail rear end and its swooping fender lines that did eternal battle against its oppressive bulk, were disasters.

Yet Mitchell and his Riviera were not alone. All car designers were mesmerized with the "classic" look of the 1930s. That decade was a period of beautiful autos, but the 1970s manifestations of that look have produced such creations as the "Mark" Lincolns, with their sprawling hoods, utterly phony rear-mount spare tire housings, and cramped passenger space; the stubby K-car "Le Barons" that look like tuxedoed midgets on stilts; and the 1980 Seville "Elegante," a bustle-backed parody of old English limousine coachwork that replaced the clean-lined original Cadillac Seville introduced by General Motors in the middle of 1975.

/////

Today, as the move toward aerodynamic efficiency increases, such styling tendencies are becoming anachronistic. Long hoods were originally designed to serve one purpose: to house long engines. Opera lights were for patrons of the opera. Landau bars were for cabriolet convertibles, which are no longer made. The illusion of glamour through such outdated trappings of elegance makes no sense in the 1980s.

The collective Detroit Mind, frustrated by the loss of this charade, has been left in a state of disorientation. *Automotive News* reported that several years ago, Henry Ford II cast his regal eyes on a new, spare-lined, aerodynamic prototype from Ford and growled, "I hope I never live to see one of those things built." He was informed that not only would he live to see it, but that the car was the forerunner of a whole new generation of more honest designs.

The flashy looks of yore remain a major distraction of industry veterans. It was as if the lament of R. K. Brown, vice president for marketing of Chrysler, still echoed through the Highland Park office. After the Plymouth Valiant had failed to weaken Volkswagen's grip on the small car market, Brown commented: "I just can't understand it. Our Valiant is bigger, faster, roomier, looks better, and is only slightly more expensive than the VW, but we just can't convince anybody."

The notion that a growing percentage of buyers was *not* looking for automobiles that were bigger, faster, roomier, gaudier, but for cars which exhibited other measurements of excellence—functionalism, quality, economy, technical innovation, handling, originality —escaped Brown and his associates for another ten years. It is only now beginning to fully penetrate the upper reaches of Detroit management.

America has no dearth of good designers. In the design studios of the major automakers are hundreds of highly trained, aesthetically keen young men from such prestigious institutions as the Art Center College of Design in Pasadena, the Design Center for Creative

Studies in Detroit, and from the best *carrozzerias* of Italy. But despite their personal taste, they are still operating under an ancient and oppressive management edict: Make them look Big!

The walls of the design studios in Detroit have long been covered with original, sleek, beautiful car concepts. There are over two thousand designers in the domestic industry and most of them possess the same aesthetic instincts, the same enthusiasm, the same training as any comparable group in Germany, Japan, France or Italy. But they have been shackled by sales experts, marketing men, upper management moguls, all of whom presume to know what makes a car "sell." Quite obviously, they do not. Otherwise, the industry would not have lost so much of its market, and its prestige, to the interlopers from overseas.

"The secret to sales is product, product, product," says Chevrolet General Manager Bob Stempel, whose eighteen month tour of duty as head of Adam Opel AG in Germany helped earn him the reputation of being a company progressive. In today's context that product must be light, efficient, nimble, and aerodynamically clean in the simple idiom of Giorgetto Giugiaro's Ital Design. Such fine examples as the Volkswagen Rabbit and the first Scirocco GT coupe, the Lotus Esprit, the Mazda GLC, and dozens of Ferraris, Lamborghinis and Maseratis have come from his drawing boards.

Giugiaro is a leader in the stark, no-trim design movement that has displaced Detroit as the world's style setter. Other Italian studios, particularly Pininfarina, operated in tandem with Giugiaro as a revolutionary vanguard in the early 1970s. Their message was simple: automobile style was more an aspect of function than form. The external shape of the automobile had to relate directly to the use of the vehicle, not to the fantasy it was trying to create. A small front-wheel-drive economy car should have an honest shape that makes it look like a small front-wheel-drive economy car, not a miniature seven-passenger limousine, a Le Mans winner or a supersonic fighter plane. The bodies should, like the first wood-and-fabric frames, do nothing more than cover the mechanical components, protect the passengers from the elements *and* slice through the air as cleanly as possible. Except for that last proviso, the mentality of automotive styling has come full circle from the first products created by the genius of Henry Ford.

A new wave of religion has suddenly swept over Detroit, one in which this "functionalism" is the credo. New General Motors and Ford cars can be found with their interiors coated with flat black surfaces punctuated with fake rivets, boltheads, and Allen screws that appear to have been lifted from the cockpit of a Stuka dive bomber. Soft velour and muted vinyls draped over bolstered bucket seats have replaced the fluffy brocades and buttoned expanses of tinted leather or replica vinyls that were once the trademark of American interiors.

The chrome (actually bright plastic) trim and instrument bezels have disappeared, to be replaced by the stark intensity of the German school, which long ago placed a premium on dash panels that were safe and contained ergonomically sound instruments and controls. However, once again, the functional appearance of Detroit cars is an illusion. In most new American-built cars, the meters and switches are fake. A majority of models feature only a speedometer and a gas gauge. The rest of the engine's vital signs are monitored by the cheaper "idiot lights" that warn only of trouble.

And so quackery still rules the day. The designers have merely shifted gears. Yesterday it was Hollywood. Today it is Stuttgart. Neither seem to be the answer. The pseudo-European designs seem borrowed and false, while the old "American" automotive style was at least homegrown. It may not have been the epitome of good taste, but it was American, and in many ways, it was a symbol of the nation's prosperity and illusions about the Good Life. That style has become obsolete, but the challenge of a new, indigenously American concept remains.

/////

The great styling excess of the fifties, sixties and seventies is almost over, a noisy memory that the automobile industry is trying to forget. The tired ploy of the annual model change seems doomed as well. It first faltered with the 1970 introductions of the smaller-sized Chevrolet Vega and the Ford Pinto, both of which were marketed with the promise that they would remain immune to annual revamps for five years, or more. The instincts of the Detroit automakers still tempt them to try to recapture the long-vanished excitement of the fall "New Car" fever, but most know it will never return. The imports introduce new models at any time of the year, and only when they have something to offer that truly qualifies as *new*. This practice has only made the old domestic autumn shell game look even more contrived than it is.

The roles of design and engineering may be returning to the more logical relationship they enjoyed before Sloan discovered his miracle of Hollywood styling in Los Angeles. If the more progressive elements of the industry gain power, styling will once again become an arm of engineering, with the responsibility of producing the cleanest, lightest, most efficient skin for the auto's internal requirements. With the passing of the old school, with their Dagmars and their Venti-Ports, must come a new breed of designers who accept the relationship of form and function in its proper sequence.

GM's Bill Mitchell is retired now, serving as an independent design consultant for a variety of firms, including those who make motorcycles, one of his great passions. His replacement is Irv Rybicki, a suave but considerably less flamboyant man who retains the same corner office in the Design Center in Warren, Michigan once occupied by Harley Earl and Mitchell. In fact, Rybicki sits behind the same curved, laminated-wood desk of the originator of GM style and has lunch in the same private dining room where a large circular table features a push-button Lazy Susan that can be operated by each of the diners.

While honoring his legacy, Rybicki—along with his peers at Chrysler, Ford and AMC—is fully aware of the new realities. "Aero" is the latest buzz-word in the design studios, and the new consciousness, as embodied by GM's crisp Camaros and Firebirds and Ford's new Thunderbird, indicates that Detroit is getting back into step with the rest of the world in viewing styling not as a marketing hype, but as a legitimate extension of good engineering.

Even the hucksters in the sales and marketing departments are begrudgingly behind the change. But the major challenge lies ahead. If sales improve and their salesmen's blood begins to percolate, they must forever be barred from interfering with the design process.

Their peddler's bags of tinware—the hood scoops, decal kits, fake louvres, imitation walnut, moon roofs, opera lights, landau bars, quad headlamps, phony wire wheels, and (God forbid) the fins— must be buried forever in the mud of the Detroit River.

Yet that is not a complete solution. By abdicating its role as styling leader to the world, the American industry has lost a major marketing advantage. For better or for worse, American style meant something. It had a vivid, often outrageous character that could not be ignored. Detroit's loss of leadership need not have happened. If, for example, General Motors had not waited until 1980 to complete its own wind tunnel (the rest of the industry rents the Lockheed Aircraft facility in Marietta, Georgia) and the design staff had been permitted more flexibility and originality, that lead might never have been lost. Tomorrow's European and Japanese automobiles might still look like they were inspired by American design, rather than the embarrassing opposite.

The industry needs a few geniuses. It aches for another Harley J. Earl. Not another Hollywood fantasizer, but a visionary designer with the same courage to forge new shapes and concepts into the cars of tomorrow. To do this, he must be released from the controls of the executive committees and marketing men who too often have bastardized beautiful automotive designs. The result may be another Chrysler Airflow, or an even more radical shape that would change the course of automobile design. As Goethe said in response to the observation that nothing new exists under the sun: "Everything has been thought of before, but the problem is to think of it again."

To achieve better car styling, unfettered thought must be encouraged in Detroit. Without it, the American auto industry is doomed to follow more daring men on other continents, and the nation forced to pay the penalty in less employment and smaller profits.

CHAPTER VI

What Happened to American Know-How?: The Technology Gap

"AMERICANS KNOW TWO THINGS ABOUT TIRES: whitewalls and black-walls," says a veteran auto industry executive. "For years, the public simply had no idea that radial tires existed. And the guys in Detroit and Akron weren't much interested in having them find out."

This comment sums up the cavalier rejection of radial tires by American automakers during the 1970s, when they were standard equipment on the better European cars. It is one of the scandals of the industry, a shameful example of the failure of vaunted American automobile know-how in the last two decades. During these techno-logically dormant years, young lions in Detroit spoke up vociferously for radial tires, but they learned to keep their radical thoughts to themselves.

First developed for the aircraft industry in 1914, the modern steel-belted radial tire was rediscovered in 1946 by researchers at the Compagnie Generale des Etablissements Michelin factory in Cler-mont-Ferrand, France. A radial tire is constructed differently than a conventional bias-ply version. The "plies," or inner material used to form the tire, run from side to side at right angles, whereas the bias tire has its plies mounted at an angle. Moreover, the radial has a "belt" of either steel or a fiber such as nylon wrapped around it like an inner tread. The use of steel, which is clearly superior, was pioneered by Michelin. It gives the tire less rolling resistance and permits less heat, which promotes wear, to build up within the body of the tire. Radial tires also handle better than the bias-ply versions, providing superior traction under all conditions, including rain and show.

The new tire's miraculous traction, durability, and wet weather handling were immediately recognized in Europe and the famed "Michelin X" brought the company to new heights of prosperity. By 1954 Michelin was producing nothing but its "cage au mouche" (fly cage) steel-belted radials; they were regarded by industry leaders worldwide as a quantum leap forward in tire technology. Yet despite their clear advantages in performance over the antiquated bias-ply tires, which dated back to a basic mid-1920s design, the radials were rejected by Detroit, whose excuse was that American drivers had sensitive derrieres. Our citizens were ostensibly too accustomed to mushy, silent boulevard rides to be subjected to such harsh treatment.

The real reasons were more complex. Radials were more difficult to manufacture than conventional tires and could not be made on the rubber industry's ancient tire molding equipment. In addition, they cost two to three times as much. The Detroit marketers maintained that it was folly to charge a premium for exotic tires that made more noise on the roads and thudded over the expansion joints.

It was best, they decided, to stick with the old stuff from Akron that could be purchased for virtually nothing. The exact cost of a typical OEM— Original Equipment Manufacturer—tire is one of the best kept secrets in American industry, but estimates place the price tag of a bottom-line bias-belt tire at something under five dollars apiece. This low cost killed the shift to new radials, even though they reduced the need for snow tires in some northern climates; would wear three times as long; produce better fuel mileage; and were infinitely safer.

Ford offered Michelin X's on some high-performance cars in the late 1960s and B. F. Goodrich experimented with the radial during the same period, but it required the imported car revolution to force Detroit to shift to the new tire in the late 1970s. Goodyear, led by its progressive chairman, Charles Pilliod, Jr., finally put America in the hi-tech tire business, but at a relatively late hour.

/////

It was not always this way in Detroit. The early 1950s was a period of technological energy in the domestic auto industry, a time when the American Big Three were still in the forefront of automotive design and manufacture. Their new overhead valve V-8 engines produced horsepower figures that were unrivaled for cost; their new automatic transmissions were without peer; Chrysler became the first major automaker to introduce disc brakes when it installed them on its 1949 Imperial; advanced ball-joint suspensions originated in Detroit, as did the mass-produced Fiberglas car bodies that first appeared on the 1953 Corvette.

By 1954 American tubeless tires were common. Chrysler was actively experimenting with turbine-powered automobiles, and it began marketing torsion-bar front suspensions in 1956. In 1957 General Motors produced its own fuel injection system for the Corvette and for certain high-performance Chevrolet models.

It was a time when Detroit deferred to no one. Competition was keen among the major American automakers and the nation, still propelled by the engineering thrust of World War II, moved ahead in a boom of optimism. Yet within five years those fires were banked. The old American know-how was replaced with smugness, and Detroit began to sink into a technological malaise which was to cost it untold billions in profits and even more in the loss of industrial status.

By 1965 Chevrolet had given up on the last courageous automotive experiment from Detroit, the 1960 Corvair, which was driven off the market by cost-cutting, compromised engineering, legal suits and a rising safety lobby. Gone as well was the urge to invest in costly experiments that did not produce quick dividends. The American automobile industry convinced itself that the big V-8 engines, automatic transmissions and chassis components which were developed in the energetic fifties would last forever.

But it was wrong. The absence of sufficient research and development during the 1960s and 1970s and the stubborn refusal to acknowledge advances made elsewhere has placed Detroit in its present embarrassing position of copying the foreign competition. Fuel injuection is one of the vital advances Detroit rejected while the determined foreign competition utilized it to impress American car buyers. To the average motorist, fuel injection is no more intelligible than the internal workings of the family refrigerator. It is seen only as some mysterious hi-tech manifestation increasingly evident in automotive advertising. But fuel injection is more relevant to the workaday driver than he suspects. It is an important advance over the traditional carburetor, that often troublesome device that mixes gasoline with the atmosphere, then introduces it into the combustion chambers of an engine.

The carburetor began life as a relatively uncomplicated device, but recent demands for emission controls and fuel economy have turned it into a nightmare of Rube Goldberg gadgetry. Fuel injection, on the other hand, is vastly simpler. Rather than mixing the air and gasoline at a central location, fuel injection uses nozzles similar to tiny shower heads to introduce the fuel charge directly into each individual cylinder, producing a more even distribution of the fuel. But fuel injection has one disadvantage: it demands higher precision in manufacture and is therefore somewhat more expensive.

Today, as exhaust emissions must be reduced without sacrificing performance, fuel injection has gained increasing favor with automobile manufacturers, especially in Germany, where it was developed prior to World War II. It is equally popular in Japan, where sensitivity to technological advances developed anywhere has become both a minor art form and a major business dogma. The United States, sadly, has lagged far behind in fuel injection research and use. American carmakers are slowly coming around to its use, but they have lost decades in experience.

Modern fuel injection was developed in the mid-1930s when the German firm of Robert Bosch worked closely with Goering's Air Ministry to perfect the process in combat aircraft. Eventually used by all the principals in the Second World War, it was first employed on a passenger car in 1954, when Mercedes-Benz introduced it in its milestone 300SL gull-wing sports car.

The energy shocks of the 1970s, coupled with the government mandates for clean air, ended Detroit's technological stagnation and rekindled interest in fuel injection. Unfortunately their early efforts to solve the air quality problem involved patchwork modifications of existing hardware. Large V-8 engines were sawed and quartered to create four- and six-cylinder versions. This was Detroit's way of producing lighter, less thirsty power plants without the billion dollar outlays needed for all-new engines. To save weight, every big-car component, from chassis bits to door handle hardware, was modified in the rush campaign to down-size. Massive outlays of cash and manpower were expended to catch up in such areas as suspension and body design, fields in which Detroit had been a leader just two decades earlier.

Fuel injection was one of the modern auto components being used in Europe and Japan that was suddenly rediscovered by Detroit. General Motors pieced together a compromise, what it called a "Throttle-Body" fuel injection system—actually a bastardized standard carburetor modified to behave like an injector. "The GM system had all the disadvantages of conventional carburetion with none of the advantages of fuel injection," remarks a GM development engineer. "In the meantime Germany's Robert Bosch had developed its own direct-port fuel-injection systems to a high level of expertise. Not only were they better suited to modern emission standards, but they provided a broader band of performance, higher fuel mileage and were easier to maintain."

A veteran engine builder who does outside development work for Buick confirms this. "The Bosch K-Jetronic and L-Jetronic Fuel injection systems are more efficient, simpler, work better under all conditions and are easier for the average mechanic to maintain," he says. "But they have one major problem—they were developed in Stuttgart and not Detroit."

"We've tried to sell the Jetronic systems in Detroit," a Bosch engineer reveals, "but they say they can develop their own that work just as well and are cheaper. Sure, their throttle body system is a little cheaper, but it's more complicated and doesn't work as well, so where's the payoff? We had some young guys at General Motors who were pushing our stuff, but they didn't have much clout. If you're a new guy at GM, you better fit in or you're a dead duck. They knew they were out in left field talking about Bosch when GM had their own divisions like Rochester Products who said they could do better, so they shut up."

GM's desire to use its own technology over Germany's is commendable— if they could do as well. But after a fifteen year hiatus in research and development, the old American "know how" that made the auto industry great has lapsed into atrophy.

/////

A sad case of American technical failure was demonstrated to me on a misty midsummer day in Central Michigan in 1966. The 4000 acre General Motors Proving Ground in Milford was swarming with strangely shaped automobiles in the final stages of testing before the traditional autumn introductions of the "new" 1967 models. In those days, when the domestic industry was selling over eight million passenger cars without apparent effort, the secrecy surrounding their new machinery was viewed as seriously as the national security. By September the advertising and promotion experts at GM, Ford, and Chrysler expected that the American public would have been raised to such a state of anticipation that they would scoop up the "new" iron without noticing that it was the same old car with a change of trimmings.

One exception was the Cadillac Eldorado, which with its sister, the Oldsmobile Toronado, was a legitimate new automobile. A small group of automotive journalists had been admitted to the proving grounds on that rather gloomy day to have a preview look at the new machine, already nicknamed "Eldo" by the engineers and public relations men who hovered nearby. It was described as one of the new generation of "personal" cars that had become popular since the introduction of the Ford Thunderbird as a four-passenger quasi-sports vehicle nearly a decade before.

The phrase "personal car" meant nothing; it was a vacuous euphemism. The Eldorado itself was another giant automobile from

Detroit, nearly 19 feet long with a 120 inch wheelbase. But there was an air of originality to the car. Both it and the Toronado were front-wheel-drive machines, a departure for Detroit. Front wheel drive had been developed before World War I, and had been used over the years with considerable success by Citroën, Cord, and Austin. Its advantages were excellent traction and a compact drive-train which eliminated the space-stealing "hump" from intruding on the passenger compartment.

The front-drive system was built under license from Ford, who had tried it in prototype Thunderbirds but rejected it because of its excessive weight and cost. Neither was a factor with the Eldorado, which was priced at slightly over $8000, an enormous sum for the time, and which weighed a few pounds shy of two and a half tons.

The "Eldo" was a typical General Motors car of the period: powerful, gadget-laden, with a feather-pillow ride. It plowed through tight corners in ungainly fashion, got only ten miles to the gallon, and would run 109 mph in a short burst like an ill-trained athlete. Aside from the lack of a transmission bulge and the fact that its power was transmitted through the front axle, the Eldorado resembled any of the oversized, overplush cars then being marketed by Detroit.

But there was one difference, a thoroughly unpleasant and dangerous one. It was the brakes. To make a panic stop in an Eldorado from 80 mph took well over a football field of distance, nearly a hundred feet more than could be considered acceptable. Exactly 386 feet were required to rein in the car from that speed, which in pre-55 mph days was a common highway velocity, especially on the open roads of the West. The question was posed to the Cadillac engineers: How can one in good conscience market a car that wouldn't stop in time?

The Eldorado was equipped with hydraulic drum brakes not unlike those commonly used on American automobiles since the mid-1920s. The drum brake, which began life on horse-drawn wagons, was exquisitely simple: a pair of curved surfaces called "shoes" riding inside a "drum," which was shaped like a square-sided pie tin. The drum was connected to the wheel and rotated with it. When the brake pedal was applied by the driver, the brake cables (then later, hydraulic pressure) caused the shoes to expand outward and rub against the inner lining of the drum. The ensuing friction slowed the rotation of the wheel.

The modern disc brake is even more rudimentary. Picture a brake on a ten speed bicycle. Two small shoes pinch the sides of the wheel rim and stop the bike. This is the identical principle used with disc brakes. A steel disc rotating with the wheel is slowed by the friction created when it is pinched by the braking material. The advantage over the old drums is that disc brakes are lighter (which enhances handling), easier to maintain, less prone to "fading" (losing stopping efficiency under hard braking), have fewer moving parts, and will not grip erratically when wet. By 1967 these more efficient disc brakes, which had originally been perfected for aircraft, had come into common use on European automobiles. In fact the Mercedes-Benz 250S sedan, then being sold in America for about $2000 *less* than the Eldorado, mounted disc brakes on all four wheels.

Rather sheepishly, the Cadillac engineers hauled another Eldorado out of hiding to show the auto journalists. It stopped better, thanks to a set of *optional* disc brakes on the front wheels. This was, they explained, a $100 option for what the engineers rather disdainfully referred to as "performance-minded customers." Presumably only this tiny segment of the market—the ones Detroit privately called "car nuts" or "buffs"—would be interested in driving an automobile that stopped in time. The vast majority of Eldorado buyers were apparently left to deal, as well as they could, with a braking system that *Car and Driver* denounced as "a treacherous, unsafe Achilles' heel."

Later that same day, the cadre of writers watched fleets of big GM sedans scrambling up a steep hill. It was hardly an unusual sight at the proving grounds, but these large cars were leaping and bucking up the incline of rough pavement with their rear tires yowling in protest.

Like the brakes they carried, their suspension systems were essentially unchanged since the 1940s, when GM had introduced independent "knee action" at the front and coil springs on the back of some models. With the exception of some modifications in shock absorbers and other components, the automobiles lurching up the hill were suspended much like their thirty year old predecessors.

In the basic suspension system of American cars, each front wheel was independently sprung to better absorb bumps. But the rear wheels were connected by a rigid steel axle, which meant that a change of attitude of the left wheel was bound to affect the right. At roughly the same time that Detroit was locking itself into this rigid, but inexpensive, suspension system, European cars were steadily switching to a setup in which each wheel was individually sprung and could react to road variations in its own way. Even the Volkswagen, as it was conceived by Dr. Ferdinand Porsche in 1931-32, had a fully independent suspension.

To be sure, Detroit has updated its system somewhat over the years. Chrysler shifted to torsion bar front springing, which was an improvement, and many manufacturers used coils to replace the rear leaf springs, which had evolved from eighteenth century horse-drawn wagons. With the advent of front wheel drive the domestic and foreign-made cars adopted more similar systems. But imported car suspensions, with their firmer shock absorber settings and stiffer springs, are still better over a broad range of conditions, simply because American manufacturers err on the side of softness. This produces an American suspension that gives a plush, silent ride on smooth surfaces but one that bucks and rattles like a donkey on rough roads, and gives the car an unstable feeling when rounding a curve. Conversely, imported suspensions generally produce a rougher ride on smooth streets, but they hold the road better on curves and are more controllable over severe bumps.

At the proving grounds, someone asked a Cadillac engineer if the bad behavior of the cars, with their rear ends hopping across the pavement, meant that General Motors was testing the Cadillac suspension system. Perhaps GM was going to upgrade their suspensions, he suggested, to match European rivals whose cars now featured fully independent suspensions, front and rear. A look of bafflement spread across the Cadillac man's face. He patiently explained that these automobiles were involved in a test of wheel bearings—totally unrelated to the suspensions. The fact that the cars climbing the hill could not keep their back wheels in contact with the pavement seemed of little import to him.

If one were to stand on the bottom of that same hill inside the Milford Proving Grounds, it is likely one would see many General Motors cars of today behaving as badly, almost fifteen years later. Although a majority of the Corporation's new cars have front wheel drive, their rear wheels are still mounted on solid one-piece axles and suspended in much the same way as the 1967 vehicles. Only an engineer could perceive any difference in the suspension of a 1982 Oldsmobile 98 and a 1967 Olds 98.

/////

The only important engineering advances to come out of Detroit since the end of World War II have been large-displacement, short-stroke, overhead valve V-8 engines and three-speed automatic transmissions. Both were, and remain, the standard of the world. Until they were made obsolete by the demand for smaller, less fuel-thirsty alternatives, the big American V-8s as conceived in the 1940s and '50s and perfected in the 1960s were the strongest, most reliable, cost-efficient, smoothest-running, maintenance-free engines in the world.

Coupled to them were the simple but effective GM Turbo Hydra-matic and Chrysler TorqueFlite automatic transmissions. Even such seekers of perfection as Rolls-Royce and Ferrari presently use the GM Turbo 400 automatic. Practically all the manufacturers in the world who build automatics either use American pieces, American technology, American patents or American inspiration to make their own versions.

But since making these acclaimed developments, Detroit has virtually stood still technologically, while the rest of the world has imaginatively forged ahead. How can this be? How can an industry which has led the world for so many years and which exists in the same superlative technological environment that produces unrivaled military hardware, aircraft, computers, electronics, and medical equipment become the new dolts of automotive innovation?

Detroit is now paying for its twenty year hiatus by having to operate almost a full engine development cycle behind the Japanese and the Germans. These two countries have tactically bracketed their products: The Germans produce clearly superior machinery on the high side of the market while the Japanese dominate the low side. While both foreign industries have produced new, lightweight, highly advanced and reliable engines and fuel injection systems, only Ford and Chrysler have developed small displacement four-cylinder engines that could be described as contemporary. (Engine size is measured in terms of "displacement," which is the total volume of the combustion chambers as expressed in cubic inches, liters, or cubic centimeters.) Although the engines are relatively new, neither company's technology is at the leading edge. General Motors has clearly lagged in this area.

Until Ford and Chrysler began building these engines a few years ago, the American industry had no useful homegrown small-engine technology. Those used on the Omni/Horizon were European by birth. While there was no secret to manufacturing powerful small engines like those on the Honda, Volkswagen, Toyota, and BMW, Detroit had contented itself with manufacturing big V-8s for too long to bother with "little" engines.

It was simple for Detroit to produce large engines with only mediocre efficiency but plenty of power and torque as long as gasoline was cheap. But as gas prices rose and smaller displacement, higher output engines were needed in America, adequate funds were not devoted to designing them or creating manufacturing facilities to make them.

When the Clean Air Acts and the OPEC fuel embargo thudded against the industry between 1970 and 1973, Detroit found itself ill-prepared. Small-engine technology, which outsiders had been warning was dangerously inadequate, was then restricted to the shoddily designed Vega engine from General Motors and the rather ordinary Pinto from Ford Motors. Both were too large, too heavy, and too crude to be of any long-term benefit. Ford, GM, Chrysler and American Motors all staggered away from the first OPEC embargo without any light, hi-tech, small power plants with which to deal with the new realities.

Many of the present American automobile engines are sawed-up, radically modified versions of the old V-8s that carried the industry through its glory days. They have been embellished with electronic gadgetry to control fuel mixtures, monitor exhaust content, and adjust idles, but they remain, in basic engineering terms, conceptually closer to the "big-banger V-8s" of yore than to the truly modern power plants from Japan and Europe.

To this day neither Ford nor General Motors has the capability to produce a wide range of top-grade engines of less than 2.5 liter capacity. Chrysler has one excellent engine for the K-car and the Ford four-cylinder used in the Escort is fairly advanced, but GM's effort with the J-car fell far short of the mark. Overall, the industry must still look overseas for the know-how to make the "little" engines it needs.

As a result, Detroit must call excessively on the past for its new cars. The base engine of the new General Motors A-cars, the machine designed to lead the Corporation into the New Era, is the venerable "Iron Duke." It is a much-modified, rather heavy, bulky and only modestly distinguished update of a power plant developed by Chevrolet for its Chevy II small cars in 1962. After being removed from the lineup and relegated to the Brazilian market and various marine applications, it was revived in 1978 under the Pontiac colors when the need became crucial. It has since ungraciously spread throughout the lineup.

Of course, the age of the engine alone should not be the basis for criticism. The Jaguar, one of the most honored marques in the world, is powered by a six cylinder engine that first appeared in 1948. The Ferrari V-12 engine worshipped by enthusiasts dates from the same era. The air-cooled Porsche 911 engine which has attained icon-like status, can be traced back to the creation of the Volkswagen in the early 1930s.

"You can't just go on reinventing the wheel," says a young engineer with TRW, a large Cleveland based company that supplies mechanical components to the industry. "Sure some of our engines have been around awhile, but you can't start out with a clean sheet of paper every time a new design is needed. Tooling is incredibly expensive and you've got the bean counters looking over your shoulder every second, trying to eliminate every last minuscule bushing, washer and extra hunk of metal imaginable. The industry is run by financial men and believe me, the Wharton School of Business teaches them how to make money, not automobiles.

"So the pressure is on to use the same tooling over and over—like the Iron Duke—to avoid the costs of new design and development. The industry's engineers have learned to make do with what they've got and to keep everything simple, not only to hold down the costs, but to make the engine reliable when they know that the basic American car consumer doesn't know how to maintain his car and wouldn't if he did. Couple that with the fact that most auto mechanics are poorly trained and you can understand the problem a little better."

American engines will probably tolerate more abuse than any others. They will run better in heat and cold, will perform without maintenance, even operate without oil or water for amazing periods of time, without complaint. In that sense they are something of a mechanical masterpiece, which bears out a claim once made by John R. Bond, a trained engineer and the former editor of *Road & Track*: "Any engineer worth his salt can design a water pump for a Rolls-Royce, but it takes a genius to design one for a Chevrolet."

All the tractorlike gutsiness of American drivetrains accepted, it cannot be denied that domestic cars are perceived by most people to be less mechanically advanced than the imports. A poll conducted by the magazine *Design News* revealed that out of 19,210 engineers questioned, 72 percent of them owned domestic cars but 37 percent of that number said they would buy an import the next time. They chastised American cars for their "poverty-stricken appearances, flimsy construction, inadequate transmissions [citing GM's late-1970s practice of putting small automatics into large cars in order to save weight] and idiot lights."

When a *Wall Street Journal*-Gallup poll asked 824 American corporate chief executives to list the poor goods and services they encountered, *half* rated their domestic-made automobiles as the worst items. The summary: "Too many business school geniuses are running things for the bottom line, with no regard for products, no regard for company loyalty, not thinking about two years from now."

The indictment is obvious. The major automakers decided in the middle-1960s that little technological improvement was necessary, either in terms of product or manufacturing techniques. Detroit reacted to extraordinary profit figures with complacency, followed by massive lethargy. "The point is that none of the major producers sought to achieve a competitive advantage through superior manufacturing performance," concludes a National Science Foundation report. "Except perhaps for economies of scale, which are affected by manufacturing decisions, the basis of competition was located outside manufacturing—in marketing, styling, and the dealerships."

"For the most part, Detroit is operating with what engineers call cover-your-ass technology," says an outsider who works for a major industry supplier. "With so many pressures to save money, the best anybody can do is get the job done with a minimum of expense. This was okay when the competition was doing the same thing, but now with the Japanese throwing new technology around like confetti, they're in real trouble."

The result of such a domestic attitude is an Oldsmobile Cutlass Royale four-door with a V-6 engine that is essentially an old cut-down V-8, suspended with the same basic engineering as its ancestors of twenty years ago. But it does have a *power-operated rear vent window*. To save weight and cost, the rear windows are fixed, but Oldsmobile engineers somehow devised a Rube Goldberg linkage of motors, shafts, and gears to make the vent window move with the press of a button. Detroit is still wedded to the past: gadgetry takes precedence over solid engineering advances. Unfortunately gadgets are infinitely cheaper to build than new engines or independent suspensions.

/////

American cars are wonderful anachronisms, somewhat like old heavyweight champions. They are the best in the world in some respects. Their heating and cooling systems are without peer. The engines may be noisy and a bit thirsty, but you can't kill them with a volley of machine gun fire. The paint may bubble and orange-peel, the bodies may rattle and rust, the brakes may fade and the trim may look like it was installed by disturbed children, but you can probably count on the thing running 200,000 miles through sand and snow with no more than an occasional oil change and an affectionate pat on its rumpled hood.

There was a day when this homespun grit was worth billions. But at a time when tiny, hi-tech Japanese automobiles will run circles around the old heavyweights, and last perhaps as long while burning gasoline by the cupful, mere hardiness that defies owner negligence is not enough.

The desire to win has not been sufficiently instilled into the engineers of beleaguered Detroit—a city which is still not aware of the gravity of its problem. "I can't believe how smug those guys are," says a physicist who has done some outside consulting work for Chrysler. "Their engineers sit in their little cubbyholes with their manuals and figure if they didn't think of it, or at least somebody in Detroit didn't think of it, it isn't worth considering."

Much of America's once-substantial lead in technology came from our young people's agility at "tinkering," a mechanical aptitude displayed by people like Henry Ford. That talent used to make up for any lack of academic training, but it now now seems to exist in short supply in the American automotive world. A young mechanical genius who worked for Ford—sans degree—on advanced engine research before fleeing to California to join an independent engineering firm, confirms this: "The young engineers at Ford could spout engineering doctrine chapter and verse. They know it all, provided it came out of a book, but they didn't know which end of a socket wrench to use. Half of them had no mechanical aptitude whatsoever. No ability to apply practical engineering. And the old guys? All they talked about was how they did it in World War II."

General Motors has done little original in the area of engine technology since the 1950s. Surely its design and engineering staffs in Warren included more than enough aggressive talent to have implemented a mandate for change. What was needed was leadership, and it was not present, especially after the Corporation lost two of its most daring thinkers. John Z. DeLorean was drummed out of the Corporation after his bloated ego and his hunger for celebrity destroyed his opportunity to encourage modern technology. Shortly after, John Beltz, general manager of Oldsmobile and an engineering progressive, died of cancer.

Pete Estes, a solid engineer before his rise to power, said to a friend as he reflected on his final years on the Fourteenth Floor: "When John DeLorean went off the deep end and John Beltz got sick, General Motors suffered a pair of blows that it still suffers from." It is a sad commentary on auto industry management that in a corporation that employed 850,000 people and grossed $35 billion a year, the loss of only two men should have virtually crippled crucial technological advancement.

Technology is no different than any other aspect of the car business. It is not software or hardware; capital investment or flowcharts; good sales promotion or catchy jingles. It is keyed to the vision of people employed to use it. As a GM engineer at the Milford Proving Grounds recently confessed: "There is absolutely nothing wrong with the American industry that a few engineers with some balls and some real feelings about automobiles couldn't fix with a clean sheet of paper and a management with enough guts to back them up."

There are indications that change may yet come. The latest generation of cars from Detroit have evidenced increased levels of quality. In a few cases they even demonstrated engineering courage and vitality: The latest Corvette sports car is a technological tour de force. In terms of suspension, aerodynamics, and body design, it is the first advanced automobile to be produced by Detroit since the late 1950s. The small Chevrolet design team which created it is made up of aggressive young engineers who crave competition. "This car is a statement," asserts Freerk Schaafsma, the Dutch-born Chevrolet engineer who was deeply involved in the chassis and suspension design of the new car. From its forged-aluminum suspension members to its Fiberglas bodywork, the Corvette represents a strong step forward. While it is only a limited production vehicle, it marks a milestone at General Motors.

A Corvette built in quantities of 25,000 is a far cry from a J-car or an Escort that must compete in the six-figure leagues with Toyota and Datsun, but it is a new beginning. Detroit is endowed with the engineering talent to create superior automobiles. The challenge lies with management to reform its outdated financial strictures, which have encouraged short-term profitability at the expense of solid technology.

Alfred P. Sloan's philosophy that GM is in the business of making money, not cars, must be modified to meet the new reality. American cars are facing competition never imagined by Sloan, and Detroit must perceive its business as one of *cars*. And in order to generate profit, those automobiles must be of superior quality. To accomplish that, the twenty-year suspension of American "know-how" must come to an abrupt end.

CHAPTER VII

The Dreaded Millionaire Car Dealer: A Disappearing Species

THE STEREOTYPE IS BRANDED on the American psyche. According to the popular image, an automobile dealer is a flashy dresser with a penchant for houndstooth sports coats, silk cravats tied in a Windsor knot and French cuffs. He probably sports a mustache and spends his days prowling the precincts of his garish, neon-and-chrome dealership in wait for the halt and the gullible who make up the ranks of the car-buying public. Should he deal in used cars, it is likely that he operates from an abandoned gas station or ragged house trailer. Should his fare be new cars, he might be disguised as a respectable member of the community, but the masquerade is clearly superficial.

In this view of automobile dealers, they have all migrated from the thieves market in Tangiers. They seem to possess the trading skills of a Phoenician, the mathematical genius of a child prodigy, the material lusts of a Vanderbilt, the ethics of a Jay Gould, the conscience of John Dillinger and the hypnotic powers of a Grigori Rasputin. To cross their threshold is to become a housefly in the parlor of a black widow.

In reality, the traditional American car dealer is more of an endangered species than a threat to our financial and moral integrity. Once a powerful individual and successful entrepreneur, sometimes correctly assumed to be a millionaire, the dealer has fallen on hard times since the boom years of the 1940s, 1950s, and 1960s. At the beginning of 1947, when Americans were buying cars in a volume unequalled in history, a total of 45,530 dealers were in business to serve, even to gouge, the public in a seller's market that was a capitalist's dream. By the beginning of 1982, that total had slipped to 21,680 domestic franchises, plus another 4,023 imported dealerships. In the intervening thirty-five years, over half the businesses devoted to the sale of Detroit-built automobiles—roughly 25,000 small, locally-owned enterprises—had disappeared.

The American car dealer is no longer wealthy and hardly involved in a growth industry. "My business has reached a point where I view sales of my Chryslers and Plymouths only as a means of buying a used car cheaply," confides a dealer whose father taught him the business. "My dad had terrific pride in his product. He was a Chrysler man. He believed. In the 1950s he'd take his fat markup, which was about $700-800 on a car, give the customer really good service, and make a good living for himself. Today it's either all volume, where you take a hundred bucks a car, or do some careful trading and hope you can make a profit on your used cars. And to the guys in the Corporation? You're just a number in their book."

The American car dealer is not the freebooter legend has made him out to be. He is a prototypical American small businessman no more honest or dishonest than the individuals who run appliance stores, or restaurants, or who practice podiatry or orthodontics. But the car dealer is more vulnerable, simply because he deals in a very expensive product, one that is important to the American public.

"We're on the firing line," says a large southern dealer who sells both domestic and imported cars. "The average guy thinks we're part of the company that makes the automobiles. He can't understand that we're independent contractors, so when something goes wrong with a product we have sold but had no involvement in making, he raises hell with us. We form a buffer for the manufacturer and there are lots of times when I'd like to say to a dissatisfied customer, 'Sir, we didn't build this thing, we just have to sell it.'"

Automobile dealers are neither fish nor fowl in the automotive world. They are, and are not, an integral part of the company system. They operate as franchised representatives of a manufacturer, but, like the public, they *buy* cars outright. Then they attempt to resell them at a profit. Once the cars are unloaded in a dealer's lot, the manufacturer is essentially no longer involved, other than to conform to whatever warranty conditions have been placed on the product and to supply spare parts, which the dealer generally marks up 40 percent for resale.

"They operate with total arrogance in Detroit, like a monarchy," says Ed Mullane, a successful Bergenfield, New Jersey Ford dealer who has been a vocal critic of the system and a nettlesome agitator for unified action in his capacity as president of the maverick Ford Dealers Alliance. "There is no bargaining power for the dealer. The sales agreement between a manufacturer like Ford and an individual dealer is a unilateral document." Mullane argues that the dealer can be overwhelmed with badly built, unsalable automobiles and be left without recourse. Once the franchise agreement is signed, Mullane stresses, the dealer must accept the cars the manufacturer sends him, with no arguments. The result is that dealers have no choice but to try to sell the cars they receive for whatever profit possible, regardless of their quality.

Mullane wants to fight back. He advocates powerful dealer groups who would "lock out" products that were unacceptable: that is, to refuse to accept them for purchase and resale to the public. "But most dealers are sheep," he argues. "They'd rather be big frogs in a small pond rather than not having any pond at all, so they go along with what the manufacturers tell them. They're hard to organize. They won't fight back. They don't know enough to save their own asses."

While the public perceives the dealer to be in a collusive partnership with the manufacturer, he is actually part of an independent system that can be traced back to the origins of the automobile business. It was Henry Ford's success with the Model T that set the basic pattern for today's dealer franchising system. At the peak of Ford's power, following the end of World War I, he had over 17,000 individual dealers, one in virtually every village and hamlet in the nation. He did not hesitate to lash them for every cent of profit. Not an advocate of consumer credit, Ford demanded cash for his cars from his dealers. He would not consider any installment buying plans for the public, even after General Motors created the General Motors Acceptance Corporation (GMAC) in 1919 and began financing purchases for 25 percent down and 12 monthly payments.

In 1920, when Ford faced repayment of a $75 million dollar bank loan and Wall Street was savoring the thought that Henry would have to make a public stock sale to raise the funds, he stunned the industry by closing his factories for six weeks and shipping 125,000 Model T's to his dealer body. The deal was simple: buy them all for cash or lose the franchise. Most dealers, like the great man himself, were convinced that the Model T was a God-given key to prosperity and the American way. They bought the glut of cars. Ford's dumping tactic worked, setting a precedent for the adversarial relationship that exists today between auto manufacturers and their dealer body.

Ford finally relented in his stone-headed insistence on cash. Following GM and Chrysler's lead, the Ford Motor Credit Corporation soon became one of the largest public lending institutions in America. By 1925 three out of every four American automobiles were being bought on installment terms.

By then the dealer system had become institutionalized. Each manufacturer had a collection of dealers to whom he sold cars, generally no more than three models in a half-dozen paint schemes and trim configurations. The dealer in turn marked them up about 25 percent and sold them to the public. It was not until the passage of the Automotive Information Disclosure Act in 1958 that the so-called Monroney sticker (named for the law's Congressional sponsor) made a list price mandatory. Before that, the dealer could charge whatever the market would bear. Dealers had sometimes marked up hot sellers almost 50 percent over what had they had paid for them.

Installment purchases had become so ingrained in the system by the late 1930s that the Justice Department intervened. Prior to that the purchaser of a new GM car was required to finance it through GMAC. The same held true of Ford and Chrysler customers, who had to use the authorized corporate credit terms or pay cash.

Arguing that this was blatant restraint of trade, the government brought suit. Ford and Chrysler capitulated but General Motors, led by the arch-conservative Alfred Sloan, Jr., refused to yield. A fierce opponent of the Roosevelt New Deal, Sloan was outraged that the government would presume to interfere in the activities of his megacorporation. He chose to go to trial in Federal Court in South Bend, Indiana in 1938. In 1941, after lengthy arguments GM was found guilty of restraint of trade and the monopolistic power of GMAC was broken. This by no means meant the end of the giant financial arm of General Motors. By the 1950s GMAC was producing an annual profit of over 18 percent and to this day, it remains a major source of revenue for the Corporation.

A shift in the method of selling automobiles came in the 1960s. Things had remained essentially unchanged since the ascendancy of General Motors in the mid-1920s, but by the early years of the turbulent 1960s two major variables had been added to the sales equation: compact cars and the influx of numbers-oriented executives, the "bean counters" who would come to dominate industry thinking on all levels.

These men, including Chrysler's accountant chief executive Lynn Townsend and Ford's McNamara, were obsessed by the financial structure of the car business and viewed the product mainly as an abstraction out of which profit or loss could be generated. Secondly, the product line was beginning to include smaller cars, which meant lower profits for the domestic dealer body. When the first wave of domestic import fighters reached the showrooms in late 1959, they carried markups in the range of 18-20 percent, rather than the traditional 25 percent. Dealers were inclined to steer customers toward their larger automobiles, where a combination of higher sticker price and higher markups produced higher gross profits. Naturally, they greeted the smaller, less lucrative machines with tepid enthusiasm.

This huge corps of old-line dealers made Detroit's repeated attempts to market European and Japanese automobiles through their domestic network—Opel through Buick, Mitsubishi and Simca through Chrysler, German Fords through Ford, Vauxhall through Pontiac, and even Renault through American Motors—futile. After the styling and engineering departments had "Americanized" the cars many of them were no longer appealing to foreign car buyers. Most important, they were being shipped into the showrooms of thousands of dealers whose minds were committed to big cars and the profits they generated.

It was not only the intrusion of small cars, but the crazed expansion of models within a single line that made the retail car market chaotic. A Lincoln-Mercury dealer was selling five different types of automobiles, four of which directly overlapped models being sold by the Ford dealer down the block. Meanwhile, a Buick and Oldsmobile dealer was merely exchanging grille sheet metal and nameplates and pretending to sell two different automobiles. Alfred Sloan's concept of upgrading car status was being perverted by financial men who cared little about the principle of brand loyalty.

With more to choose from, the public taste grew more fickle. And as automation and computerization became more refined, the manufacturers believed they could instantly accommodate the shifts in the public mood. If intermediate hardtops were suddenly a hot item, a giant effort would be made to supply that market. If big cars were being replaced by "personal intermediates," a quick fix was made at the assembly line. This response to market trends was viewed by Detroit as an advantage for American carmakers. Mercedes-Benz or Toyota, American manufacturers patronizingly pointed out, were much slower in getting new models to market and less flexible in being able to match fluctuations in consumer moods.

In reality, Detroit and its dealers were playing a dangerous game of immediate gratification—and eventual self-destruction. Meanwhile the foreign car makers were establishing long-term marketing objectives. If American big car sales slowed for a ten day period (the standard interval for computing sales), Detroit marketing executives began to urge a shift in production to intermediates or compacts. If those faltered, the instant cry was for more subcompacts, convertibles, four-barrel or two-barrel carburetors or anything else that might pick up the last few sales from a wavering public.

By riding these short-term public fancies, there is no question that the dealers generated more profit and the car makers achieved greater sales volumes, at least temporarily. But both parties eventually suffered grievous damage. Longtime brand loyalties were being destroyed by constantly shifting product lines and overlapping products.

Says a big urban Buick dealer: "If you want to know the truth, car dealers are chameleons. They change color by the hour, depending on the moods of their public. The salesmen are constantly pressuring for different product mixes, based on the whims of their floor traffic. This information gets passed on to the sales manager, then to the dealership owner and on to the company's zone and district managers. Pretty soon the guys in Detroit are trying to adjust production to meet the so-called demand. In a lot of cases by the time they make the shift the mood has changed on the street, and what was hot last month is a dog this month."

"The goals of a car dealer and a manufacturer are basically opposed," states Robert J. Sinclair, the president of Saab-Scania of America and one of the most respected automotive executives. "Dealers by nature have to take a short-term view of the business. They want to multiply their capital within their own careers and hopefully cash out at a relatively young age and buy that yacht or castle in Spain they've always dreamed about. On the other hand, a manufacturer has to look at things over a longer span of time, making sure that product developments, years down the road, are on track and that the shareholders get a reasonable return on investment."

Because they operate much smaller companies, the management of firms like Saab, BMW, Porsche, Jaguar, Honda, Subaru, and Mazda, have to approach the development of a new automobile with great caution. Capital restraints prevent them from haphazard flings in the market, whereas in its glory days General Motors could shrug off a disaster like the Corvair and Ford could bounce back after an Edsel debacle. But a miscue by a smaller car builder can mean oblivion, as it nearly did for Mazda when it overcommitted to the Wankel rotary engine in the mid-1970s, or for Porsche with its somewhat overengineered 928 coupe.

Most imported car dealers built their selling tactics around a relatively constant product lineup. They understood that if their company did not have a hot, sporty car to sell, it was improbable that one would be pieced together out of existing bits and pieces, as was recently done with the Ford and Lincoln Mercury EXPs and LN-7s, which were created out of Escort parts to exploit a short-term trend. "You Americans are too impatient," said an old Italian automobile executive years ago. "The Europeans are more inclined to take a longer look at the future. To shift constantly is never to grow roots."

The constant urge to pump up sales over the short haul is an overriding passion for all American manufacturers, whose executives are rewarded according to the bonus system based on annual profits rather than on decade-long growth patterns. The result is that the entire car-selling system has become one ruled by cynical opportunism.

/////

The ultimate perversion of this system came with the infamous "sales bank" instituted by Chrysler Corporation during the 1960s and 1970s. Created by president Lynn Townsend and carried on by his protege and successor, John J. Riccardo, the sales bank was an accounting fan-dance designed to produce annual high-volume sales figures borrowed from the future. Both Townsend and Riccardo were accountants, with backgrounds in the major firm of Touche, Ross, Bailey and Smart. They came to the automobile industry convinced that proper business methods were far more important than hard knowledge about cars.

Their "sales bank" was quite simply a euphemism for overproduction, often at the expense of the dealer. It was a general practice in the business to produce cars on the basis of dealer orders and to keep the assembly lines running in general harmony with consumer demand. Not so with Chrysler, where automobiles poured out of the Highland Park and Hamtramck plants like homeless waifs. Often with no specific dealer orders to justify their existence, they were carted off to marshaling yards, where they would sometimes sit for three or four months while harried district and zone sales managers tried to dragoon dealers into purchasing them.

During the spring and early summer of each model year all Chrysler Corporation products—Dodges, Plymouths, and Chryslers alike—would be overproduced and stored for later sales. It was not uncommon for giant parking areas all over Detroit, including the immense Michigan State Fairgrounds on Woodward Avenue, to become filled with Chrysler-made cars. By the time July and August arrived, the sales and accounting staffs would be working under intolerable pressure. They were being pushed by their superiors to unload the surplus automobiles in any legal way possible, including fire sales to leasing agencies and rental car fleets, through registration transfers to Corporate Zone offices, through sales contests and giveaways and most important, through head-knocking assaults on their dealers.

"It was crazy," recalls a prominent Chrysler-Plymouth dealer whose family has held the franchise since the 1930s. "The whole system was built on fear, coercion, and pressure. The phone would start ringing and wouldn't stop. I'd get calls from the zone guys in the middle of the night trying to get me to buy more cars. They had so many contests, rebates and bonuses that nobody could keep track of them, and if they didn't work, the zone guys would plain threaten you. They had terrific leverage. Without their cooperation, specially ordered cars might get lost, warranty claims wouldn't be processed, parts inventories might slip, and truckloads of weird colors and body styles might show up on your lot. The dealers hated the system because they knew the sales bank cars were slapped together. Most of them had sat out in the sun and rain for months. Added to that was the fact that they'd been built so fast that the quality was terrible and the mix in body styles and options sometimes created totally useless cars.

"We fought and complained but in the end they had us. If we wanted to stay in business we had to take the cars. It made Chrysler look good at the end of the year, but it put a lot of dealers out of business, or weakened them so badly they never really recovered. Worst of all, it gave the company a reputation for building junk that we're still fighting."

The sales bank is long gone, but the essential elements of the system remain in place throughout the industry. "It's a little bit different now because the major manufacturers—domestic and imported alike—let the dealers work as their sales bank," says a small town GM dealer. "They use rebates, bonus programs, and flashy contests to get you to buy more cars than you really need. Therefore, you end up storing their excess inventory and paying the interest on the floor plan instead of them."

"It gets a little nasty sometimes," says a big city Buick dealer. "The zone manager is in here two or three times a year pushing some major sales contests, dealer promotion campaigns and rebate deals. ["Rebates" to the dealers or to the public permit the companies to sell their cars at reduced prices without actually cutting the list price. In this way a price increase is not necessary if demand increases.] A lot of the stuff is hokey. If I buy a hundred extra Skyhawks, I might be eligible to win a trip to Bermuda for me and my wife. Hell, if I wanted to go to Bermuda, I'd just buy the tickets and avoid all the hassle of trying to sell a bunch of extra cars I don't need. But do I play? Sure I do, because like the zone guy says, it's *'franchise insurance'*. If I buy a few hundred extra cars that are slow sellers this month, I am more likely to get extra consideration when I try to order more of a really hot item next month. This is a tough business and anybody who thinks a dealer and a manufacturer are working together is crazy."

/////

It was in this dealer climate that the foreign imports began to set up their own American franchises. "There isn't any appreciable difference between the domestics and the imports," says Ford dealer Ed Mullane. "The imports tend to give their dealers more breathing space by separating them geographically and therefore increasing their market potential, but the general philosophy is the same."

"The Japanese were damned clever," remarks a Buick-Toyota dealer. "In the beginning they tried to dual with front-line General Motors dealers in the big markets. This was done to gain instant credibility and it worked. In the beginning they were damned accommodating, but when they got in a strong position, things changed. Now they're as tough as anybody. There's no negotiation on warranty claims anymore and the guys at Toyota and Datsun can be just as effective in strong-arming you to buy a few extra dogs in the lineup as the guys at Buick or Chevrolet."

There has been a major shift in the selling atmosphere of an automobile showroom, one which benefits imported cars. At the base level of the system, in the trenches where the automobile salesmen work on a pure commission basis, the word is out that more money can be made on imports than on domestics. The mathematics are simple: The gross profit margins for a dealer range between about 11 percent of the retail price for cheaper, low-line cars to about 20-22 percent for high-line, upscale models. A mid-range automobile costing about $10-11,000 will generate about 18 percent gross profit for a dealer, which means that he and his salesmen have an $1800 to $2000 margin of flexibility with which to "deal" with a customer.

Consider the example of a successful large southern dealer who has a dual Honda and Ford franchise. Assuming he has a Ford Mustang and a four-door Honda Accord with retail prices of $10,000 each, he has paid the manufacturers about $8200 for each of the cars. Once his interest payments for "floor planning" (holding the car in inventory) plus salesmen's commissions and such other costs as trade-in allowances on used cars have been totaled up, the profits on the two cars differ significantly. "We'll gross about $400-500 on a Mustang, but a four-door Honda will bring us between $1400 and $2000, depending on the options we sell. It's a simple matter of supply and demand. People want Hondas more than they want Mustangs and they are prepared to pay more to get them," the dealer says.

If there is one thing car salesmen can do, they can count. Since the early 1970s, it has been an article of faith in the business that a salesman can make more money per sale in an import dealership than in a domestic one. This has had a snowballing effect. It has produced a situation in which import dealerships can generally choose from among the best available salesmen, selecting younger, more intelligent, more car-oriented men and leaving the sharpies to the domestic franchises. "My salesmen are all college graduates, wear Brooks Brothers suits and Gucci loafers, and make between $45,000 and $75,000 a year," explains a Florida Mercedes-Benz and Porsche Audi dealer. "What am I going to do with one of those silver-tongued hustlers in a polyester suit?"

Secondly, the strong market for imports has led dealers with both a domestic and a foreign franchise to segregate the two because the American brand was ignored by salesmen seeking higher profits. "My salesmen all wanted to sell Hondas instead of Fords," says an Alabama car dealer. "I finally had to build a separate building for the Hondas or else my Ford sales would have collapsed completely."

The Big Three irrationally responded to such shifts in buying habits by increasing the cost of financing a competitor's automobile through their credit organizations. Ford Motor Credit, for example, charges an extra 1½ percent interest to anyone who seeks a loan on a new non-Ford car, and Chrysler Credit and GMAC instituted similar penalties. "It didn't do a damn bit of good," says one dual franchise dealer. "The import buyer just went someplace else to get his loan and the Detroit guys lost all the income from the extra loan business. You might call that cutting off your nose to spite your face."

On the front lines in the war between the automakers and the dealers are the zone and district representatives: junior and middle-grade executives serving "in the field" before being called back to the home office in Detroit, and promoted. They have one job: to move cars. Each of them recalls how a brash engineer named Lee Iacocca grabbed an obscure truck salesman's job in Chester, Pennsylvania and through a series of brilliant sales campaigns used his diamond-bright personality to ride it to the very pinnacle of the business. Iacocca first established his visibility in Dearborn with a clever regional "$56 for '56" Ford sales campaign that encouraged the purchase of a 1956 Ford for $56.00 per month. The legend was born. To this day every junior zone sales representative dreams of being plucked from obscurity and rising to power.

Their actual work life more often entails endless trips around the state cajoling dealers into buying more cars. "Here I am," says a veteran domestic dealer, "sitting with a business that involves well over a million dollars in property, building, staff, new and used car inventories, and spare parts, and every month this thirty-two-year-old guy making thirty grand a year and driving a company car comes into my office and tries to cram more cars down my throat. He is essentially altering the way I do business. That's what he's been trained to do. And if I don't cooperate, I can guarantee you I'm looking for trouble on filling warranty claims and getting the right mix of models that are selling well.

"My only real contact with the manufacturer is with a low-level, low-line executive who will stay in the job for a few years and if his prayers are answered, will be transferred through a series of zone and district assignments until he finally reaches Detroit as the assistant marketing or sales manager. And you know what? The *closest* he will have ever gotten to the real car business is when he was sitting in dealership offices like mine!"

"There are no dealer-based people in the domestic industry," says a highly respected imported car sales executive. "The men who are running the sales and marketing functions in Detroit have no real understanding of how to sell cars. Their careers have all been one-sided, based purely on the function of selling automobiles in the biggest volumes possible, with absolutely no regard for either the dealer or the customer, both of whom he considers to be replaceable."

A model illustration of the system's failure can be seen in the Cadillac dealerships. Since the 1930s the leading American prestige car has been the Cadillac. It has become part of the language ("It's the Cadillac of vacuum cleaners"), and until the 1970s the ownership of a "Caddy" was the symbol of success. It has been replaced by the Mercedes-Benz, a vehicle whose appeal does not lie in glitter and bulk but in technological excellence and a spartan demeanor.

Until recently a Cadillac dealership was a license to print money. Franchises were sought with the fervor usually reserved for entry into the National Football League. But today several dealers have lapsed into bankruptcy and the classified section of *Automotive News* commonly lists Cadillac dealerships for sale each week. Although a majority of them are non-exclusive (only 270 out of a total of 1595 sell Cadillacs alone), the fact remains that the great old icon of American conspicuous consumption is cracking.

In 1981 a total of 224,458 Cadillacs were sold. Nearly half were the obsolete five-year-old DeVille models, a full-size leviathan with a 121.4 inch wheelbase and a 221 inch overall length, which itself was "down-sized" by nine inches from its oversized predessor. The average dealer's gross profit was about $700 per unit on the 144 cars he sold in 1982, which produced gross revenues of about $100,000. Contrast that with Mercedes-Benz, which has slightly more than 400 dealerships. They accounted for 63,059 sales during the same period. With average sales per dealer numbering 154, and gross profits per car nearly *$5000*—or about *seven times* the profit on a typical Cadillac—the average Mercedes-Benz dealer took in some $770,000. That gross came on a sales volume less than 30 percent as large as Cadillac's. The Mercedes-Benz dealership has obviously become the single most desirable franchise in the United States.

This did not happen by accident. "The Mercedes-Benz dealer representatives are the best in the business," says a prominent Florida M-B franchisee. "They are extremely professional and operate with a battery of facts and information. They care about the product and there is never any of the conventional pressure to hustle cars. Sure, they have a hammerlock on the way things are run and they have rigid standards on everything from the size of the mechanics' washroom to the number of sales brochures you keep in stock. The entire system is set up to produce sales and profit for everybody. Nobody is trying to dump cars, or come up with quickie fixes to exploit short-term shifts in the market. Everything is done very cautiously, with an eye to the future. When a new model comes out we know we'll have it for seven or eight years minimum and the primary goal of everybody in the sales organization is to maintain the *credibility* of the product before and after the sale."

If there is anything that has become a rarity in the American dealer network, it is credibility. As the drive for pure volume became the obsession of the domestic manufacturers (in the seven boom years between 1958 and 1965, domestic car sales more than doubled from 4.2 million to 8.7 million), the motivation, much less the ability, to maintain quality or customer satisfaction became secondary.

The 21,000 domestic dealers remaining in America are an enervated group. They are tired and bored with the constant bombardments of Sweepstakes, Sales Carnivals, Sell-a-thons, Dollar Days, Red Tag Sales, Tent Sales, Discount Days, that have brought little more than a load of mechanical headaches and a profit of as meager as $50 per car over the invoice price.

If there is a central force in the movement for reform, it is Ed Mullane, whose Ford Dealers Alliance has openly pressed for change in the setup. In an address to his organization in January 1982, Mullane attacked the American automakers system head on for their mismanagement:

"The Stanford Study prepared for Congress indicates that... machine uptime on our assembly lines is 60 percent. In Japan it's 80 percent. We get five defects a car to their one. That's where I'd go to work. Ford Motor is far from biting the bullet when it comes to trimming down their operations. They haven't even touched layers of middle management.

"I can tell you there is a lot that could be done and I hope it will be done. The ideal solution is to lick the imports with improved technology in material, manufacturing and product. This can only be done by leapfrogging the market by two to three years—and that doesn't appear to be happening. The cold economic facts tell me that instead of being hopeful, this is the worst time in the history of our careers."

The prevailing sentiment in Detroit is that things work best when supply exceeds demand, provided of course that the dealers buy and pay for that excess supply. Mullane wants to correct that. He advocates a much more independent stance for dealers who should operate as a tougher, more cohesive bargaining force. With the kind of strength in numbers he seeks, the dealers could resist the force-feeding of massive inventories. They could pool their resources and merge dealerships where there are too many within a small geographic area.

"By their past actions they [Ford] have forfeited all rights to loyalty, tradition, and respect. Make it a straight business arrangement," Mullane argues, "where Ford levels with us, offers competitive products, allows us economic opportunity without overcrowding and provides technical assistance to keep our service current. All we want is a straightforward business relationship with the Ford Motor Company. In the past, it's been a contrived, controlled relationship. But the days of Big Daddy are over."

Not everyone in the business is as angry as Ed Mullane, but only a few confirmed Pollyannas believe that a big turnaround is in sight. Even Bob Lund, the former general manager of Chevrolet, a tub-thumper who promised the 5430 Chevy dealers an annual sales total of ten million cars that never materialized, is losing faith. "When you look back, it never should have happened the way it did," he says.

CHAPTER VIII

Labor, Quality Control, Management, and Other American Mysteries

AT SOME POINT IN ITS MIDDLE INDUSTRIAL HISTORY, perhaps around 1960, America began the long descent in the quality of its manufactured goods. It was hardly an overnight transformation, but there was a period in which the rush to exploit the quickening demand for consumer goods swept aside pride-of-workmanship in the name of quick profit.

During these get-rich-quick 1960s, this cult of New Greed infected American industry. As sales volume increased, once-sturdy appliances were built with their internal workings fabricated from the cheapest of stampings. Furniture appeared with flimsy fiberboard backings and drawer bottoms. Staples replaced nails, metal screws were substituted for nuts and bolts, cheap die-castings made forgings obsolete and suddenly everything, from the grilles on our automobiles to the clock radios at our bedsides, was made of plastic.

In the egalitarian rush to create a society of plenty, America became junk-maker to the world. The discount store, that miracle of modern merchandising, was one step in that direction. Designed to satisfy consumers otherwise denied new gadgetry at affordable prices, the items it carried had to be radically cheapened but still had to maintain the appearance of luxury. How can one build a well-designed television set to sell for $200 that might otherwise cost twice as much? The obvious answer was to cut back on quality of the electronic innards, manufacture a cabinet of pressed wood or plastic and gear up the assembly lines.

This discount mentality seized the automobile industry at roughly the same time that it was proliferating throughout the shopping centers of America. Volume became the primary goal. The American automobile industry was capable of producing nearly ten million cars a year in the middle 1950s, but euphoric analysts envisioned sales approaching fifteen million in the immediate future. Three and four-car families were universally predicted; an incredible auto-borne prosperity was just around the corner.

In the rush to meet the demands of the burgeoning marketplace, quality and quality control were left far behind. It was as if every automobile that was manufactured in Detroit had some degenerative disease; as if the molecules of metal began disintegrating the moment the hapless customer rolled his new car out onto the street. To many, it was an agonizing battle of rattles, rust-outs, recalls and screaming matches with service managers that often ended with a trip to the nearest imported car dealership.

The situation reached ludicrous heights in 1978, the last boom year for Detroit (9.3 million car sales). The Big Two and the Little Two (Chrysler and AMC) pumped out automobiles at a furious rate, with negligible regard for quality. At the same time, the companies were making a major effort to meet stringent government emission control and safety regulations and to launch a new generation of down-size automobiles. With the best engineering talent focused on the future, little attention was paid to the briskly-selling machinery that was pouring off the assembly lines. The result? Some of the shabbiest automobiles in the history of the industry.

Such popular cars as the Oldsmobile Cutlass and the Ford Thunderbird were officially recalled no less than nine times during 1977 and 1981 to correct defects in the steering, suspension, fuel and electrical systems. The GM X-cars that were thrown onto the market to meet the imported front-wheel drive threat were recalled no less than *four* times in 1980 alone to repair factory-built brake, suspension, fuel system and transmission flaws. Hardly a day passed without an announcement issuing from Detroit that one or more of its products was being summoned back to the dealerships to make special repairs.

There is considerable evidence that the public's perception of quality is closely related to the car's finish—the look of a well-painted, well-trimmed car that makes it seem strong and substantial even if it is not. Regardless of the subtleties of their construction, most modern American automobiles deserve to be flayed for their dreadful fit and finish, the sloppiness with which the paint, trim, upholstery and bodywork have been applied to the frames. Some stories verge on the absurd, as in the case of the American Motors dealer who reported receiving cars without window glass or the many Corvette dealers who automatically repainted the $18,000 Chevrolet sports car before putting it in the showroom.

Many of the automobiles, especially the Fords, had long had a widespread underground reputation for rusting, while most Chrysler cars appeared to have been painted with a broom and left out to dry in a dusty field. General Motors automobiles created a better first impression, thanks to their flashier styling and better finish. In fact, they had been favored by many body men and mechanics as the best designed and best fabricated of the domestics. But when compared against the top of the imports, they too were deficient.

As more and more soft-fascia urethane nosepieces and rear end treatments were employed, color matching between the metal and plastic surfaces became difficult, which further aggravated a nettlesome problem: American paintwork looked inferior to that on Japanese and European cars. That, coupled with the poor fit of body panels and doors, the wavy chrome trim, and badly stitched interiors, erected a massive psychological barrier in the marketplace.

"Paint was a terrible problem for us," confides a GM engineer. "We had three or four different painting processes within the Corporation, and nothing was standardized. We were using two different kinds of paint, acrylic lacquer and urethane enamel, on the metal and plastic portions of a lot of cars. Moreover, the Environmental Protection Agency was pressuring us to shift to water-based enamels to reduce plant emissions. They and OSHA [Occupational Safety and Health Administration] forced us to stop using chromates in our paints because of the health hazard to workers, which means you've seen the last of those wonderfully vivid red, yellow and green colors we used to have.

"Nobody realizes how difficult it is to paint a car, or how expensive it is to design and build a modern paint shop that will produce first-class results and still be environmentally clean. This is a factor that isn't quite as stringent for the European and Japanese competition. We are slowly converting to a process whereby our cars will be painted in a fashion similar to, say, Mercedes-Benz. It's called a base-coat, clear-coat method, and it involves two wet-on-wet coats of high-solids urethane enamel that are cured, after which two coats of clear enamel are applied and cured. Why didn't we do it before? Because the old ways were good enough. And by the time you get through building a paint shop, which is three stories high and includes monstrous air and water pumping and filter systems, you will probably have spent nearly $40 million! We're catching on, slowly. In a couple of years, you'll see American paint jobs equal to that of anything in the world. And chrome? Forget it. We're following the European example. The new Corvette, for example, has one piece of chrome on the entire car, and that's a door key flap the size of a fifty cent piece."

/////

Over the last fifteen years, the quality of American-built cars has become a national embarrassment. The recall of automobiles mandated by the federal government's National Highway Traffic Safety Administration involved 6.5 million domestically manufactured vehicles in one year alone, 1979. Both American-made and imported cars were recalled in the same proportion, with the exception of Japanese cars. They accounted for only 3.8 percent of the recalls, despite the fact that they represented over 14 percent of all car sales in America that year. (However, safety officials are quick to point out that although Japanese cars may suffer less mechanical defects, they are not as crashworthy as American cars. Ben Kelley of the

Insurance Institute for Highway Safety says: "Japanese cars are more prone to producing injury than small American cars.")

The list of domestic car recalls ordered by the government is reassuring in the sense that these defects are being located. But it is also depressing to contemplate the magnitude of Detroit error. From September 1966 through July 1978 there were a total of 2447 recalls involving 71 million cars, some of which were called back several times. The implicit danger is frightening: 185,000 1978 Ford Fairmonts and Zephyrs were called in to repair a connection that could cause the loss of electrical power; 1,225,000 Chrysler-made Aspens, Volares, and LeBarons were recalled because of a defective component that could cause the loss of front braking; 782,111 Chevrolets, Pontiacs, Oldsmobiles, and Buicks were called back because the "front upper control arm inner bushing retainer nuts" could loosen and fall off, causing the control arm cross shaft to break, resulting in loss of control of the automobile.

Recalls have involved inadequate steering clamps on Pintos and Mustangs; the danger of fire from missing carburetor O-rings on Thunderbirds; defective brake vacuum power boosters in Chevrolets; power steering hose failure in Gremlins and Hornets; flawed rear axle shafts in the 1977 Pontiac LeMans and Grand Prix, as well as several Chevrolet, Buick, and Oldsmobile models; even faulty fuel hoses in 133,419 Cadillacs built from 1975 to 1978.

The cost of these recalls in money and reputation has finally prompted Detroit to become more careful. Ford has tested all the first 5000 engines of its new front-wheel-drive Escort, tearing them apart to study the effect of being driven up to 50,000 miles. "We've never done this before," says Joseph Macura, Ford's engine project manager. "We want these engines to be the very best we ever built."

Chrysler has road-tested not just isolated models, but the first one thousand production units of its K-cars to insure better quality, and General Motors has begun similar upgrading programs. Recalls, however, still plague the industry. In June of 1982, Ford had to recall 140,000 Escorts and Lynxes to replace a defective electrical component in the air conditioner blower motor that could cause a fire. General Motors has recalled 519,000 of their 1982 A, J, and X body lines to replace clamps on the fuel filler and vent pipe hoses. These clamps could break, causing potentially dangerous fuel leakage when the gas tank is being filled or even while driving when the tank is over three-quarters full.

A recent quality problem involves the already much-recalled 1980 X-bodies, the first line of GM cars to feature front wheel drive. The cars had an alleged tendency for the rear wheels to lock when heavy brake pressure was applied, possibly forcing the car into a dangerous spin. In 1981, GM recalled 47,000 early production models of the Chevrolet Citation and other X-body cars, and installed a valve that would allow less of the brake pressure to reach the rear wheels during a stop. General Motors thought it had corrected the problem but an investigation by the National Highway Traffic Safety Administration has led the agency to recommend the recall of 320,000 of the X-cars for the same braking failure.

The result has been a public perception of domestic car quality as inferior to that of foreign makes. This has long been a source of bafflement to American automakers, who have pointed out that domestic power plants are the most trouble-free in the world and that American-made automatic transmissions have unprecedented durability. Many executives, principally Lee Iacocca of Chrysler, have reminded us that because of their products' greater vulnerability to rust, no Japanese manufacturer will offer a five-year/50,000 mile warranty. But the public is insistent; poll after poll indicates that Americans believe Japanese and European cars are better built.

One major villain was the industry decision to cut out weight in order to increase gas mileage. Its plan to meet government-mandated CAFE (Corporate Average Fuel Economy) standards triggered a massive slippage in quality. "You can see it in all the cars after the mid-1970s," relates an expert body repairman. "They saved weight on the infrastructure, where the public couldn't see it. Pop rivets were used where they used to use quarter-inch nuts and bolts. Lightweight braces and gussets, plastic and thin aluminum were used in place of steel, and epoxies were used to hold things together that used to be welded or bolted. The unit bodies are so flimsy that when you use a Port-a-Power [a hydraulic repair tool used to twist bent frames back into place]the steel is so light that it bends in all the wrong places. Frankly the Japanese cars are the worst of all in terms of inner body strength, but they look the best on the outside, and that's why people think they've got better quality. Let them work in my shop for a few days and they'd see that all of 'em, with the exception of a few of the more expensive European models, are junk."

/////

The marginal standards of American cars began to concern consumers in the 1970s who singled out the domestic auto worker and his sloppy workmanship for criticism. Up to that point auto workers had been viewed merely as an overpaid, somewhat strike-prone segment of the labor force. But as soon as the appearance of American automobiles was contrasted with that of German cars, and even less expensive Japanese cars, the auto worker became the lightning rod for national frustrations. He was the lazy, loutish, generally absent sluggard who was thought to be mainly responsible for the haphazard way in which cars were being built in Motor City.

In some cases it was true. Before the great reforms that swept through the industry during the early eighties, low performance by the average autoworker was more the rule than the exception. "We worked half an hour on, half an hour off," recalls a young man who spent two and a half leisurely years with General Motors in one of its assembly plants before becoming a victim of the mass layoffs of 1981-82.

"That way we could make the work last until maybe a couple of hours before our shift ended. If we worked too fast, it was a problem dodging the foremen and supervisors. To be honest, I'm not the most ambitious guy in the world, but I could easily have done the work for myself and the two men next to me in an eight hour shift and still have had an easy day. Based on what I saw, I'd estimate the entire plant could have operated easily with less than two-thirds of the work force it had before the layoffs began."

The best estimates place the basic cost advantage of Japanese small cars at about $1500 under comparable American built models, with some $500 of that traceable to higher American labor costs. The real advantage of Japanese manufacturers lies not only in lower wages but in higher productivity. Recent figures published by the National Science Foundation indicate that 112.5 employee hours are required to manufacture the average Ford vehicle, while those built by Toyo Kogyo (Mazda, of which Ford owns 25 percent), require only 47. Even when allowance is made for the numerous Ford models versus Mazda's comparatively simple product line, the hours required to produce a Mazda only increase to 56, or roughly half that expended on a typical American car.

The Nikko Research Center in Tokyo conducted a survey which revealed that of the 49 Japanese firms which have plants in America, fully two-thirds of them rate productivity lower than in their homeland. Takashi Ishihara, the tough-talking president of Nissan, which makes Datsun cars and trucks, has frankly stated that his firm will be building only small pickups in its new Tennessee factory simply because they are less complicated than automobiles and it is less likely that American laborers will fabricate them badly.

Japanese cars are not only built with roughly *half* the man-hours, but their laborers make roughly half as much money. The UAW wage scale is approximately $19 in wages and benefits compared with $10 to $12 for the Japanese autoworker. But once again management is an important factor in the wage difference. While admitting that his workers make twice as much as their Japanese counterparts, UAW President Douglas A. Fraser retorts that the typical American auto executive outearns his Japanese counterpart by almost 700 percent.

Much of the Japanese myth involves their use of robotics and the subsequent elimination of the human factor. It is true that the Japanese auto industry employs about 10,000 sophisticated robots to America's 4,300 (with another 10,000 on line by 1990), but that is not at the core of the problem. Most experts agree that the physical capabilities of Japanese auto factories are no better, overall, than ours. The difference is in the human factor. A Harvard professor who studied the Japanese auto industry found that one Toyota assembly plant was fifteen years old, substantially older than many American facilities. Yet the factory was producing at *twice* the capacity with *half* the employees. If the Japanese do have an advantage in manufacturing equipment, it is in their superior body-stamping presses—which are made in the United States.

With typical American fervor, the domestic auto industry decided in the late 1970s that quality was a major problem. It moved toward a solution with manic energy. Much of the early effort was window dressing: television ads trumpeting Ford's contention that "Quality is Job One" or General Motors' "Quality of Work Life" program which was begun on a limited basis, accompanied with some skepticism on the part of management. But ad campaigns and luncheon speeches by Detroit executives could not obscure the problem this time. As more was revealed about the efficient, creative way in which Japan was producing automobiles, the blame for shabby American workmanship could no longer be laid solely on the blue-collar work force. In fact, an examination of the manufacturing techniques used in Germany and Japan disclosed an entirely different culprit: the uncaring, generally bloated management in the upper levels of the American automakers.

James W. McLernon, a former Chevrolet executive, and until recently the president of Volkswagen of America, commented on VW's recently opened assembly plant in New Stanton, Pennsylvania, where the products rolling off the line were equal, if not superior, in fabrication to those being made in Wolfsburg, West Germany. He made it very clear where the responsibility lay. "Quality is a management decision," McLernon declared, silencing the aging Detroit bleat that the rattles and the rust in their automobiles were solely the fault of the UAW and its members.

Ironically it was a small group of Americans who identified this as a problem. Indeed, Americans wrote the book for the Japanese on quality control in the first place. Men like W. Edward Deming and Dr. Joseph M. Jurand, now both in their late seventies, are prophets who have long preached the benefits of statistical quality control. While Deming was being idolized in Japan, where the Deming Award for quality is considered the nation's most coveted industrial honor, he was largely ignored in his homeland. Finally both he and Jurand, as well as other experts in statistical quality control, are being belatedly accorded recognition in America.

Deming is outspoken about the failure of quality control in Detroit, and where the fault lies. "Populating management with financially oriented people has ruined the country," he stated recently. "Management jobs rob the hourly worker of his right to be proud of his work. Quality is of no great concern to management, since no manager lost a job because he didn't act on quality."

What little quality control Detroit historically employed involved assembly-line inspectors randomly sampling products as they moved between work stations. In the noisy, steaming workplaces shoddy workmanship was not only ignored, it was subtly encouraged by management exhortations to produce more at all costs. The problem was exacerbated by the performance of outside vendors, more than 5000 private contractors who build everything from ashtrays to tires for the auto industry. They were often guilty of atrocious workmanship, in some cases encouraged by the stingy price-bargaining of the auto companies which left no margin for upgrading quality.

Today, Detroit—in the wake of its disaster—is beginning its first sincere effort to improve quality. But it will be futile if outside suppliers do not keep pace. "The first real effort we made to improve our quality came when we started the Escort line," recounts a Ford executive. "I can remember the first shipment of interior door panels we got from a vendor for our two-seat EXP, which was made on the Escort platform. There were 7500 panels in the shipment. We rejected nearly 5000 of them. The vendor was in a state of shock. He'd been using the same quality standards for years, but suddenly they didn't apply anymore. Frankly we'd been making do with second-rate work for years."

The frantic search for quality goes on. Some observers note that it took the Japanese nearly twenty years to perfect their statistical methodology of quality control and to train a work force to operate within that system. The American industry has no such luxury of time; if it is to remain competitive, a massive shift in policy must be accomplished within five years.

Serious pilot projects such as the new GM Corvette are already underway which offer interesting contrasts with the past. The Corvette is considered to be an "image car," a vehicle that will represent the Corporation's best efforts in engineering and performance. In recent years the automobile had become a travesty.

Between 1968 and 1982 the Corvette was produced in a crowded, inefficient plant in St. Louis, Missouri. In certain years the assembly line, which was designed to produce about 30,000 units a year, pumped out over 40,000 sports cars that demonstrated shamefully poor workmanship.

In 1982 Chevrolet opened a new factory in Bowling Green, Kentucky to build its all new version of the Corvette. Not only does the car now contain few compromises in technical excellence, but the new factory is a model of efficiency. "For the first time we've painted the floors of an assembly plant white," says a Chevrolet spokesman. "That will give you an idea of how we feel about creating a clean, constructive working environment." Moreover, the men and women who build Corvettes will wear coveralls—in the Japanese manner—with the car's emblem attached.

Poor quality is expensive. Some estimate that there is a retail penalty of 25 percent on each automobile for poor quality, extra thousands of dollars in claims, parts replacement, depreciation, and scrappage. The financial incentive to make this obvious connection has finally penetrated the stubborn Detroit Mind. Yet the matter of the man on the line—the much-maligned, much-misunderstood blue collar foot soldier—has yet to be resolved. After seventy years of warfare between the white and blue forces, the dispute cannot be reconciled with slogans and hollow pledges of good faith, or even by well-intentioned pilot projects.

/////

The American automobile worker has the reputation of being a malingerer whose work on Mondays and Fridays is so shoddy that wary consumers refuse to purchase automobiles made on those days. It was not always so. The earliest days of automaking are filled with stories of craftsmen of German, English, and Scandinavian background hammering, filing, and forging automobiles out of steel and wood with pride.

It was Henry Ford's twin revolutions of the assembly line and the five dollar a day wage in 1913-14 that changed things, for the better and for the worse. In moves some historians believe have had a greater impact on the twentieth century than Marxism, this quirky but intuitive farm boy from Dearborn altered the way automobiles were made and the way the western working man lived. Acting on the advice of an engineer, Clarence W. Avery, Ford worked out the primitive elements of assembly line manufacture by reversing the disassembly techniques used in the Chicago and Cincinnati meat-packing business. By doing this, he was able to reduce the time required to assemble one of his new Model T's from 12.5 hours to 5 hours, and thereby radically reduce its selling price.

But the strange new world of repetitive assembly-line work at his Highland Park factory triggered high worker turnover and discontent. This prompted Ford to adopt the suggestion of another associate, James Couzens, a Detroiter who ten years earlier had become fascinated with Ford's special vision and talents. Couzens had borrowed $2500 to invest in the Ford Motor Company and rose to become the founder's second-in-command and a prince of finance. He proposed a stunning idea: to double the going wage in the industry from $2.50 to $5.00 per day. This was not only the highest wage ever paid unskilled labor, but it was more than the average British workman earned in a week.

Despite the outraged disapproval of his fellow industrialists, Ford persisted and his wage policy produced an instant upturn in worker loyalty and productivity. Jobs at Ford became so desirable that rumors of hirings attracted crowds that had to be dispersed with fire hoses. Eventually, Ford's wage policy forced other manufacturers to slowly upgrade their wage scales. Relatively high wages, plus the powerful Detroit Manufacturers' Union, managed to keep labor union organizers outside the borders of the Motor City for nearly twenty more years.

Henry Ford did not invent the automobile. In 1886, when Ford was still a wandering field engineer for the Westinghouse Company, a pair of Germans, Gottlieb Daimler and Karl Benz, fielded the first practical motorized vehicles. But it was surely Ford who put "America on wheels." By 1920—only thirty-four years after Daimler and Benz wobbled their vehicles onto the streets of Mannheim and Cannstatt—ten million automobiles were registered in America alone. Ford, who had just cut his price for a Model T from $575 to

$440, could take the credit for half of them.

The five dollars a day that Ford was paying workers was creating a revolution but it did not come without strings attached. The high wage was paid only if a worker was considered "worthy" after six months' employment. Moreover, his newly established Sociological Department, run by a blue-lipped Episcopal clergyman, probed into the employees' lives to insure their commitment to the high moral standards espoused, if not always observed, by their leader. (Ford was a womanizer of some renown and died with a Detroiter loudly claiming, with considerable conviction, to be his illegitimate son.)

Ford's five-dollar day was, in retrospect, the only creative act of labor relations ever recorded in Detroit's history. From that moment to this, the industry has been scarred by a succession of unrelenting adversarial contests between labor and management, with the periods between massive strikes punctuated by constant bickering, mutual recriminations and sagging productivity.

The national labor revolts of the 1930s produced fierce fights in Detroit and its environs. The first great battle occurred in Flint, Michigan, in 1937, and involved the fledgling United Auto Workers, a part of the rebel Congress of Industrial Organizations (CIO) which had seceded from the more conservative American Federation of Labor. The AFL itself had made repeated but timorous attempts to unionize the auto industry, but without success.

With fewer than one hundred and fifty original members, including the famed Reuther brothers, Roy, Victor, and the titan of the Union, Walter, the tiny UAW managed to light a fire in Flint, the company town in which 50,000 of its 160,000 inhabitants then worked in General Motors plants.

General Motors was run by those who John L. Lewis, the flame-throated leader of the United Mine Workers called "economic royalists...who have their fangs in labor." He was referring to the Du Pont family, which controlled a large block of GM stock and specifically to GM's chairman, the ironbound capitalist, Alfred P. Sloan, Jr. It was Sloan who let Flint policemen and Michigan state troopers club down workers who attempted to strike in 1930 at Fisher Body's Plant Number One. Along with Walter Chrysler, Henry Ford and other industry leaders, Sloan chose to ignore the

National Labor Relations Act, which guaranteed collective bargaining. As late as 1936 Sloan hired fourteen private detective agencies to infiltrate the work force and block any attempts to unionize.

Until 1936 the major auto companies held the tiny UAW at bay, but sympathy for the union within the work force was growing. Finally, its leaders decided on a strategy to discredit the dogma of the "open shop" that had been so religiously defended by Sloan and General Motors. It was the "sit-down strike," a tactic used with success by Italian and Greek factory workers, as well as by Welsh and Spanish miners. The tactic was also employed in 1936 in France, where widespread sit-downs amounted almost to a general strike, and at several American plants that made accessories for the auto industry. Never had it been tried against a business titan like General Motors.

On December 30, 1936, after the Corporation had rejected the union's request to bargain over pay scales, seniority rights, job security, the despised speed-ups of the assembly line and the recognition of the UAW itself, the workers of the two main Fisher Body plants in Flint sat down at their places and refused to leave the factories. This audacious act triggered strikes throughout the GM empire and brought 136,000 men streaming onto the picket lines.

Although the workers in the two Fisher factories in Flint numbered only 1400, their role was pivotal. If a strike could succeed in the heart of the GM empire, the existence of the UAW would be assured. While the corporate public relations machine ground out copy that "the GM family" was threatened by a minority of workers involved in a "Red plot," and Chairman Sloan grumped about "labor dictators," the strike brought General Motors to its knees after forty-four days.

Finally, after intense bargaining that centered on executive vice president William Knudsen and union representative John L. Lewis (not a UAW member, but the finest orator on labor's side), General Motors agreed to let the strikers return to their jobs and to recognize the union as its workers' sole bargaining agent.

Three months later, Chrysler collapsed after a short but similarly effective sit-down. The major independents—Hudson, Packard, Studebaker, Willys-Overland—quickly eased into line. Within months the UAW's membership had grown to nearly 400,000 and the only remaining target was Ford. Furious that his largesse of 1914 was not still being appreciated, old Henry became nasty. Employing his personal thug, Harry Bennett, whose notorious internal security force was whimsically called the "Service Department," Ford's bat-wielding heavies clobbered the union members in the famous Miller Road "Battle of the Overpass" on May 26, 1937 outside the River Rouge factory complex.

It took nearly four more years and the hard-nosed leadership of union president Walter Reuther to smash through Bennett's wall of toughs. It also took the full power of the federal courts to open the way for the UAW. The strong internal efforts of Henry Ford's progressive-minded son, Edsel, also helped to make the breach. Finally, after a decade of conflict and bloodshed, Ford and the rest of the automobile industry were organized. The tense pattern of labor-management relations of the next forty years was established.

While the brass knuckles and swinging fists have long since been forgotten, until very recently the relationship remained as contentious as when the Reuthers were trading insults with Sloan and Ford. It has been a history of wild pendulum swings of power, of prejudicial acts on both sides, and of selfish, essentially self-destructive policies.

By 1978 the union had reached the zenith of its power with 760,000 members. But within its power was an internal weakness: it had too long pursued a policy of demanding more pay for less work, a stance which would contribute to the destruction of the industry. Over the years Detroit lived in an environment of constant bargaining based on respective claims of poverty by both labor and management, a battle that evolved out of a refusal by either side to accept any alteration in the lines drawn in the crucible years of 1937-41.

Operating under the watchful eye of the courts and the National Labor Relations Board, a recalcitrant management, still smarting from its defeat, hammered out a series of agreements simply described in labor-management circles as wage-effort bargains. These provided for highly regulated, heavily structured work environments, with direct, linear relationships between hours worked and compensation, plus consideration for such variables as seniority and working conditions. They were rigid packages in which the only variations came through formalized grievance procedures and new contract negotiations—all of which were carried on in an atmosphere of mutual suspicion and mistrust.

Many of the management old-timers saw the union men as nothing more than a gang of thinly-disguised Communists and fellow-travelers seeking to undermine the foundations of the free enterprise system. The UAW members, on the other hand, wondered if every negotiation session was about to be broken up by Harry Bennett's strike breakers or GM's private detectives and Michigan state police lackeys.

World War II had barely ended when the Union called a 119 day strike that was settled only by a shaky one-year truce. That ended in 1947, with another strike being avoided only by hours. Finally a mutual urge to exploit the booming car market of the postwar years brought peace in 1948. Recognizing that General Motors could not fully meet the residual demand for automobiles created by five years of war without a stable labor situation, management and the UAW forged the first multi-year union contract. It permitted the Corporation to engage in long-range product planning while giving the worker job security and an opportunity to share in the great automotive prosperity that lay ahead.

The most significant and far-reaching component of that 1948 agreement was the wage escalation clause, a formula by which workers' wages were linked to current price levels. This would come to be known as COLA, or the Cost of Living Allowance, and through simple inflationary pressures it has enabled UAW wage scales to expand by about 130 percent since the contract was signed.

The system creaked along until the middle-1960s, when a new breed of auto worker began to replace the aging vets. Many of the older breed were first-generation immigrants and displaced southerners who could remember the pitched battles and the empty plates of the 1930s. These men had settled nicely into the structured system created by the bronze-cast agreements of the 1940s and 1950s, but their sons and successors—many of them blacks and disillusioned youngsters—took a more cynical view. The result was a steadily declining level of worker loyalty and involvement with the manufacturing process. The schizoid mood of the 1960s, with the Vietnam War and the counterculture tugging at their consciences, turned the younger UAW workers into an indifferent, often absent, totally uninvolved work force. Drugs, racial struggles, abominable workmanship, tardiness, absenteeism and work stoppages began to reach epidemic proportions.

By the late 1960s the industry began to take notice of the changing attitudes of its work force. But Detroit was hobbled by the hidebound notion that its employees were little more than a group of unruly children who could be mollified by more liberal work rules, ever-escalating fringe benefits, more paid holidays, thirty-year retirement packages, and more and more pay per hour. Despite these inducements, productivity had not increased. If anything, it declined.

Management, roaring through the prosperity of the 1960s and early 1970s that many expected to be perpetual, tended to view this fattened compensation as a form of blackmail. Not only did it keep the work force relatively docile, but it kept the union from pressing its new demands for a four-day workweek, increased holidays, and profitsharing. The result was doubly negative: it radically increased the cost of doing business while stimulating mass disloyalty and cynicism in the labor force.

/////

All that is now changing. The rising tide of Japanese imports, a sagging economy, the oil crisis and the ensuing near-collapse of Chrysler and fiscal convulsions of Ford and even General Motors, have brought new religion to the industry and its labor unions. UAW President Douglas Fraser, the crusty Scotsman who succeeded Leonard Woodcock as UAW President, scanned his membership rolls and found that by 1982 he had lost about 237,000 workers to unemployment in less than four years.

By 1979 it was clear that the Chrysler Corporation was not faking when it cried poverty as its UAW contract came up for renewal. The perpetual number three in the business was on the verge of becoming number zero. It placed Fraser in the unique position to call thumbs up or down, Nero-like, on the dying company. Despite first aid from the nation's lending institutions and the federal government and a virtuoso performance by its president, Lee Iacocca, Chrysler's survival was still dependent on a deal with the UAW. Unless Fraser could convince his 84,000 hourly workers to give up a healthy pay raise and the hallowed cost-of-living allowance—which would, along with other concessions, amount to savings totaling over one billion dollars during 1979-80—bankruptcy was assured. To do this, Fraser had to break a union rule: collective bargaining agreements with the car manufacturers had to be thematically identical. No company was to receive terms not available to the other. In this way union unanimity was assured.

Fraser was successful in persuading his fellow members. Unless concessions were made specifically for Chrysler, 100,000 more union men (including employees of Chrysler suppliers) would be on the street. The Chrysler UAW membership consented, and the first break in the forty years of street fighting that had characterized labor relations in the automobile industry had arrived.

More concessions followed for Ford and General Motors, although the cutbacks at GM were passed by a skintight margin. The union's easing of annual wage increases, the elimination of nine paid holidays, and the deferral of three cost-of-living increases was estimated to have saved General Motors over $2.5 billion through September 1984. The Corporation's powers of persuasion were somewhat compromised when, during the pontifications about the need for mutual sacrifices, Chairman Roger B. Smith made that now famous announcement that he was deducting *$135 a week* from his estimated $35,000 a month compensation. When the screams of anger from the union and the guffaws from the business press subsided, Douglas Fraser commented, "It would have been better for him to do absolutely nothing."

The ink was barely dry on the new General Motors pact when its board of directors infuriated the union and the public by announcing that its top executives, including Mr. Smith, would benefit from an expanded bonus plan, plus additional stock options and incentives. "I've never seen a situation where the workers felt more upset,"

Fraser told the press. The blue-collar men and women, who had just backed down in the face of threatened plant closings, were livid at what they believed had been a barefaced betrayal.

Their anger was directed at Chairman Smith. During the early negotiations, Smith had announced to the public that any savings wrung out of the union would be passed along in the form of lower car prices. This instantly removed from the market thousands of potential GM customers, who decided to wait until the deal was struck.

And so it went. While the advertising agencies cranked out ads proclaiming improved labor relations and conversions to such programs as GM's "Quality of Work Life," it was essentially business as usual. As Chrysler seemed to be returning to profitability, Fraser's seat on the Chrysler Board of Directors appeared to some hard-line union members to be causing him to bank his old antimanagement fires. But this was not the case. As he neared retirement age, Fraser's final assault involved a quixotic attempt to lobby a bill through Congress that would force major sellers of automobiles in the United States to manufacture as much as 90 percent of their component parts in the United States and Canada.

But as Fraser pressed for his bill and his impatient colleagues began to cry for a resumption of the old adversarial bargaining techniques, General Motors announced a plan to purchase 200,000 subcompacts in 1984 from Isuzu Motors of Japan, in which it holds a 34.2 percent operating share. GM also opened talks with Toyota and Suzuki Motors to discuss joint ventures, adding to the impetus of car manufacturers worldwide to seek out alliances that will, some predict, produce six or eight major international consortiums that will dominate the business by 1990.

While the UAW and its allies in Congress were fulminating about local-content laws, Honda was going ahead with its Marysville, Ohio, facility, where its existing motorcycle assembly operation would soon be joined by a full-scale car-manufacturing plant. Like Nissan in Tennessee, Honda openly resisted the advances of the UAW, noting that the accomplishments of its nonunion, corn-fed Buckeye State laborers were on a par with its hometown employees in Hamamatsu. "There is no difference," flatly stated a Honda vice president. His company's wariness toward the UAW clearly implies that the Japanese believe that the quality of their American-made cars could change for the worse with the UAW's presence.

Sadly, Fraser and his colleagues are part of a decaying system. It is a system born of the days of strife when workers needed powerful collective action against the exploitations of tycoons like Alfred P. Sloan, Jr. (Sloan, incidentally, became the posthumous victim of an ultimate irony: The factory which propelled him to his heights in General Motors, the Hyatt Roller Bearing Company of Clark, New Jersey, was sold by GM to a consortium of UAW workers for $53 million. Sloan would have been amused by the fact that the workers immediately slashed their pay by 30 percent after taking command.)

Both the Sloans and the Frasers now seem like relics of another age. As automotive consultant John B. Schnapp observed in the *Wall Street Journal*: "The problem Mr. Fraser faces is the classic one of a runaway industry fleeing a labor force whose costs have drifted away from reality and whose union leadership may not be able to make the creative leap to a policy position that will insure the health of the industry on which its membership depends."

Union myopia is only part of the problem. Management ranks are also filled with men like Mr. Smith who speak of reforms through automation and robotics, and rhapsodize about the advanced technology of their Japanese rivals, when in fact the physical capabilities of most Japanese automakers are not radically superior to their own. The Japanese advantage lies not in machines, but in managing the men who operate them. As auto consultant James E. Harbour warned at a recent *Automotive News* World Congress, the U.S. industry has no more than five years to adapt to modern management techniques. Otherwise, in ten to fifteen years, he prophesized, America will be operating with an industrial base so eroded that "the only thing we will be exporting is free enterprise rhetoric."

Harbour has repeatedly said that the domestic automakers must, among other things, carve out half of their middle-management fat. They must utilize the creativity and skills of their hourly production workers in the planning and management process and create a zero-defects system that radically reduces scrappages and warranty costs in order to survive.

This problem cannot be solved by new robotics or by lip service to the Japanese method. Dr. Kim B. Clark, the Harvard Graduate School of Business Administration professor who prepared the report, "The Competitive Status of the U.S. Auto Industry" for the National Science Foundation, says: "In the case of productivity and product quality and the role of the workforce, we are talking about something close to a *cultural revolution*, about fundamental changes in the way the business is managed, and the ways people at all levels participate in the enterprise."

Nothing less than a revolution in management and labor attitude, with productivity and quality as its criteria, will save the American auto industry.

CHAPTER IX

The Government: For Better or Worse

AMERICAN AUTOMOBILES ARE DIFFERENT. Unlike most others in the world, they have been produced under the close scrutiny of a non-industrial partner—the United States Government.

The presence of the federal government has been the source of general unpleasantness between a recalcitrant industry and an aggressive bureaucracy. A Congressional report describes the regulatory environment of the automobile as "an inherently adversarial process." Detroit, the report says, is seen as "the bad guy," and suggests that "some members of Congress and their staffs typically operated on the assumption that, if the industry does not oppose it, it must be too lenient."

Fifteen years and billions of dollars after this confrontation between Washington and Detroit began, the average American is driving an automobile that is cleaner by nearly 90 percent in terms of air pollution and is also marginally safer. On the minus side of the ledger, it is several hundred pounds heavier than similar cars being sold elsewhere in the world. It runs less smoothly, is more expensive to maintain (due to complicated electronic emission control gear), has substantially less acceleration and passing power. Most important in the competitive world market, it delivers about 15 percent less mileage per gallon than might otherwise be possible. It also costs more, perhaps as much as $400.

In essence the contemporary American automobile is the result of a series of political decisions intended to achieve certain social objectives. One expert recently determined that since 1960 all cars and light trucks sold in America have been subject to no less than 237 federal regulations. Guidelines set out design and performance criteria for everything from exhaust emissions to headlight candle-power, to dashboard padding to bumper heights and tire pressures. Some of these regulations are quite useful, still others are of negligible impact, and still others are actually counterproductive.

Detroit executives still privately curse the government and growl openly when they speak of Ralph Nader. (The large safety research laboratory at GM's Milford Proving Grounds is ruefully referred to as "the House that Nader Built.") They are proud that their cars generally rate better in crash testing and insurance company accident data than their Japanese competitors. They grudgingly admit that the safety and emission-control legislation has benefited society, but they grouse about its massive costs to themselves and to the consumers.

They also conveniently fail to recognize one salient fact: All the government interference could have been avoided if the industry had demonstrated some social responsibility during the 1960s. Had the leadership at General Motors, Ford, and Chrysler been less fascinated with the big-car, big-profit merry-go-round, the over-reaction from Washington could have been avoided. Bad automobiles came before bad laws. To be sure, federal bureaucrats have since swung the regulation pendulum too far, but that too was an inevitable response to Detroit's witless excesses.

/////

The regulation of automobiles has found a welcome constituency among those who believe in social engineering, who see the automobile as a tool of potential anarchy. It is true that the car provides the kind of mobility that defies orderly planning. A population riding obediently on carefully scheduled trains or buses makes for order; multitudes riding over the landscape in millions of cars seems to invite social upheaval. The unruly auto has even stimulated such fulminations as *Autokind versus Mankind* in which Kenneth R. Schneider inveighed, "The social malignancy underlying automobility, *tyrannus mobilitis*, draws men into inescapable dependence. Dependence arises from a vicious circle in which the charm of the car and the remaking of the environment reinforce each other. Automobility gradually permeates the daily behaviour of people, the purpose of institutions, and the structure of the cities and countryside. This tyranny has been promoted under the cunning popular myth of expanding freedom and affluence."

Mr. Schneider chooses to ignore two facts: first, that the automobile has contributed enormously to the level of American affluence. Second, this "tyranny" is so successful that it has mesmerized not only a perceptive American population but has won total acceptance in every developed country on earth.

The car as cultural villain is an attractive intellectual image to those who imagine they would otherwise be lolling on the banks of a thousand Waldens or trundling *en masse* on state-regulated railroad cars. John Jerome was so persuaded by this notion when he wrote his *Death of the Automobile* in 1972. His summary of the coming automotive apocalypse was as follows:

"The automobile will die when it becomes unbearable... When the moment comes—as it will, as surely as tomorrow's polluted dawn—when movement threatens, when to go carries a greater psychic cost than to stay, then we will stop. The automobile has made a powerful beginning in the creation of an environment in which such a threat is integral. Every day new elements click into place: the risk, the cost, the delay, the bother, the crowding, the congestion. The rage."

Jerome's obituary was premature. Ten years later, following a pair of oil crises, a major recession, mass-transit funding, the public still bears up under the delay, the bother, the *rage*, as it were, in order to enjoy the personal freedom and privacy uniquely afforded by the automobile.

The anti-car lobby has a leader, a somber lawyer from Winsted, a seedy mill town in western Connecticut. His name is Ralph Nader. A graduate of Princeton University, where he graduated magna cum laude in 1955 before entering Harvard Law School, Nader carries with him an open contempt for the elitism he believes infests American life. As the editor of the *Law Record* he vocally defended the rights of American Indians and in his third year, he wrote a long, detailed paper critically dealing with automobile design and product liability.

It was during this period that his interests branched toward what would later be described as "public interest law" and his antagonism toward Detroit deepened. Some biographers have traced it to a number of severe automobile accidents the young lawyer witnessed while hitchhiking between Fort Dix, New Jersey, and Connecticut during a six-month army reserve tour in 1960. After moving to Washington, Nader trained his sights on Detroit, lecturing and writing articles on auto safety for *The New Republic* and *The Nation*. He operated as a free-lance consultant and researcher for Daniel P. Moynihan, who was then assistant secretary of labor. Moynihan, now a U.S. senator from New York, had produced several position papers on auto safety in the late 1950s as an aide to New York Governor Averell Harriman.

Until Ralph Nader arrived on the scene, the subject of automobile safety was little more than periodic fodder for the Sunday supplements, a "potboiler" that could be recycled endlessly. But Nader's approach was different. Rather than bring his case to the popular press, he made his assault through the corridors of government.

Abraham Ribicoff—then the junior senator from Connecticut— opened his subcommittee hearings on automobile safety in March, 1965, at a time when little concern for the subject had been shown in Washington. As the chairman of the Senate Subcommittee on Executive Reorganization, Ribicoff decided to examine the problems surrounding both the driver and the automobile in the hope of developing federal legislation in the area of traffic safety. With him on the subcommittee were Fred Harris and Robert F. Kennedy, two senators with overt presidential ambitions. Ralph Nader was his star witness.

Into this lair of governmental lions the spoiled and arrogant carmakers of Detroit marched for the committee hearings, where they were eaten alive by the politicians. Kennedy was the most aggressive of the attackers. During an exchange with James M. Roche, the president of General Motors, and Frederic G. Donner, the chairman, on July 13, 1965, Kennedy managed to get the two executives to admit that out of the $1.7 billion in profits generated by GM the previous year, only *one million dollars* had been spent on safety research.

The admission electrified the Washington establishment. Suddenly they had snared a villain—lumbering, provincial and inept— but a villain nonetheless. Roche and Donner, the loyal corporate monks who seldom revealed themselves to larger public gatherings than the annual stockholders' meeting, were suddenly the targets of a hectoring press and an enraged Congress. Baffled and chagrined, they hurried back to Detroit to lick their wounds, and to further compound their ineptness.

Washington could now play pious. Columnist Nick Thimmesch, then a *Time* magazine staffer, recalled an anecdote which illustrates the contradictions of the battle. Driving back to McLean, Virginia with Senator Robert Kennedy one evening after the automobile safety hearings, they ripped along the Beltway at 75 mph in Bobby's massive Lincoln Continental convertible, discussing the day's assaults on the unprincipled Detroit moguls. Thimmesch also recalled that the safety belts lay unused on the leather seats of the speeding car.

No one in Detroit truly understood what all the outrage was about. The executives naively believed they were building safe automobiles. Oversized, overpowered, with soggy suspensions, vague steering, weak brakes and low-grade tires, the average Detroit automobile of the day was a true ocean liner of the road. It was smooth and relatively stable when proceeding in a straight line, but it became a slave to inertia when asked to stop or change direction. Ironically almost all these safety hazards were ignored in the Ribicoff hearings. The senators, aided by lawyers like Ralph Nader, who acted as a voluntary, unpaid adviser to the subcommittee, were unschooled in automobile engineering. (Nader could not even drive a car.) They paid little attention to the prevention of accidents caused by the awful handling and braking of American cars and concentrated instead on their crashworthiness—their ability to protect passengers *after* the collisions.

Up to that point, the safety campaign had been limited to slowing down the "speeder." Now a new emphasis was created. The *automobile*, not the driver, was to be the target. This posture would produce widespread dividends: First, by identifying "someone" else as the culprit, it placed the government with the voting public, not against it. Anti-speed and anti-drinking programs, even if ineffective, carried the political risk of labeling the populace themselves as the enemy. But to make Goliaths such as General Motors and Ford culpable in the name of the public welfare was the stuff of political heroism.

By placing the blame on the automobile itself, the emphasis was shifted away from the theory that accidents could be avoided through improved highway design and marking, lighting, licensing, better tires, steering, braking and suspensions. Europeans generally believed that these components, plus the creation of automobiles engineered with what they called "evasive capability," were the key to accident prevention. But the chief priority of the American safety lobby was now quite different. They wanted Detroit to build automobiles that were invulnerable: four-wheel padded cells in which witless drivers could bash into each other without fear of injury.

Shortly after Nader's book *Unsafe at Any Speed*, which was published in November 1965, became a best-seller, Congress passed two bills—the Highway Safety Act and the National Traffic and Motor Vehicle Safety Act. They put the federal government squarely in the automobile business. With that came the National Highway Traffic Safety Administration (NHTSA) which was mandated to draw up Federal Motor Vehicle Safety Standards (FMVSS) intended to (1) reduce accidents by setting performance standards for brakes, lights, tires (2) eliminate the "second collision," that is, the impact of passengers against the car's interior, by padding and restraint systems, and (3) create a vast body of data through required record keeping by the manufacturers, suppliers, and the government.

Overnight the complexion of the industry was changed. Although the manufacturers complained that they had been offering seat belts both as options and standard equipment since the 1950s to an indifferent public, critics assailed the industry for shortcomings in steering column design, dashboard panel configurations which were dappled with spearlike switches and knobs, and faulty design and placement of seat belt mountings. Within months after President Lyndon Johnson signed the law in September 1966, the NHTSA legions went to work to implement it. Their first results were among the most useful: better seat belt mountings, improved shatterproof windshields, and collapsible steering columns—all of which the industry was clearly remiss in not installing on its own.

From the beginning, the small agency was pushed by both sides in the conflict. Nader, now a national figure heavily funded by private donations, was constantly charging that the NHTSA was poorly staffed and not sufficiently aggressive in policing the industry. Detroit meanwhile viewed the government as an interloper into its private domain and decried the implementation of the standards. In the words of Henry Ford II, the most visible auto mogul of the day, the government regulations were "unreasonable and arbitrary," a position parroted by every executive in the industry.

Within a decade, the bureaucrats generated over fifty FMVSS standards, some of which, like those that required reinforced side door beams and improved seat/shoulder belts, were constructive. However, the infamous ignition interlock system of 1974, which required that the front passenger's seat belts be fastened before the engine would start, was regarded as such an impertinence in a free society that it was rescinded by a special act of Congress. The 5-mph crashproof bumpers turned out to be ineffective safety devices and more expensive to replace in *6 mph-plus* crashes than the originals. They also added unnecessary weight at a time when manufacturers were attempting to lighten their products to improve fuel consumption. And to meet the increasingly stringent demands for lower exhaust emissions, mileage suffered approximately 15 percent just at the time that OPEC imposed its 1973-74 embargo and gasoline mileage was of the essence.

There are those in Detroit who lay the entire problem of slow sales and low profits at Washington's doorstep. Conversely there are those who insist that the industry would have saved itself had the government regulated automobiles even more stringently. In many cases Detroit undoubtedly dragged its feet in complying with federal standards, as they did with the installation of the catalytic converter. But in some cases the industry was proven correct and the government over-aggressive. The 1970 Clean Air Act, for example, required cars to emit exhaust gases that, in a broad chemical sense, were *cleaner* than the ambient air. Equally ineffective have been the 85-mph limit speedometer and the 55-mph speed limit, which has now become the most universally ignored law since the Volstead Act.

The 1970s was an absurd decade during which government and industry butted heads and the general public gained little. Washington and Detroit were battling each other while the Japanese and the Europeans quietly moved ahead toward compliance. The foreign auto firms often worked on a cooperative basis to meet American government standards, something that our anti-trust laws foolishly forbid. While Americans argued, some of the foreign manufacturers even appropriated American technology, prompting the 1976 lawsuit by General Motors against Toyota for using engine emission data developed under its patent. The claim of infringement was upheld by a federal appeals court in 1981, but the case has not been finally resolved.

The government not only failed to make compliance with air pollution regulations a national cooperative project, but the Justice Department and the new Environmental Protection Agency maintained a sharp eye to ensure that no *cooperation* of any sort was being carried on between the companies. The auto firms were thus forced into a decade of costly, overlapping research to seek their joint goals of low emissions and higher gas mileage. Had cooperation been permitted in a common industry effort for the public good, as was done in Japan, billions would have been saved and the goals reached earlier.

Sadly, the entire episode of government regulation of the automobile industry has led to excesses on both sides. The 1970 Clean

Air Act, as spearheaded by Senator Edmund Muskie, was pure government overkill, placing more stringent requirements on Detroit than the Japanese or Common Market nations did on manufacturers in their own countries, where pollution was, if anything, worse than in America. Some Washingtonians operated with insufferable arrogance. When informed that the massive investment in the research and development of emissions equipment might drive faltering American Motors out of business, Senator Muskie observed, "So be it."

Had the Clean Air Act of 1970 and its subsequent escalations of emissions standards been more technically meaningful, the agony that resulted from the thirsty, inefficient automobiles of that decade might have been avoided. The provisions of the law included a "cold-start" standard which required that engines produce low emissions during the first thirty seconds they were running. During this short period, the engine's reciprocating parts are not at operating temperatures and are therefore very inefficient. To develop the technology to make engines clean during this brief period cost uncounted millions and reduced efficiency over the entire running range of the engine. The standard was so impractical that the Japanese, whose air quality problems are much more critical than the Americans, rejected the "cold-start" when formulating their own laws.

On its part, Detroit has reacted badly to governmental pressures, even when those pressures were reasonably applied. Their early attempts to tack exhaust emission plumbing on existing large-displacement engines was a grave error. The automakers did not recognize—until much too late—that smaller, more advanced designs were needed rather than patchwork fixes on existing hardware. Too much time was consumed in legal foot-dragging and whining that the standards could not be met, which further eroded public confidence in Detroit, and added to the industry's image as a pack of obstructionist profiteers. This included some extraordinary blunders such as Ford's fudging of test data during 50,000 mile reliability tests when the company performed such forbidden maintenance procedures as changing sparkplugs. This brought public censure, a $7 million dollar fine, and the general perception that the industry cared little about air quality.

Legitimate advances in safety stimulated by the government are praiseworthy but have sometimes been perverted by an overzealous bureaucracy. For example, NHTSA has created a set of tire evaluation standards designed to make it easier for consumers to appraise products in the disorderly tire market. But instead of clarifying the issues, the government only added obfuscation and confusion. By concocting an abstruse set of standards based on tread wear, traction and temperature resistance, the government managed to produce information that was based on performance indexes that nobody understood.

These Federal standards have no bearing on real world experience and are overbalanced toward tire mileage rather than safety. In reality, the ability of a tire to grip the road is unrelated to its longevity. A tire can provide awful traction yet wear like iron. On the other hand, a tire can produce excellent adhesion and not be very durable. Because the tire companies were involved in the testing, and because some of the more prestigious brands—Michelin, Goodyear, Pirelli—denounced the entire program as technically specious and refused to cooperate fully, the results were a farce. The NHTSA-sanctioned ratings imply that many second-rate brands are superior to top-flight, state-of-the-art Pirelli, Michelin, Goodyear, and B.F. Goodrich steel-belted radials. The only victims of this ridiculous program are the consumers.

/////

As the battle over regulation between Detroit and Washington intensified, both sides became intransigent. The government insisted that the industry was uncooperative and, in the words of NHTSA administrator Douglas Toms, could only be stimulated by holding those very feet "to the fire." Brock Adams, Secretary of Transportation during the Carter administration, went even further. He demanded that Detroit "reinvent" the automobile. For its part, the industry claimed with one voice that the avalanche of government standards was both capricious and unattainable.

Both sides were wrong. The government, in the form of both the

Environmental Protection Agency and NHTSA, openly distorted data to support its campaign for lower-than-practical emission levels, the usefulness of air bags (virtually ineffective and dangerous in anything but head-on collisions), the value of the 5-mph bumpers, the fuel and life-saving benefits of the widely ignored 55-mph speed limit (independent studies *repeatedly* confirmed negligible results on both counts) and the presumed ease with which 50 mph crash-proof cars could be manufactured. As for the Detroit community, it never avoided an opportunity to denounce the government as a swarm of ignorant gadflies, and went to court to impede the implementation of even the most valuable standards.

The public paid dearly for all this, in cash and in having to drive automobiles in the mid-seventies whose performance was dismal. But there is little disagreement that the government's escalating CAFE standards forced the industry to produce lighter, more fuel-efficient automobiles. Moreover, the Clean Air Act, while based on environmental overkill, has essentially eliminated automotive emissions as a factor in air pollution. The 1981 EPA standards reduced hydrocarbons and carbon monoxide to about 4 percent of their 1960 levels and oxides of nitrogen have been reduced to about 24 percent of their original level.

GM now complains that achieving the last few percentage points of emission reduction has added an additional $480 to the cost of each car in terms of pollution control hardware. Other manufacturers agree that the problem has essentially been solved and that further reductions are simply not cost effective.

Some of the intense pressure on the auto industry eased when the Reagan administration took office. NHTSA has since set out to modify the safety standards in seventeen areas, a campaign that can save the industry $1.5 billion in development costs and consumers over $9 billion in reduced auto prices. Part of that effort involves the cancellation of the controversial air bags, a device which the safety lobby believes can save up to 9000 lives a year, but which the industry feels is overrated and ineffective when compared to the compulsory use of seat belts.

Critics of air bags note that GM had offered them as $400 options on Cadillacs, Buicks, and Oldsmobiles. The bags incurred a massive development cost and were sold at a sizable loss; only 10,000 customers ordered them. "We might as well have sold the bags and given away the cars," mused a GM spokesman. General Motors dropped the program in 1976.

The air bag war continues. General Motors says it will cost them $300 million dollars to equip all of its cars with them. Ford estimates the cost at $200 million. Raymond Peck, Reagan's NHTSA Administrator, has decided that the device is of dubious value and has rescinded the original mandate of the Carter administration. Peck speculates that the air bag would prove even less popular than the ill-fated interlock system and that a great many of them would be disconnected. His supporters claim that many drivers have expressed loud reservations about riding around with an explosive charge capable of accidental discharge mounted in the steering column.

In 1982, a federal Appeals Court judge overturned Peck's decision and ruled that the air bag provision be implemented on schedule. His decision was subsequently reversed, which has left the outcome in the hands of the Supreme Court, where it is as of this writing.

The debate between the government and the car industry has obviously not subsided. The anti-speed, anti-crash advocates have found a permanent niche in the world of the American automobile. They defiantly vow that they will not rest until the automobile has claimed its last victim. Such success is unlikely, unless they can successfully cancel the laws of physics. But the safety lobby and Washington's emphasis on cleaner air and less gasoline usage has succeeded in achieving at least three vital goals: they have helped to reduce pollution created by cars, they have focused national interest on car safety, and they have shaken a lethargic Detroit out of the insular, truculent position that has helped to make it a supine target for the more imaginative, more aggressive, more flexible foreign competition.

CHAPTER X

The Good, The Bad, and the Indifferent:
THE TEN BEST AND TEN WORST SEDANS

THE DECLINE OF AMERICAN AUTOMOTIVE POWER and the rise of foreign imports has changed the shape of the marketplace. Where once the great majority of superior cars were made in America, quality is now a worldwide function. There are literally hundreds of industrial operations around the world that describe themselves as automobile manufacturers, including the Turkish Tofas, Sta Matilde of Brazil, Hindustan Motors of India, and Taiwan's YLN-YUE Loong Motors Company. However, only fifty major carmakers are presently doing serious business internationally, ranging from the five largest—General Motors, Ford, Toyota, Nissan, and Volkswagen—to such relatively minor players as East Germany's Trabant, and Sweden's Saab-Scania.

In addition to the five principal automakers who manufacture and sell cars in the United States (GM, Ford, Chrysler, American Motors-Renault and Volkswagen of America) about twenty-five carmakers from Europe and Japan regularly import models for the American market. These range in magnitude from such giants as Toyota and Nissan (Datsun), which sell approximately 500,000 cars each, to custom automakers such as Ferrari, Lotus, and Maserati, whose combined sales total about one thousand annually.

The situation is further confused by the growing internationalization of the business, which blurs the distinction between a "domestic" and an "imported" automobile. Such brands as Chrysler Corporation's Colt, Champ, Challenger, and Sapporo are built by Mitsubishi in Japan. Until recently Ford marketed the Fiesta, which was made by West Germany's Ford Werke AG. The new AMC Alliance is essentially a French car being manufactured in Kenosha, Wisconsin. Hondas are now being built in the heartland of Ohio, while Volkswagen Rabbits have been assembled for some time in New Stanton, Pennsylvania.

This interchangeability is rapidly compromising the old tradition of automobiles with pure national roots. Perhaps the ultimate absurdity is a "Buy American" sticker on a Plymouth Horizon or a Dodge Omni, cars which are powered by German-made engines and French-designed transmissions.

Despite this internationalism, many automobiles still reflect the personalities of the nations which produce them. German cars are uniformly fast, spartan, and purposeful; Italian cars have a faint aroma of the sublimated, frustrated racer about them; while French cars contain a dollop of *outre* and a sort of bumptious flair for the unconventional. Japanese cars are just beginning to develop a national character. It is one of fussy concern with detail and a stern, disciplined streak of efficiency overlaid with a sometimes frivolous preoccupation with microprocessing.

American automobiles remain a combination of Model T and bogus Rolls-Royce: still trying futilely to be all things to all men, the suburban housewife uncomfortably masquerading as a streetwalker. British cars (what few remain) are a strange gumbo of the Victorian and the hi-tech—automobiles that courageously grope their way toward the future with their bumpers chained to the musty glories of Empire. Swedish cars exhibit a strongly Teutonic, somewhat blunt-edged fixation with function at all costs, an urge which perhaps arises from their snowbound environment.

Contemporary purchasers of automobiles are lashed by doubts from all quarters. Is there one perfect automobile on the market? The answer is "No." Are there any good automobiles at all? Emphatically "Yes." Should one make a buying decision based on other factors besides price and availability? "Yes." How important is the dealer and distribution system backing him up? "Critically important."

Very few consumers know a good automobile from a bad one, or how to choose between the two. Word of mouth is often the best source of information, but it can be larded with specious hearsay. This chapter is an attempt, however limited, to explain some of the factors—and cars—that should be considered by an astute buyer.

/////

The modern automobile, regardless of its origin, is stronger, more reliable, safer and more functional that any of its antecedents. There is a wider selection of types—from four-wheel-drive four-door sedans to front-wheel-drive hatchback coupes or two-seater roadsters, from fifty-mile-per gallon minicars to 150 mph road-burners —than ever before. In fact, the biggest problem facing a potential buyer is to sift through the nearly two hundred different automobiles presently available in the United States, what one marketing expert has desparingly described as "the agony of choice."

Inevitably that choice is subjective. Seldom is a car purchase made on purely rational grounds. For example, academics have driven Volvos and Saabs as a matter of course since the 1960s. Indeed, the Volvo has been called "the car for people who hate cars." A Saab executive has quipped, "One of our biggest problems was designing the pedals so the car could be driven in earth shoes." Volvos and Saabs seemed somehow the ultimate in Bauhaus automobiles—stark, functional, safe. Sadly, until very recently, the cars of Sweden were cursed with bad workmanship. They were, in fact, a terrible choice for a social class that is, for the most part, mechanically ignorant. Fortunately, the problem has been solved and both Swedish car makers now produce excellent cars.

Mercedes-Benz diesels also have been purchased by the wrong people on the basis on rationalizations. These are marvelous automobiles, capable of operating for years at a time with virtually no maintenance. The advantages of a diesel, which is noisy and sluggish at low speeds, can be realized only in steady-state long distance operations, hence their application in large trucks, boats and tractors. Yet the 240D Mercedes sold in the United States is mainly used to putter around fashionable suburbs by housewives who would have to live for several hundred years before they could accumulate sufficient mileage to make the car an economical choice. It was estimated that a Mercedes-Benz 240D sedan, costing about five times as much as a $6,000 gasoline-powered Citation, would have to be driven at least 600,000 miles before any savings in fuel cost could be realized. Still the car is perceived as the ultimate in good sense and rationality, a sort of rich man's Volvo.

We are all slaves to fashion. The young computer programmer who sinks himself in debt for forty-eight months to impress a willowy fellow worker with his new Pontiac Trans-Am is no more driven by peer group pressure than the Sierra Clubber who *has* to own a Subaru four-wheel-drive station wagon, a Fairfield County advertising executive who would face the public pillory before buying an American car, a Des Moines insurance salesman who considers his Cadillac DeVille the final testimony to his success, or a Beverly Hills matron whose Mercedes-Benz 450SL roadster serves as a navigational beacon in the shoal waters of her overly competitive local society.

There is nothing original in the notion that automobiles are extensions of the personalities of their owners. The crucial fact is that the consumer's passionate involvement with his car, and its impact on American society remains as strong as it was twenty years ago. Worldwide, the power of the automobile has increased as the new middle classes everywhere overwhelmingly choose private automobile travel over public transportation. Automobiles provide some of the only truly private moments for harried modern individuals. This sense of precious solitude, coupled with the unlimited options for independent action provided by the auto, will always make it an object of human affection, even a therapeutic tool.

But buying a car requires more than love. Judgment is necessary. Today, for example, fuel mileage has become an overemphasized determinant in car-buying decisions, often causing a customer to ignore a more suitable automobile simply because it gets a few miles less per gallon. Pure gas mileage can become an obsession by which all other benefits of a car are obscured in a mad rush to save a few cents at the pump.

A car driven ten thousand miles in a year that gets twenty miles per gallon will only cost its owner about $280 more for fuel than one that gets thirty-five miles per gallon. Therefore, for about $23 per month more, one can drive an automobile that might provide more acceleration, passing power, long-range comfort, interior room and carrying capacity. Moreover, range is as important a factor as mileage in times of gas shortage. A car with a twenty-four gallon tank that gets twenty miles per gallon will travel over a hundred miles farther between gas stops than a car with a ten gallon tank that gets thirty-five miles per gallon.

The overall function of the car must also be considered. If it is to be used solely for short-haul commutes, a tiny maneuverable sub-compact is ideal. If the mission involves long trips on the Interstate system, a larger, smoother-running machine with a greater load capacity is better. Front-wheel-drive, with its higher traction capability is preferable in hostile climates and relatively useless in the warm, dry South. Manual transmissions are more efficient than automatics, but they require more skill and attentiveness to operate.

Each brand and type has its advantages and shortcomings. The Mercedes-Benz 380SEL, for instance, is generally considered to be the most perfect mass-produced automobile in the world. It is strong, powerful, abundantly safe, and endowed with high technology and craftsmanship. But it costs about $50,000. Still, it is a brisk seller among those who can afford it because of its excellent resale value and enormous owner satisfaction. At the other end of the price scale is the Ford Escort and its identical sister, the Lincoln-Mercury Lynx. For the loyalist American who refuses to patronize the Japanese, the Escort is an ideal little machine: quite reliable, well-fabricated, economical and easily serviced. That car, along with such Far Eastern brands as the Honda Civic, Mazda GLC and Toyota Starlet provide the small car customer with a broad selection of truly excellent automobiles from which to choose.

In the middle range of cars there is also a large assortment of solid values. They include the dazzling Honda Accord, the outstand-

ing Nissan Stanza, the older but respected General Motors intermediates (Buick Regal, Oldsmobile Cutlass, Pontiac Grand Prix,
Chevrolet Monte Carlo), the Chrysler K-cars and the new Ford
front-wheel-drive entries.

At the next echelon, where people have acclimated themselves to
spending over $12,000 for a family sedan, a number of excellent
machines can be found, ranging from the occasionally overlooked
but value-laden Nissan (Datsun) 810 Maxima and Toyota Cressida
to those fine Swedish twins, Volvo and Saab. The German representatives include that powerful status symbol, the BMW 528, plus the
excellent Audi 5000 series. At the upper levels of status and price
(from $30,000 up), we have the radically improved Jaguar, a number
of Mercedes-Benz models and the somewhat underrated BMW 733i.
Within the specialty car categories one can find such gems as the
Chevrolet Z-28 Camaro, and its sister, the Pontiac Firebird Trans-
Am, as well as the Ford Mustang, Toyota Celica, Datsun 280ZX,
Mazda RX-7, Mitsubishi Starion, Porsche 944 (as well as the more
expensive 911SC and 928), and a variety of light trucks and four-
wheel-drive vehicles from both Detroit and Japan.

The market is filled with good automobiles, but it is incumbent
upon a well-informed consumer to seek them out. They cannot be
found by entering the nearest dealership and haggling over price and
trade-in value. Often a smaller, more conscientious dealer cannot
match the bottom line of a major, high-volume outlet, but may be a
much better choice in terms of service, warranty claims, and customer service.

The ownership of an offbeat brand with very few dealerships—as
is the case with most French and Italian cars (excluding Renault)—
can be risky. However, if one patronizes a reliable dealer with an
adequate parts supply, there is reduced risk. One should beware of all
Italian cars—except Ferraris—which have now fallen on hard times
in terms of overall reliability and quality levels.

The last bit of advice requires either courage or foolhardiness.
Calling on both, I have set forth my list of the ten best and ten worst
sedans in the world. A word of caution: all selective lists include
injustices, omissions, prejudices, and generalizations. This one is no
exception. By focusing on normal-duty sedans that carry four or five

passengers, the list arbitrarily excludes such specialty items as sports and GT cars, four-wheel-drive vehicles, light pickups, and vans. Being subjective, the selections are based on a broad evaluation of cost, reliability, safety, resale value and the ability to meet the design objective as compared to the competition. Neither the "best" nor "worst" lists are ranked in any particular order. Rather all ten represent, in my opinion, the high and low points in various segments of the market, from top to bottom.

The Ten Best Sedans

MERCEDES-BENZ 123-SERIES 300DT SEDAN

Mercedes is the oldest automobile manufacturer in the world and, in the opinion of many, the best. The top-line 380 SEL is an engineering marvel, but at nearly $50,000 it appears to have reached the upper limits of practicality versus price—especially for a rather severely styled sedan, whose looks border on the mundane. A far better value, it would seem, are the less expensive (by $20,000) but slightly smaller and somewhat older 123-series sedans, especially the splendid five-cylinder 300D Turbo Diesel model. The cars are built like anvils, will run forever, have superb handling and crashworthiness, and enjoy an excellent resale market. The only drawbacks are their rather spartan interiors and exceptionally steep maintenance costs on the occasions when things need fixing. The four-cylinder 240D diesel is the best-selling model, but it is too sluggish a performer to justify its high price. A new Mercedes-Benz small sedan about to be introduced in the United States is expected to set new standards of performance and finish for subcompacts. Unlike many of its rivals, Mercedes-Benz has eschewed front-wheel-drive for its new generation of automobiles (as have Porsche, BMW and Volvo), an indication that not all advanced automobile thinkers are in agreement as to its advantages.

TOYOTA COROLLA

At the bottom of the market, where the competition is keenest, this somewhat aged machine (its new body style was introduced in 1980, but its drivetrain is over ten years old) reigns as the largest-selling single model in the world. It is surpassed by several other cars in terms of engineering, sophistication, styling, performance, and fuel mileage, but for overall low-cost, workaday urban transportation it is difficult to beat. Its reliability record in the merciless world of rental cars is superb, and it is available in a variety of body styles and trim options. The Corolla is hardly the ultimate highway status symbol, but it is a supreme value in terms of low price, modest maintenance, and durability that borders on the bulletproof.

HONDA ACCORD

The recipient of more universal plaudits than any other single make beside the Mercedes-Benz, this second-generation car, in three-and four-door sedan configurations, is slightly larger and plushier than the first, but it remains a high-water mark in small passenger vehicle design and packaging. American loyalists can buy the four-door in good conscience because it is being manufactured—with the same exceptional standards of quality—in Honda's new Marysville, Ohio plant. Within its league of high economy medium-sized sedans, it is without peer and ranks at or near the top in terms of overall value, regardless of price. The Accord can be recommended without qualification.

AUDI 5000S

With a wheelbase of 105 inches and a length of 188.9 inches, this is a perfectly sized four-door sedan. It is built to high standards of German craftsmanship, with an advanced five-cylinder engine in both gasoline and diesel varieties. The 5000S is hard to beat for carrying up to five passengers and luggage in safe, long-range comfort without apparent effort while delivering economy and a high level of reliability. This car is a complete turnabout for Audi, which fell on hard times with its earlier, mediocre 100LS and Fox sedans. It now serves as a baseline for all mid-range four-doors that are forthcoming from Detroit. Not cheap at $13,000 to $18,000, but bulging with value.

HONDA CIVIC

This third incarnation of the famed front-wheel-drive miniature that nudged the world into accepting truly tiny automobiles has increased somewhat in size and splendor. In fact, it rather closely resembles the first-edition Accord in accommodations and performance. Its fabrication and general level of quality are among the best in the industry. Unlike in its early years, however, it now has serious rivals, principally the Mazda GLC. Many experts believe the Mazda GLC is the equal of the Civic in most areas, although it is slightly more expensive and does not generate the incredible miles-per-gallon numbers attributed to the 1300FE Civic—an EPA rating of 55 mpg on the highway. Another top contender in this minicar league is the Dodge Colt and its twin, the Plymouth Champ. Made by Mitsubishi for Chrysler, these little boxes are solidly fabricated machines built on the same theme as the Civic and GLC. Both are worthy competitors, especially with their optional larger 1.6 liter engines.

SAAB 900 APC TURBO

This car is built by an aerospace manufacturer and its somewhat bizarre appearance reflects a daring approach to transportation. A front-wheel-drive four-cylinder car with a highly-developed turbocharger system that not only enhances performance but increases fuel mileage, the Saab 900 Turbo is available as a conventional four-door and a sports-coupe-mini-wagon-three-door combo. Like its sister Swede, the somewhat heavier Volvo (whose new 760 Turbo Diesel sedan is drawing rave reviews), the Saab is in the forefront of durability, engineering, all-weather operation and crashworthiness. Both Saab and Volvo have corrected the quality control problems that blighted their cars in the mid-1970s and now offer machines with fabrication levels equaling the best from Germany and Japan. Not cheap at about $16,000, the Saab 900 Turbo has come out of limbo in recent years to gain a much-deserved ranking among the best automobiles in the world, regardless of price.

FORD ESCORT/MERCURY LYNX

These automobiles, which are identical save for minor details of trim, were introduced as part of Ford's "World Car" program and were at first met with universal jeers from the motoring press. While the general concept of the automobile was lauded, a sloppy ride and handling setup and only mediocre engine performance were the central points of criticism. Happily, those deficiencies have for the most part been corrected, although the cars still remain a notch or two below the Honda Civic and Mazda GLC. However, Ford is diligently striving for excellence with this model and its future is bright. For those who will not buy an imported car, yet desire its benefits, the Escort is a solid bet in the small car group. A vast Ford dealer network, good resale value, its sturdy construction, and a five-door hatchback version are all points in favor of the Escort/Lynx.

OLDSMOBILE CUTLASS SUPREME/BUICK REGAL

This is what America does best. One questions the wisdom of GM's planned dumping from the lineup of such a traditionally effective, reliable and salable commodity as the so-called G-cars, the Cutlass and Regal (along with their sister cars, the Chevrolet Malibu and Pontiac Grand Prix) in a panicked conversion to front-wheel drive. On the market since 1978, these cars have undergone steady improvement to the point where they are now strong, silent, reliable performers in the American idiom. The coupe versions can be criticized for limited rear seat room, trunks that are too small and hoods that are too long, but they have a proven American audience. The Cutlass Supreme and Buick Regal sales have been one of precious few bright spots on the GM profit sheets of late. They can hardly be described as state-of-the-art automobiles, but the relatively low maintenance, surprisingly good economy, ease of service, solid fabrication, and good resale value make them excellent choices for traditional American car buyers.

JAGUAR XJ 6

This automobile has long been like the fabled little girl with the curl in the middle of her forehead. When it was good, it was very, very good. When it was bad, it was a mechanical abomination. Long considered to be the most beautiful yet functional four-door sedan shape ever produced, the Jaguar was cursed for many years by poor workmanship that kept it in the maintenance shop and more than nullified the advantages of its sophisticated running gear. Now a reorganized company is manufacturing Jaguars with a newfound devotion to craftsmanship. The result is a silky four-passenger sedan with superb handling and performance encased in a body of timeless grace.

MAZDA 626

When it is recalled that Toyo Kogyo nearly went out of business after its Mazda rotary-engine cars received bad publicity for poor reliability and high gas consumption, its recovery seems nothing short of miraculous. First came its excellent Mazda RX-7 sports car, then the GLC, and now the second edition of its larger 626 sedan. Designed as a competitor for the Honda Accord, and available in a five-door hatchback as well as a two-door coupe and four-door, the latest 626 embodies striking styling, leading-edge front-wheel-drive technology, and eight more horsepower than the Accord. Priced in the $8,000 range, cars like the Accord and the 626 represent the heart and soul of the family-size car market in the United States. This is a market the J-cars from General Motors failed to penetrate, and one which the GM A-cars and the Ford Escort have bracketed by design. It is within this area that the Japanese are proving that they are capable of building more than bare-boned econoboxes. They are doing as well in the upscale $10,000 to $12,000 market with such cars as the Datsun Maxima and Toyota Cressida. Detroit must effectively meet this challenge if it is to regain its old dominance. So far, automobiles like the 626 still stand unchallenged by either GM, Ford or Chrysler.

The Ten Worst Sedans

Because this list includes some of the true sacred cows of the automotive world, an explanation is in order. "Worst" in this case does not imply overtly poor quality and performance as much as it does value. Some of the automobiles mentioned here would not qualify as "worst" or even "bad" if they were not so blatantly overpriced. Others would be cited no matter what the criteria. It is to the credit of the entire industry that the list is so short.

RENAULT LeCAR

Despite its size as an automobile manufacturer, France has never enjoyed long-term success selling cars in the United States, and LeCar (called the R-5 elsewhere) is a prime example of the problem. Tall and boxy and riding on skinny tires, LeCar looks as if it was accidentally squeezed between two dump trucks. Its interior is a melange of plastic and vinyl that baffles all but the most quirky Gallic mind. Thanks to a supple suspension, it is a frisky traveler on bumpy roads, but its excessive body lean can convince the faint of heart that it about to tip over when rounding corners. Acceleration is brisk but noisy, maneuverability in heavy traffic is good, but the general level of workmanship is ragged. Whenever LeCar is discussed, it is equated with French whimsy. Said one road tester in summary, "Minimal motoring with a sense of humor. We're not laughing."

BMW 320i

The selection of this vehicle as one of the "worst" may earn this writer a place on a fanatic BMW owner's hit list, but it cannot be avoided. BMW had a triumph of high performance and low price with its earlier 2002 series, and its larger sedans and coupes are among the best in the world. But its small 320i series has declined steadily in quality since its introduction in 1976 while its price has escalated to absurd heights. The naive and the slavish seekers after status have not yet gotten the word: the 320i is grossly overpriced in the $15,000 range (some loaded versions nudge $20,000) while providing skittish handling and some notably weak internal quality levels. The grotesquely overpriced 320i remains a status symbol, but little else. A new and improved version of the 320i has been announced and may offer the quality one expects from BMW.

ROLLS-ROYCE SILVER SPUR

A number of years ago, *Car and Driver* magazine described the then-fashionable Rolls-Royce Silver Cloud III as "an example of what modern technology and a spare-no-expense philosophy can do for a 1939 Packard." Sadly, the evaluation still applies. Beneath all the walnut veneer, the matched cowhide, the hand-rubbed lacquer, and the fitted metalwork lies an overweight (5,000 lbs), fussy, compulsively-engineered old lady whose $120,000 price tag is so ridiculous that today it attracts dope peddlers, punk rockers and tasteless Hollywood producers to its once-haughty ranks. Rolls-Royces have long since lost their legendary reliability and are, in fact, decidedly finicky, save for their American-built GM Turbo Hydra-matic transmission—the same unit that can be found on a Chevrolet Caprice for less than one tenth of the price. What Rolls-Royce has successfully sold for the past thirty years is a famous radiator grille with a rather frumpy automobile hooked on the back. The present sag in sales appears to indicate that the game has finally caught up with them.

GENERAL MOTORS J-CARS

These automobiles have been treated in substantial detail elsewhere in these pages. While improvements have been made in recent models, the J-cars remain heavy and are still cursed with noisy engines, particularly in comparison to the competition. Perceived as being too costly by the public, they have become a major problem for General Motors. While quite reliable and workmanlike, the J-cars have been blighted with a loser's image.

RENAULT 18i

Yet another blow struck for the French Republic that went wide. As part is its major assault on the American market through the wobbly offices of American Motors, Renault briefly tried to convince the American public that this was a low-priced BMW alternative, but soon gave up. The 18i is, in fact, a somewhat frumpy version of the Honda Accord without any of its performance, good looks, or quality. Like so many French automobiles, it appears to have been styled out of ice cream that is beginning to melt around the edges. With front-wheel drive and both gasoline and diesel options, the 18i acquits itself well in a technical sense, but it has a noisy engine. The new AMC-Renault Alliance, a well-designed "Accord" size competitor made in the U.S., has a much better chance of major consumer acceptance.

CHRYSLER IMPERIAL

A classic, old-line Detroit con job. Underneath the rather flashy exterior lies a Chrysler Cordoba, complete with its wheezy 318 cubic inch V-8 and outdated chassis. The Imperial carries a long-term warranty and is reputed to receive a major massaging before leaving the factory, but the fact remains that this is a counterfeit car, selling the same collection of "luxury" items that one can find on a Cordoba at half the price. Fortunately, the new realities of the car business will cause this brand of all-frosting automobile to disappear, although there are unrepentant marketing types in Detroit who remain convinced that this is the one true way to sell cars.

CADILLAC SEVILLE

When the first Seville hit the market in 1976, it was quickly identified as a much-improved and modified Chevrolet Nova. No matter. It was a solid, traditional attempt to market a down-size Cadillac, and its squared-up contours had a muted, enduring quality. Then came the new Seville in 1980: a bustle-backed creation intended to sweep nostalgia buffs back to the 1940s, and the days of elegant English coach builders. The new Seville borrowed its front-wheel drive from the Eldorado-Riviera-Toronado class and should presumably offer additional passenger room. It does not. Its sprawling hood consumes most of the available space and leaves the Seville a four-passenger machine with modest trunk space. In diesel form this two-tonner is a flabby performer. With its fuel-injected aluminum V-8, it is no less thirsty than one of the old Caddy battleships of yore. Tastelessly bechromed in its Elegante form, a heavily optioned Seville can reach the rather heady plateau of $30,000, which butts it up against such vastly superior automobiles as the Jaguar XJ-6 and the BMW 733i, which belongs on an expanded "Best Buy" list.

NISSAN (DATSUN) SENTRA

This is not a truly bad automobile, but it is simply outmatched by the Honda Civic, Mazda GLC, Toyota Tercel, and a host of other small front-wheel-drive cars at the bottom of the market. If there is one company that deserves a rap for manufacturing tinny, lightweight small cars in recent years, it is Datsun (now Nissan). While some of its more expensive models—the new Stanzas and Pulsars as well as the Maxima sedan and 280 ZX sports car—are well made, its little machines seem flimsy, cramped, noisy, and not a little stark when compared to the competition. For an extra $1,000 Nissan fans will be much happier with their Stanzas.

PEUGEOT 505

Despite a massive advertising campaign patterned after the wildly successful Mercedes-Benz newspaper ads of the 1970s (both by the same agency, Ogilvy & Mather), in which Peugeot is reputed to be investing over $600 per car, the 505 is hardly driving the managers at BMW, Saab, Volvo, or Audi into fits of despair. Its Turbo Diesel model is rather sprightly as such machines go, but its normal four-cylinder gas engine is somewhat underpowered in a car weighing over 3,000 pounds. It delivers modest mileage. The general fit and finish for a sedan in this price range is not up to competitive standards. Another major weakness is a spotty dealer and parts-maintenance network which can mean grave difficulty if one breaks down in the hinterlands. A car for Francophiles only.

LINCOLN TOWN CAR AND MARK VI

A glorious hodgepodge of American glitz. This is one of the final convulsions of old-line Detroit ostentation and deserves an early demise. Decked out in various "signature" getups from such noted arbiters of taste as Bill Blass, Pucci, Givenchy, and Cartier, these vinyl-roofed, opera-windowed luxury liners (both of which are virtually the same 4,100 pound monsters with slightly different levels of cut-pile carpeting and velvet) are soft to the touch and to the gas pedal. They float down the road like runaway soap bubbles and are the ultimate expression of Detroit's obsession with the superficial trappings of elegance. Possessing no redeeming social value, they represent a worst-case example of the crude, exploitative thinking that has placed Detroit in its present difficult position.

/////

Owning an automobile is a unique twentieth century experience. They are marvelous devices, affording more freedom of movement to a wider segment of humanity than any invention since the shoe. But to the careless, the uninformed, or the indifferent, they can be loathesome encumbrances, capable of shattering the composure of a Buddhist monk. To avoid such misadventures, one must be equipped with a modicum of knowledge. The modern, internationalized automobile penalizes consumer ignorance.

CHAPTER XI

The American Automobile Industry: Can It Be Saved?

AS AN AUTOMOBILE EXECUTIVE rises he moves inexorably into a world where cars become an abstraction on sales charts and income projections. His exposure to the product comes through a series of perfectly tuned and groomed test vehicles garaged in the basement of his office building and brought to a state of unreal perfection by teams of mechanics. He drives a new model in from his Bloomfield Hills suburban home and leaves it in his parking space where he will find it that evening washed and primped for the ride back home. "They never drive a piece of junk," says a Chevrolet insider. "They never have one that doesn't start, or one with a rattle in the dashboard or with a hunk of chrome trim that looks like it came from another car.

"I remember when Bob Lund was general manager at Chevrolet," this GM executive continues. "Bob used to take dozens of trips out into the field, where he thought he was finding out what really was happening. You know, really getting his finger on the pulse. Those trips involved a plane flight, and being picked up by the zone manager or some flunky in a brand new Caprice. From there he'd be driven to the nearest Hyatt Regency, where he'd hold a few meetings before being driven back to the airport for the trip to Detroit. That was how Bob and most of the other guys of his rank found out what was going on."

Edsel Ford II, the son of Henry II and heir to the throne of the Ford Motor Company, is considered to be a legitimate automotive progressive. ("All of his old man's good sense with none of his ego problems," says an associate.) He has told a story that illustrates the distance his father had eventually put between himself and the company's products. During the 1960s, the Ford Motor Company invested millions in the development of racing cars designed to win the Le Mans twenty-four hour endurance race held each June in France. The event was considered vital in developing Ford's image as a performance-oriented, high-technology car company. After two years of failure, the company finally won the big race in 1966, with Henry Ford II in attendance, sporting sideburns that, in the words of *Car and Driver*, "would have gotten him fired at General Motors." The corporate publicity machine profusely praised its boss as a patron of motor sport, despite the fact that a rare $20,000 Maserati Ghibli grand touring car he had bought for his wife was rusting away in a Dearborn parking lot.

Long after Ford had ended its Le Mans efforts, Edsel II fully restored one of the beautiful, low-slung Ford GT40 racing cars for his personal collection. Edsel II had moved into a new house with his young wife and he invited his father for dinner. Proudly he took his father to the garage where he revealed the glittering classic which had brought so much international glory to the family company. Henry II eyed the machine for a few moments and then huffed, "What the hell kind of a car is that?"

The senior Ford's hermetic separation from the real world of cars lends a new dimension to the famed remark of Charles F. "Boss" Kettering, the General Motors chief of research whose credits include the perfection of the electric self-starter, quick-drying paint, and leaded anti-knock ethyl gasoline. It was Boss Kettering who summarized the latent sentiments of the industry when he grumbled: "It isn't that we build such bad cars. It's that they are such lousy customers."

It is true that many American auto customers are spoiled and ill-informed, and care little about either the mechanics of their cars or the art of driving. But rather than try to correct consumer ignorance, the industry has cynically exploited it. The buyers blame the manufacturers for sloppily made products while the automakers counter that they are merely meeting the demands of unsophisticated customers interested only in high gas mileage and glitter.

American car consumers have finally awakened to the reality of the situation. They now want *superior* products from Detroit. Not products that are equivalent to foreign makes, but superior products. But is it possible?

One fact is obvious: the automobile remains the most viable form of mass transportation for a free society. Barring complete social chaos, it will remain an integral part of our culture for the foreseeable future. The American passion for the car may have waned since the 1960s, but the nation's need for the automobile cannot be eliminated through anything short of a cataclysmic shift in circumstances. Cars must be built in annual units of millions. The question is: Will they be built in America or elsewhere? And in what quantities?

One important trend is the growth of multinational alliances, which will intensify over the next twenty years. Seemingly improbable unions have already been consummated: Fiat with Lancia, which is in turn tied to Sweden's Saab-Scania; Volvo with Renault which is linked to American Motors; Citroën and Peugeot; Daimler-Benz with Alpine, which has ties with Volkswagen; Porsche-Audi with NSU; Ford with Japan's Toyo Kogyo; Italy's De Tomaso and Innocenti, which is tied to British Leyland; General Motors with Isuzu and Suzuki; Chrysler with Peugeot and Simca.

The trend is clear. No single corporate entity has the manufacturing capability, much less the marketing, research and development skills, to operate alone in the world market. Joint ventures of all types will have to be created, even involving such arch-rivals as General Motors and Toyota, who may combine to manufacture small cars in Fremont, California. Many experts are convinced that within ten years no more than six major automakers will have survived, and each will be a multinational consortium capable of producing and distributing on a worldwide basis.

Does this mean that America's venerable Big Three are doomed as independent entities in the car business? Will they go the way of hapless American Motors? Is Ford fated to follow Chrysler's path to Washington to become an indentured servant of the banks and the government?

Not necessarily. After reaching the brink of financial disintegration, Chrysler—or more correctly, "the new Chrysler Corporation" of Lee Iacocca—is a stronger, leaner operation than it has been since before World War II. It seems capable of producing a carefully tailored lineup of automobiles with a radically down-sized management. The same is essentially true of Ford, which ran up billions in losses in the early 1980s, then turned itself around with strong international sales and a new series of aerodynamic, fuel efficient cars. Perhaps more important, Ford is now run by an internationally oriented management, trimmed in size by 25 percent and freed of the psychological tethers imposed during the impetuous reign of the world's last monarch-mogul, Henry Ford II.

Ford's drive for increased productivity and worker involvement in the manufacturing process has produced early dividends. Its future as a carmaker seems assured, but some analysts believe that both Chrysler and Ford will eventually meld into one of the monster multinationals.

What of General Motors? By traditionally dominating the automobile market in the United States with at least a 50 percent share of sales, it remains the single largest carmaker in the world. Since the 1930s, General Motors has been *the* American automobile business in terms of model lineups, pricing structures, and organizational concepts. For years Ford and Chrysler have been operating as mini-GM's, merely aping the giant. Each autumn they obediently wait until General Motors announces its list prices on various models, then quickly parrot numbers that are competitive. Each time Chrysler's or Ford's profits slumped, an executive vice president gallantly announced that they had every intention of remaining "a full-line car company" determined to compete with GM on every front.

American Motors gave up playing this futile game in 1957, when it stopped building its big Ambassadors and concentrated on the compact Ramblers. Had the cars been better designed and fabricated, American Motors might have survived intact. Chrysler pressed its toe-to-toe competition with GM until its final hour of agony in 1979-80, at which point it too pinned its future on smaller, more timely automobiles. Ford carries on with its fantasy that it can somehow find parity with GM in the American market, but that is not possible. Even its major sales successes—the Mustang, Maverick, Fairlane, and the present Escort—have not enhanced its share of the market.

General Motors still calls the American tune. Through the mystical formulas of the Sloan System, GM was one of the key forces in the colossal elevation of American living standards in the postwar period. Its billions in profits over the years fueled the economy through workers' wages, stock dividends and the ever-widening circle of satellite industries that serviced the monolith of West Grand Avenue. However, like those of so many prophets whose impact is tied to a single moment in history, Sloan's dictums have now lost much of their meaning.

In its later manifestations the Sloan system of management rewarded the ordinary and penalized the dissidents who might have charted a new course for GM. The myopic accountants and engineers who had drifted into control of GM ignored one simple fact: The convulsions in the marketplace were being influenced by social forces as much as by economic reality.

The new "team players," comfortable within the blandness of their Detroit Mind, missed two facts: (1) Modern social trends start at the top echelons of society, not at the bottom, where Detroit's marketing power was concentrated, and (2) By the 1970s, the world had forsaken styling glitter for a fascination with modern technology, or the appearance of it. The tragedy of the industry is that most of its leaders still do not understand what has taken place.

Old-line American engineering and production types scoff at hi-tech foreign imports and claim—quite correctly—that traditional pushrod engines, beam axles, drum brakes and conventional carburetion can be made to operate as effectively as the most abstruse and expensive gadgetry. American cars were once sold with this image of solid reliability and simplicity, but fashion has made obsolete all that gabble from Motown about ease of manufacture, low cost, and utility. Those concepts have as much relevance as the 1910 argument that a good horse never had a blowout. Times have changed, and Detroit has ceased to be a source of automobiles that carry strong *perceived value* in the world marketplace.

Perceived value is what has raised the imported cars to their present lofty position. Of course it is impossible to justify a Mercedes-Benz 380SEL as being nearly three times as valuable as a Cadillac DeVille. Nor is a Honda Accord necessarily more value-laden than, say, a Chevrolet Caprice. But such a perception exists among the opinion-makers of society and that is sufficient to make it a fact of life. Detroit can struggle for better mileage, lower costs, and more effective manufacturing techniques until the square wheel is perfected. As long as it continues to be exclusively preoccupied with the meganumber, low-end market segment, the imports will continue to grow in power.

What Detroit desperately needs is a new generation of automobiles that lead, not follow: cars that embody daring technological and design advances that surpass anything Europe or Japan is producing. It is imperative that Detroit develop original designs featuring advanced, powerful, light, efficient engines and superlative brakes and suspensions that are intended not for the average consumer and his Chevettes and Escorts, but for the top end of the market, where the Mercedes-Benz and BMWs dominate.

Once Detroit is capable of vying at that level, with automobiles that represent the highest state of technology, styling, and finish, market credibility will return. Moreover, once that philosophy of no-compromise, ultimate-effort engineering becomes a constant in the American industry, not only will it impress customers and dealerships, but their own engineering, design and sales staffs will also be imbued with a new spirit.

An example of how that once vibrant, if misguided, Detroit hubris has fallen away was provided in the summer of 1982 when the first Detroit Grand Prix was held on the streets surrounding the city's towering testimonial to urban renewal, Renaissance Center. It was an international motor race for Formula One automobiles, the theoretical outer limit of vehicular design. The race was dominated by Europeans: *European* drivers, *European* teams and *European* manufacturers—in Detroit.

The only American representatives were from the accessory companies: Goodyear Tire & Rubber, Valvoline Oil, Champion Spark Plugs. The automobile companies participating in Formula One were purely foreign—Renault, Alfa Romeo, Ferrari (now a part of Fiat), BMW, the English Lotus team, and Talbot. As they displayed their advanced auto technology in the front yard of the American industry, Detroit not only stood in silence on the sidelines, but actually gave the race its support. This entire event was as logical as the Red Army asking the U.S. Navy Blue Angels aerobatic team to perform at its May Day Parade, but it did prompt one alarming thought. Is Detroit resigned to its fate? Has it accepted the role of subordinate in the world of cars?

Barring an industry revolution, much of America's losses may never be recovered. A recent poll of 200 experts conducted by the University of Michigan and Arthur Andersen & Company concluded that even with a $60 billion outlay by 1990 to produce new plants with higher levels of automation, the average American car will still cost from $700 to $1500 more than comparable Japanese models. The result? From 21 to 24 percent of the domestic market will remain in foreign hands. Like so many reports published by sources essentially sympathetic to Detroit, this one tends to focus on cost and thus relieve top management of culpability. Outsiders, including Wisconsin Democratic Congressman Les Aspin, have laid the blame more directly at Detroit's doorstep.

"Detroit, in its truly alarming insularity, has forgotten that automobiles are sold one by one," says Michael H. Dale, the vice president of sales and service for Jaguar in America. "Automobiles are not sold in lots of ten thousand, like blocks of stock or tons of steel. Quite to the contrary, ten thousand individual buying decisions are made, and in the case of General Motors and their J-cars, for example, they forgot that individuals, as opposed to demographic profiles, have to like them. To produce that sort of appeal requires a management that is in tune with the needs of its customers. That simply does not seem to be the case with the top management in Detroit at the present time. Contrast that situation with the Japanese cars, most of which are *interesting* for individuals to look at, to sit in, and to drive."

Although it is minute by Detroit standards, Dale's parent company, Jaguar in Britain, recently passed through an ordeal that illustrated many of the same ailments currently vexing American automakers. A respected manufacturer of high-performance sports cars and saloons beginning with 1922, Jaguar had operated on the edge of chaos since 1966, when it was amalgamated with the large, confused British Motors Corporation. This in turn became the infamous British Leyland, a monstrous government-subsidized firm and the source of some of the worst-made automobiles in the world.

Despite the graceful aesthetics of the Jaguars, they gained a worldwide reputation for sloppy workmanship that bordered on the treacherous. Yet the historic Jaguar mystique transcended reason and provided a base for its survival. Said *Car and Driver* in 1966, "There's something so sensual, so elemental about the appeal of that car that few men can resist its siren song. It's like that woman you used to love, the one you'd never waste another minute on. You can avoid her for months, but one night she calls and you'd crawl naked across three hundred yards of flaming gasoline and broken bottles to get to her. Obviously, a car that can excite such primitive urges is bigger than a non-synchro first gear or bad oil consumption."

Yet by the late 1970s the Jaguar had changed from a charming temptress into an irascible, four-wheeled harlot. There was talk that Jaguar would collapse, as did its old British Leyland stepbrother, the once-loved Triumph. Its Coventry factory was judged to be antiquated, its labor force mutinous, and its automobiles insanely overcomplicated. Sales were plummeting, especially in the important American market, and Jaguar seemed on the verge of becoming yet another casualty of the British industrial tragedy.

Then in 1981, Sir Michael Edwards, the feisty leader of BL, appointed a former auto-parts marketing specialist named John Egan to the chairmanship of Jaguar. As the new man entered the patchwork of low brick structures that makes up the Jaguar factory, he faced annual losses of $80 million dollars, annual sales of fewer than 12,000 automobiles, and the prospect of wildcat strikes coming with the regularity of the noon whistle. Despite the obstacles, within twelve months Egan had Jaguar back on the road to profitability. "We're not out of the woods yet, but definitely in a clearing," he said recently.

"What John Egan did was devastatingly simple," explains Mike Dale. "To begin with, he provided leadership with a vision of the future, much like Lee Iacocca did with Chrysler. He took the same people and got them to perform, mainly by establishing communication between the workers and the management, so they all understood what was needed of them. He initially showed them videotapes of themselves and their coworkers rushing for the gates ten minutes before quitting time and of people in the financial department sitting around reading novels during working hours. By communicating with these people, mainly through monthly video reports and establishing quality circles in which the workers could actually contribute to the manufacture of the cars, productivity increased radically and the labor unrest eased.

"We took a Mercedes-Benz and a Jaguar apart and compared them. We found that the Jaguar was deficient in one hundred and fifty areas. We divided up the problems among crises teams formed of workers and management, and we discovered one simple thing: People will bust their asses if they feel there is a future."

Egan's "new" Jaguar organization is presently operating with only 60 percent of its former work force, but it is producing *twice* as many automobiles of significantly higher quality. A recent poll of luxury-car owners indicates that Jaguar has supplanted Cadillac in third place in terms of perceived quality, behind Mercedes-Benz and BMW. Sales have doubled from their 1981 nadir. The turnaround has been miraculous but the methods, as Dale says, are "devastatingly simple."

The situation at Chrysler has its parallels with Jaguar. Here too, the company was in a terminal malaise, foundering in a sea of inefficiency and self-loathing. Then Lee Iacocca arrived in November 1978. Within hours he was injecting powerful doses of personal dynamism into the ranks. Within the four years Iacocca has been at Chrysler he has returned it to profitability, has removed the creditors from its doorstep, has increased its domestic share of the market by about two percentage points. Most important, he has given the entire work force a new sense of mission and purpose. That labor group, reduced by roughly 40 percent, is now producing cars at almost double the rate of the old days.

There are men at General Motors who will sniff imperiously at the examples set by operations like Jaguar, dismissing them as minor-league curiosities. The magnitude of the General Motors operation and the attendant economy of scale invalidate any such analogy, they say. The example of carmakers like Jaguar (or Volvo or Saab or any one of a dozen other minor players) or even middle-sized Chrysler (present rank in the world is thirteenth, just behind Lada of the USSR) have little relevance, GM leaders claim.

Yet one cannot help but wonder if they are not wrong. What if General Motors was headed by a charismatic leader, rather than a former accountant? What if that megacorporation was suddenly being run by a rank outsider, like an Iacocca or an Egan? What if the next president and chairman of General Motors were not products of the Corporation's seamless, faceless infrastructure?

/////

The American industry must upgrade its automation in order to compete in world markets, but ten thousand new robots will not save Detroit. Nor will more computers and laser beams, nor Japanese-style "just-in-time" inventory control. Massive wage concessions by the labor unions are not the key to salvation. Neither is the answer more modern American factories, which are already collectively equal to any in the world. The industry will not be saved by front-wheel drive, a fresh generation of small cars, or imaginative advertising and marketing campaigns. While all this can contribute to greater industrial health, there is but one true lever to prosperity for Detroit and America: new corporate leaders of sophistication and strength.

They must be men whose dreams go beyond the lakefronts of Bloomfield Hills. They must be men who are obsessed with making great automobiles, not just good automobiles. They must be able to fire the imagination of audacious juniors under them. There is nothing that ails the American auto industry that cannot be rectified by the presence of a few lions, preferably hungry ones, in Detroit.

The American mystique assumes that the impossible can be made to take place. It has often proven true, but it usually happens only after a period of self-criticism. If the automakers can understand the reasons behind their failure and be made to appreciate the necessity for drastic—even revolutionary—change, they may yet be able to salvage an indispendable industry, one that has been tied, pocketbook and soul, to the American experience.

Index

ABOUT THE AUTHOR

BROCK YATES, one of the nation's outstanding automotive journalists, has for the past twenty years been a keen observer of American carmakers and their consumers. His writings on automobiles have appeared in such leading publications as *Esquire, Sports Illustrated, Playboy,* and dozens of automotive magazines. Mr. Yates is editor-at-large and a columnist for *Car and Driver* magazine, a publication for which he has been managing editor and editor. He has written several books including a non-fiction work, *Sunday Driver,* published in 1972 by Farrar, Straus & Giroux and a novel, *Dead in the Water,* published in 1976. The author is also editor and publisher of a widely-circulated automotive industry newsletter. Mr. Yates has received several honors for his writing including an award from the International Motor Press Association. He was born in upstate New York, where he now lives, and is a graduate of Hobart College.